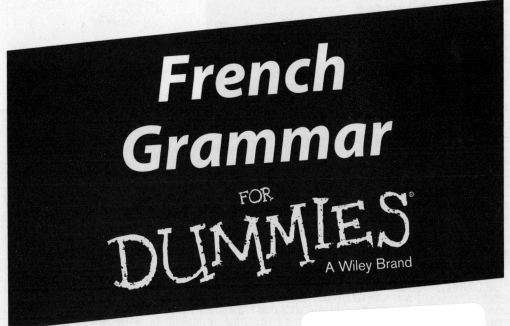

French Grammar

FOR DUMMIES®

A Wiley Brand

by Véronique Mazet, PhD

D1627931

French Grammar For Dummies®

Published by
John Wiley & Sons, Inc.
111 River St.
Hoboken, NJ 07030-5774
www.wiley.com

Copyright © 2013 by John Wiley & Sons, Inc., Hoboken, New Jersey

Published simultaneously in Canada

For general information on our other products and services, please contact our Customer Care Department within the U.S. at 877-762-2974, outside the U.S. at 317-572-3993, or fax 317-572-4002.

For technical support, please visit www.wiley.com/techsupport.

Wiley publishes in a variety of print and electronic formats and by print-on-demand. Some material included with standard print versions of this book may not be included in e-books or in print-on-demand. If this book refers to media such as a CD or DVD that is not included in the version you purchased, you may download this material at http://booksupport.wiley.com. For more information about Wiley products, visit www.wiley.com.

Library of Congress Control Number: 2013933935

ISBN 978-1-118-50251-8 (pbk); ISBN 978-1-118-50248-8 (ebk); ISBN 978-1-118-50250-1 (ebk); ISBN 978-1-118-50324-9 (ebk)

Manufactured in the United States of America

10 9 8 7 6 5 4 3 2 1

About the Author

Véronique Mazet, PhD, is a professor of French, adjunct, at Austin Community College in Austin, Texas. She's the author of two other French grammar books: *Correct Your French Blunders* and *Advanced French Grammar* (both published by McGraw-Hill).

Dedication

To my students of all ages: Thanks for believing in the beauty of the French language, and thanks for trusting me.

Author's Acknowledgments

Thanks to my agent, Grace Freedson, for calling me, and to my husband, for his super support.

Publisher's Acknowledgments

We're proud of this book; please send us your comments at http://dummies.custhelp.com. For other comments, please contact our Customer Care Department within the U.S. at 877-762-2974, outside the U.S. at 317-572-3993, or fax 317-572-4002.

Some of the people who helped bring this book to market include the following:

Acquisitions, Editorial, and Vertical Websites

Senior Project Editor: Georgette Beatty

Acquisitions Editor: Michael Lewis

Copy Editor: Caitlin Copple

Assistant Editor: David Lutton

Editorial Program Coordinator: Joe Niesen

Technical Editors: Eric Laird, Jessica Sturm

Editorial Manager: Michelle Hacker

Editorial Assistant: Alexa Koschier

Cover Photo: © James Gately/iStockphoto.com

Composition Services

Senior Project Coordinator: Kristie Rees

Layout and Graphics: Carrie A. Cesavice, Joyce Haughey, Erin Zeltner

Proofreader: The Well-Chosen Word

Indexer: BIM Indexing & Proofreading Services

Publishing and Editorial for Consumer Dummies

    Kathleen Nebenhaus, Vice President and Executive Publisher

    David Palmer, Associate Publisher

    Kristin Ferguson-Wagstaffe, Product Development Director

Publishing for Technology Dummies

    Andy Cummings, Vice President and Publisher

Composition Services

    Debbie Stailey, Director of Composition Services

Contents at a Glance

Table of Contents

Introduction

*I*deas, needs, and feelings are expressed with words. If you want to express yourself in any language, you need to know the right words, but words alone are not enough. If I say **dehors** (*outside*) to you, you can't guess if I want you *to go outside*, *look outside*, or something else. I need to add a verb like **allez** (*go*) and use it in the correct way to make my meaning clear.

In order to put words together in a coherent way, you need grammar. Unlike the English language, in which you can often string words together with minimum linking, French requires more formal structure. In this book I show you how the parts of French grammar work together so you can express what you need, how you feel, and even what you think, in French.

About This Book

French Grammar For Dummies tackles specific French grammar topics in detail, with plenty of examples and practice problems. An answer key at the end of each chapter allows you to check your work.

I start you off with basic French grammar on nouns, articles, adjectives, numbers, dates, and times. Then you move to verbs so you can build simple sentences in the present tense. From that point, you find out how to embellish simple French sentences with more detailed phrasing that makes you sound like a native speaker, thanks to adverbs, prepositional phrases, and pronouns. Then you're ready to move in time with different verb tenses, like the past and the future.

You don't have to read this book from cover to cover; you can simply read the sections or chapters that interest you. Put the book away until you need it again — it'll be ready and waiting for you!

Conventions Used in This Book

I use the following conventions to make this book easier for you to navigate:

- ✔ French words and sentences appear in **boldface**.

- ✔ English equivalents in *italics* follow French words and sentences.

- ✔ I usually present the English equivalent of French expressions, which is not always the literal translation. For example, you can translate the French phrase **de rien** literally as *of nothing*, but in English, the correct equivalent is *you're welcome*. This book usually gives you the *you're welcome* version of the translation, but in some spots, I provide the literal translation as well.

- ✔ An answer key at the end of every chapter provides the correct answers to all the practice questions in the chapter.

To make verbs stand out, I usually present verb conjugations in tables like this one:

aimer (to like, to love)	
j'aime	nous aimons
tu aimes	vous aimez
il/elle/on aime	ils/elles aiment

The top of the table notes a French verb and its English translation, followed by six verb forms that vary according to who or what is performing the action: *I*; *you* (singular informal); *he*, *she*, or *one*; *we*; *you* (singular formal or plural formal and informal); and *they* (masculine and feminine plural).

Note: This book doesn't feature pronunciations after French text (with the exception of Chapter 2, which is about sounding out French words). It concentrates on grammar and written communication. Be sure to check out a French dictionary for any pronunciation questions you have.

What You're Not to Read

If you don't have a lot time, or if you need more help with certain grammatical topics, you can skip around to stuff that most interests you. For instance, if you're already familiar with the gender of nouns but would like to put them in action with verbs, skip directly to Chapter 6.

If you know right away what an exercise wants you to do, you can skip the examples and just dive into the exercise questions themselves. Also, if I present several examples to illustrate a particular grammar rule and you understand the rule after reading the first example, you don't need to bother with the rest of them. After all, this book is here to help you go at your own pace.

Foolish Assumptions

As I wrote this book, I made the following assumptions about you, dear reader:

- You want to be able to communicate more creatively in French, especially in writing — even if you already have a background in French and can carry on a conversation.
- You want to practice French grammar so you can be sure you can retain your newly acquired knowledge.
- You love French and find grammar fascinating . . . maybe?

How This Book Is Organized

French Grammar For Dummies is divided into six parts. The following sections introduce the parts and their contents.

Part I: Getting Started with French Grammar

This part is for beginners, or those of you who want a brief refresher on French basics. Here you find out how to pronounce French words; handle gender and number with nouns, articles, and adjectives; practice counting and telling time; and brush up on dates, days of the week, and months of the year.

Part II: Constructing Sentences, Saying No, and Asking Questions

In this part you find out how to put together a subject and a verb in the present tense to create a basic sentence, express reflexive or mutual actions with pronominal verbs like **se lever** (*to get up*) and **se parler** (*to talk to each other*), say *no* using words like **jamais** (*never*) and **rien** (*nothing*), and ask questions.

Part III: Beefing Up Your Sentences

In this part, I explain how to make sentences more informative by adding adverbs and prepositional phrases. You discover how to compare all kinds of things and how to replace nouns with pronouns to avoid repetition. And you find out how to use gerunds to explain how something is done and use the passive to insist on the doing rather than the doer of an action.

Part IV: Talking about the Past or Future

In these chapters I show you how you can move a sentence in time by changing the conjugation of the verb from present tense to past tense and future tense. French has many more verb tenses than this book covers, but I limit the tenses to the ones that you're the most likely to use daily. Here I focus on the present perfect, the imperfect, and the future.

Part V: Expressing Conditions, Subjectivity, and Orders

In this part, I present the conditional, the subjunctive, and the imperative.

- Conditional statements go something like this: **Je viendrais avec toi si j'avais le temps.** (*I would come with you if I had time.*) The conditional allows you to express a daydream, a wish, or a hypothetical situation.

- The subjunctive and its triggers allow you to express surprise, fear, or joy at something. For example: **Nous sommes contents que vous veniez nous voir.** (*We are happy that you're coming to see us.*)

- The imperative is what you need to give orders or forbid things, just like signs you see in a park: **Ne marchez pas sur la pelouse.** (*Don't walk on the grass.*)

As a bonus in this part, I explain how to use the auxiliary verbs **avoir** (*to have*) and **être** (*to be*) to form tenses called *compound tenses* like the pluperfect, the future perfect, and the past conditional.

Part VI: The Part of Tens

Every *For Dummies* book has a Part of Tens — why break with tradition? In this part, you find ten typical French grammar mistakes (and how to avoid them) and a list of ten French idioms to help you sound like a native French speaker.

Icons Used in This Book

The following icons make certain kinds of information easier for you to find.

This icon points out information that you should recall long after you finish reading this book. If you read anything here, it should be the text marked with this icon.

This icon highlights pointers for understanding French grammar quickly and more easily.

This icon points to the pitfalls of French grammar — beware!

This icon highlights practice problems that you can use to sharpen your French grammar skills.

Where to Go from Here

Beginners and anyone else who wants a refresher on French grammar basics can start with Chapter 2, on sounding out French words, or Chapter 5 on numbers, dates, and times. Chapters 3 and 4 help you make sure your nouns, articles, and adjectives all agree in gender (masculine or feminine) and number (one or more than one). If you're ready to start composing sentences, jump to Chapter 6, where you'll find out how to put subjects and verbs together.

Otherwise, feel free to dive in wherever you'd like. Every chapter is a stand-alone module. The more modules you complete, the more fluent you'll become in French grammar. **Bonne chance** (*good luck*)!

Part I

Getting Started with French Grammar

In this part . . .

✔ Discover how to sound out French words.

✔ Get the scoop on nouns, including their gender and the articles to use with them.

✔ Match adjectives to the nouns they describe and place them properly in sentences.

✔ Start counting with cardinal and ordinal numbers, and then talk about dates and times.

Chapter 1

French Grammar in a Nutshell

....

In This Chapter

▶ Getting to know French parts of speech

▶ Building and embellishing sentences

▶ Moving through verb tenses and moods

....

French grammar is somewhat complex, and this book gives you plenty of material to dig into, little by little. I start you off easy in this chapter, providing an overview of what's to come so you'll feel a little more familiar with the topics throughout the book. If you take the time to read this chapter, you get a good grammar primer to help you through the journey you're about to embark on.

The Parts of Speech

Learning a language is easier if you know what it's made of. To grasp the fundamentals of any language, your native language as well as French, you need to recognize the *parts of speech,* the various types of words that compose a language and how they work. The following sections give you the scoop.

Nouns

You should know three essential things about a French **nom** (*noun*):

✔ It refers to people, places, things, or concepts.

✔ It has a gender (masculine, *he*, or feminine, *she*), and a number (singular or plural). You need to know the noun's characteristics to make other elements of a sentence match it. That's called *agreement in gender and number.*

✔ It can have different roles (called *functions*) in a sentence:

  • It can be the *subject* of the verb, as the noun **professeur** in this sentence: **Le professeur parle.** (*The professor speaks.*)

  • It can be the *object* of the verb, as the noun **lune** in: **Nous regardons la lune.** (*We watch the moon.*)

See Chapter 3 for full details on French nouns.

Articles

An *article* (**un article**) is a small but essential little word that introduces a noun and takes its gender and number. Articles come in three types:

- ✔ The definite articles: **le**, **la**, **l'**, and **les** (*the*). For example: **les enfants** (*the children*).
- ✔ The indefinite articles: **un** and **une** (*a/an*), **des** (*some*), and **de** and **d'** (*no/not any*). For example: **un chat** (*a cat*).
- ✔ The partitive articles: **du**, **de la**, **de l'**, and **des** (*some*). For example, **de l'eau** (*some water*).

Chapter 3 covers these articles in more detail and explains how to choose the correct article for any sentence.

Adjectives

An adjective adds some color to a noun. For example: **un étudiant <u>sérieux</u>** (*a <u>hard-working</u> student*). To use **les adjectifs** correctly in French, you need to know a couple of things:

- ✔ An adjective is a chameleon; it changes to match the noun it describes. It can be masculine singular, masculine plural, feminine singular, or feminine plural. Matching an adjective to the noun it describes is called the *agreement* of the adjective.
- ✔ Most French adjectives are placed after a noun, not before like in English. For example you say **une voiture <u>rouge</u>** (*a <u>red</u> car*). **Rouge** (*red*) goes after **voiture** (*car*).

Get the lowdown on adjectives in Chapter 4.

Verbs

Verbs (**les verbes**) are the core element of a sentence because they provide essential information. They take many different forms to do so. They indicate:

- ✔ What action is being performed, through the choice of the infinitive
- ✔ Who performs it, through the choice of the subject
- ✔ When it is performed, through the choice of the tense

Identifying the infinitive

The *infinitive* is like the name of the verb. It also tells you the type of a verb: regular verbs are grouped into three types, according to the ending of their infinitive. They are:

- ✔ Verbs ending in -**er**, like **parler** (*to talk*)
- ✔ Verbs ending in -**ir**, like **finir** (*to finish*)
- ✔ Verbs ending in -**re**, like **vendre** (*to sell*)

And then there are the irregular verbs, like **avoir** (*to have*), **aller** (*to go*), **faire** (*to do, to make*), and **être** (*to be*), to name only a few. These verbs follow different patterns when they're *conjugated* (changed to reflect the subject and tense). (See the later section "Starting with a conjugated verb" for more information.)

Establishing subject-verb agreement

To start putting a verb into action (to conjugate it) you need a *subject* (who or what is doing the action). In French, you always say who the subject is, except in commands (English is the same way).

Each subject corresponds to a matching form of the verb. These differences in the forms happen at the end of the verb itself. For example, you say **tu chantes** (*you* [singular informal] *sing*) but **nous chantons** (*we sing*), changing the form of the verb on the ending, according to the subject.

Moving an action in time

An action can be expressed in a variety of tenses, such as the past tense, future tense, conditional tense, and many more. Here are some examples of different tenses for **parler** (*to speak*):

- Present: **nous parlons** (*we speak/are speaking*)
- Imperfect: **nous parlions** (*we used to speak*)
- Future: **nous parlerons** (*we will speak*)

Tenses come in two types: *simple tenses* and *compound tenses*.

- A simple tense is a one-word verb form, like **vous parlez** (*you speak*).
- A compound tense involves two words, like **tu as parlé** (*you spoke*).

Some tenses express a mood, like the conditional and the subjunctive. But to simplify, you can just look at those so-called moods as other tenses. See the later section "Many Tenses and Moods" for more information.

Conjunctions

Conjunctions (**les conjonctions**) are small invariable words used to link parts of a sentence or just words. For instance, in **Tu sors ou tu rentres?** (*Are you going out or are you coming in?*), **ou** (*or*) is a conjunction.

Adverbs

An *adverb* (**un adverbe**) is a little word that can modify a verb (usually), an adjective, or another adverb by telling you how the action in question is done: *slowly, quickly, seriously* (**lentement, vite, sérieusement**). Here's an example of what adverbs can do to a sentence:

- Without adverbs: **Julie parle et Paul écoute.** (*Julie talks and Paul listens.*)
- With adverbs: **Julie parle lentement et Paul écoute attentivement.** (*Julie talks slowly and Paul listens attentively.*)

Get the scoop on adverbs in Chapter 10.

Prepositions

A **préposition** (*preposition*) is a little word placed between a verb and a noun or between two nouns to indicate a relationship of space/direction, time, or manner. A preposition introduces a prepositional phrase that adds information to the sentence, as in **Nous allons au cinéma** (*We go <u>to</u> the movies*). In this example, **au** is the preposition.

A French preposition keeps its meaning, no matter what surrounds it, unlike English prepositions that can adopt a different meaning with different verbs. For instance, the English preposition *after* indicates time — unless you join it to the verb *to look*, and *to look after* has nothing to do with time!

Check out Chapter 11 for help with using prepositions.

Pronouns

A pronoun (**un pronom**) can replace a noun when you want to avoid repetition. A pronoun is also a chameleon word that must match not only the gender (most of the time) and number of the noun it replaces but also its *function* in the sentence: subject or object. Here's a list of all the pronoun types you may come across in this book:

- The *subject pronouns* precede a conjugated verb, like this: <u>**tu**</u> **parles** (<u>*you*</u> *speak*) and **nous écoutons** (<u>*we*</u> *listen*). They are **je** (*I*), **tu** (*you* [singular informal]), **il** (*he*), **elle** (*she*), **on** (*one*), **nous** (*we*), **vous** (*you* [singular formal or plural formal and informal]), **ils** (*they*, masculine), and **elles** (*they*, feminine).

- The *direct object pronouns* replace nouns that are the direct object of the verb. For example: **je <u>l'</u>ai vu** (*I saw <u>it</u>/<u>him</u>*). The DOPs are: **me** (*me*), **te** (*you*), **le** (*him/it*), **la** (*her/it*), **l'** (*him/her/it* before a vowel), **nous** (*us*), **vous** (*you*), and **les** (*them*).

- The *indirect object pronouns* replace nouns that are indirect objects of the verb. For example: **tu <u>lui</u> parles** (*you speak to <u>him</u>/<u>her</u>*). They are: **me** (*to me*), **te** (*to you*), **lui** (*to him/her/it*), **nous** (*to us*), **vous** (*to you*), and **leur** (*to them*).

- The direct object **y** replaces a noun that indicated a place (most of the time). For example: **elle <u>y</u> va** (*she's going <u>there</u>*). **Y** is alone in its kind.

- The object pronoun **en** replaces a noun that was the object of the verb and indicated a quantity. For example: **tu <u>en</u> manges beaucoup** (*you eat a lot of <u>it</u>*). **En** is also one of a kind.

- The *stress pronouns* replace nouns that refer to people, after certain prepositions. For example: **viens avec <u>moi</u>** (*come with <u>me</u>*). They are: **moi** (*me*), **toi** (*you*), **lui** (*him/it*), **elle** (*her/it*), **nous** (*us*), **vous** (*you*), **eux** (*them*, masculine), and **elles** (*them*, feminine).

- The *reflexive pronouns* help conjugate pronominal verbs that express an action done to oneself. For example: **elle <u>se</u> regarde dans le miroir** (*she looks at <u>herself</u> in the mirror*). The reflexive pronouns are: **me** (*myself*), **te** (*yourself*), **se** (*himself/herself/itself*), **nous** (*ourselves*), **vous** (*yourselves*), and **se** (*themselves*).

Chapter 13 has more information on most of these pronouns; in addition, check out Chapter 6 for details on subject pronouns and Chapter 7 for details on reflexive pronouns.

The Basics of Composing Sentences

After you know the parts of speech in French, you can put them together to compose a sentence. The following sections explain how to start with a verb and then add embellishment.

Starting with a conjugated verb

To function properly in a sentence, a verb needs to be *conjugated,* which means:

✔ Matching the subject in person (first, second, or third) and number (plural or singular)

✔ Expressing when the action takes place through the use of a tense (now, in the past, in the future, and so on)

To do either one of those two operations, you need to know the *pattern* of conjugation for your verb. It is usually made up of a *stem* and an *ending.* Here's an example: To get the present tense pattern of a regular verb with an **-er** infinitive, drop the **-er** and replace it with the following endings that correspond to the subjects:

✔ For **je**, add **-e** to the stem.

✔ For **tu**, add **-es** to the stem.

✔ For **il/elle/on**, add **-e** to the stem.

✔ For **nous**, add **-ons** to the stem.

✔ For **vous**, add **-ez** to the stem.

✔ For **ils/elles**, add **-ent** to the stem.

Here they are for the verb **danser** (*to dance*).

danser (*to dance*)	
je **danse**	nous **dansons**
tu **danses**	vous **dansez**
il/elle/on **danse**	ils/elles **dansent**

All regular **-er** verbs follow this pattern for the present tense, so if you memorize it, you've mastered about 80 percent of French present tense conjugation, because **-er** verbs count for over 80 percent of French verbs. For regular **-ir** and **-re** verbs, the endings to use for the present tense are different but their stem is formed the same way, by dropping the infinitive endings **-ir** and **-re**. (Check out Chapter 6 for the scoop on the present tense.) Other tenses, like the present perfect, the imperfect, and the future, use different stems and endings but also follow conjugation patterns. Parts IV and V talk about the conjugation patterns of other tenses in detail.

Adding details

You can develop your sentences by adding as much information as you want. Saying **les enfants chantent** (*the kids sing*) is a good start on conveying information, but it's lacking in detail, don't you think? *What* are they singing? *Where*? And *when* exactly do they sing?

- To say *what* they sing, use a *direct object* like **une chanson de Noël** (*a Christmas carol*) and place it after the verb, like this: **Les enfants chantent une chanson de Noël.** (*The kids sing a Christmas carol.*)

- To say *where* they sing, use a prepositional phrase like **à l'école** (*at school*), or an adverb like **ici** (*here*): **Les enfants chantent une chanson de Noël à l'école.** (*The kids sing a Christmas carol at school.*)

- To say *when* they sing, use a prepositional phrase like **après le goûter** (*after the afternoon snack*), or an adverb like **maintenant** (*now*), like this: **Les enfants chantent une chanson de Noël à l'école, après le goûter.** (*The kids sing a Christmas carol at school after the afternoon snack.*)

You can also beef up the nouns with adjectives, but make sure they match the nouns they describe in gender and number. For example: **Les petits enfants chantent une jolie chanson de Noël à l'école, après le bon goûter.** (*The little kids sing a pretty Christmas carol at school after the good afternoon snack.*)

Fun Stuff You Can Do with Your Sentences

You can jazz up your French sentences in a few more ways. You can make them negative, turn them around to ask questions, and compare all their elements.

Going negative

To make a negative sentence in French, you don't need to change or add anything to the verb (like I just did in English with *don't*). All you need are two little negative words: **ne** and **pas** (which together mean *not*) in basic negations, or a more specific one, like **jamais** (*never*), **rien** (*nothing*), **personne** (*no one*), or **nulle part** (*nowhere*) instead of **pas**. Here are a few examples that illustrate where these words go in the sentence.

Pierre **n'**écoute **pas** le prof. (*Pierre doesn't listen to the teacher.*)

Tu **ne** prends **jamais** le bus. (*You never take the bus.*)

Elle **ne** fait **rien**. (*She doesn't do anything.*)

Nous **n'**irons **nulle part** pour les vacances. (*We will not go anywhere for the holidays.*)

Chapter 8 has more information about negative words and expressions.

Asking questions

Like in English, you can ask a simple yes-no question like **Aimez-vous les huitres?** (*Do you like oysters?*). If you need more information, use question words like **quand** (*when*), **qui** (*who*), **où** (*where*), **pourquoi** (*why*), **comment** (*how*), or **qu'est-ce que** (*what*).

Both types of questions can be phrased in two ways:

✔ Inverting the normal word order of subject-verb to verb-subject (called *inversion*), as in **Aimez-vous les huitres?** (*Do you like oysters?*) which doesn't exist in English, as opposed to **Vous aimez les huitres** (*You like oysters*).

✔ Keeping the normal word order and using the tag **est-ce que** at the beginning of the question or right after the question word, if there is one. For example: **Est-ce que vous parlez français?** (*Do you speak French?*) or **Où est-ce que vous parlez français?** (*Where do you speak French?*)

Check out Chapter 9 for more on handling questions.

Making comparisons

French makes the same kinds of comparisons that English does.

✔ Comparative of superiority: For example, **Il est <u>plus</u> grand que moi.** (*He is tall<u>er</u> [<u>more</u> tall] than me.*)

✔ Comparative of inferiority: For example, **Il est <u>moins</u> intéressant que toi.** (*He is <u>less</u> interesting than you.*)

✔ Comparative of equality: For example, **Il est <u>aussi</u> grand que moi.** (*He is <u>as</u> tall as me.*)

Flip to Chapter 12 for more about making comparisons.

Many Tenses and Moods

When you need to move beyond the present, you need new tenses! French has about 18 tenses/moods to choose from. In this book I focus only on the ones you will use the most: present, imperfect, future, conditional, subjunctive, and imperative for the simple tenses; and the present perfect, pluperfect, future perfect, and past conditional for the compound tenses.

The past

To express a past action, French has two main tenses to choose from. The **passé composé** (*present perfect*) names past actions that occurred, and the **imparfait** (*imperfect*) describes what it was like when the past action occurred. The **imparfait** also describes how things used to be, in your childhood for example, without focusing on a specific date. Here they are in action:

✔ **Passé composé:** Naming a past action: **Hier nous <u>sommes allés</u> au ciné.** (*Yesterday we <u>went</u> to the movies.*)

✔ **Imparfait:** What it was like when something happened: **Quand je suis sorti ce matin, il <u>faisait</u> beau.** (*When I went out this morning, the weather <u>was</u> nice.*)

✔ **Imparfait:** How things used to be: **Quand nous <u>étions</u> petits, nous <u>jouions</u> au parc.** (*When we <u>were</u> little, we <u>used to play</u> in the park.*)

Head to Chapter 15 for more about the present perfect and Chapter 16 for more about the imperfect.

The future

The future tense (**le futur**) describes what will probably happen down the road, like **Je <u>finirai</u> ça plus tard.** (*I <u>will finish</u> this later.*)

To describe a future event that is certain to happen, and is almost imminent, French uses the **futur proche** (*immediate future*). For example: **Il est 6h30, elle <u>va préparer</u> le dîner.** (*It's 6:30; she's <u>going to prepare</u> dinner.*)

The future is probably the easiest tense to conjugate because its stem is the infinitive. The future endings are: **-ai**, **-as**, **-a**, **-ons**, **-ez**, **-ont**. Here's the complete conjugation of a regular **-er** verb in the future.

manger (*to eat*)	
je **mangerai**	nous **mangerons**
tu **mangeras**	vous **mangerez**
il/elle/on **mangera**	ils/elles **mangeront**

Chapter 17 has what you need to know about the future tense.

The conditional

The conditional is a simple tense, and its stem is derived from the infinitive, like the future tense (see the preceding section), so it's a fairly easy one to conjugate, too. The conditional endings are: **-ais**, **-ais**, **-ait**, **-ions**, **-iez**, and **-aient**.

French uses **le conditionnel** (*the conditional*) to express:

✔ Daydreams/hypothetical situations, in combination with the imperfect (see the earlier section "The past" for details). For example: **S'il pleuvait, je <u>resterais</u> à la maison.** (*If it were raining, I <u>would stay</u> home.*)

✔ Friendly advice, using the verb **devoir** (*must*). For example: **Tu <u>devrais manger</u> moins de sucre.** (*You <u>should eat</u> less sugar.*)

✔ Polite requests, using the verb **pouvoir** (*can*). For example: **<u>Pourriez</u>-vous m'indiquer la poste s'il vous plait?** (<u>*Could*</u> *you please show me the post office?*)

✔ Wishes, using the verb **vouloir** (*want*) or **aimer** (*like*). For example: **Nous <u>aimerions</u> gagner le loto.** (*We <u>would like</u> to win the lottery.*)

✔ The future in a past context. For example: **Sherlock pensait qu'il <u>découvrirait</u> l'assassin.** (*Sherlock thought he <u>would discover</u> the murderer.*)

Check out more of the conditional in Chapter 18.

The subjunctive

Le subjonctif (*the subjunctive*) is commonly used in French to say that you want someone to do something, that you're happy or sad that something is happening, or that you fear something may happen. The subjunctive may seem difficult to native English speakers because it pretty much doesn't exist in English. Here are some examples of the **subjonctif**:

> **Pierre veut que vous <u>partiez</u>.** (*Pierre wants you <u>to leave</u>.*)

> **Il faut que tu <u>prennes</u> une décision.** (*It's necessary that you <u>make</u> a decision.*)

> **Les enfants sont contents que l'école <u>finisse</u>.** (*The children are happy that school <u>is over</u>.*)

A sentence with a verb in subjunctive begins with a trigger phrase and has two different subjects.

✔ In the three preceding examples, **veut que**, **Il faut que**, and **sont contents que** are examples of triggers for the subjunctive. There are quite a few different triggers, and I give you a long list of the most useful ones in Chapter 19.

✔ The three preceding examples are sentences with two *clauses* (parts) and two different subjects: **Pierre** and **vous** in the first example; **il** and **tu** in the second, and **les enfants** and **l'école** in the third.

Chapter 19 has the full scoop on the subjunctive.

The imperative

Use the imperative to tell one or several persons what to do or what not to do. It is not a regular tense, because the subject is not expressed, and it has only three forms that are borrowed almost exactly from the present tense conjugation for most verbs. (For details and exceptions flip to Chapter 20.)

For example, here are the three imperative forms for **-er** verbs:

- ✔ From the present tense **tu** form (*you* [singular]) of **parler**: **Parle!** (*Speak!*)

- ✔ From the present tense **nous** (*we*) form: **Parlons!** (*Let's speak!*)

- ✔ From the present tense **vous** form (that is, the plural *you*): **Parlez!** (*Speak!*)

The negative commands are formed the same way. You just add **ne** before the imperative and **pas** after it, like this:

- ✔ From the affirmative command **parle** (*speak*) to **ne parle pas** (*don't speak*).

- ✔ From the affirmative command **parlons** (*let's speak*) to **ne parlons pas!** (*let's not speak*).

- ✔ From the affirmative command **parlez** (*speak*) to **ne parlez pas** (*don't speak*).

Compound tenses

French compound tenses are two-word verb forms that always express an action that is more past than the main action. For instance, in *He had already gotten up when his alarm finally went off*, the pluperfect verb phrase is *had gotten up*. French has several compound tenses, and the most commonly used are: the *present perfect*, which I discuss earlier in this chapter, the pluperfect, the future perfect, and the past conditional.

A French compound tense is formed by putting together a conjugated form of one of the two *auxiliary verbs* (also called helper verbs) — **être** (*to be*) and **avoir** (*to have*) — and the past participle of the main verb. (Chapter 15 has full details on how to form past participles.)

English and French compound tenses are different in their form (English may use three-word forms) and in their usage. They occur more strictly and frequently in French. Here are some examples of compound tenses in French, with nonliteral English translations:

- ✔ The pluperfect: **Il était déjà allé à la boulangerie.** (*He had already gone to the bread shop.*)

- ✔ The future perfect: **Je m'amuserai quand j'aurai fini mon travail.** (*I will play when I am finished with my work.*)

- ✔ The past conditional: **Si elle avait su, elle aurait choisi l'autre solution.** (*If she had known, she would have chosen the other solution.*)

See Chapter 21 for full details on compound tenses.

Chapter 2

Sounding Out French Words

In This Chapter

▶ Pronouncing vowels and consonants

▶ Adding accents and cedillas in the right places

▶ Getting the hang of the liaison

▶ Understanding French stress and syllables

French and English share the same alphabet, but the way each language pronounces letters, especially vowels, is very different. When you learn a language, mastering the pronunciation is crucial because all the vocabulary in the world won't mean a thing if it isn't pronounced correctly! The main challenges of French pronunciation are

✔ The articulation of the vowels, including **u** and the nasal sounds

✔ The relationship between spelling and sound, including how the same sound can have different spellings and how accents and other diacritical marks can change the way some letters are pronounced

✔ The rhythm of a sentence, or how syllables are grouped and how words link to one another through sounds that sometimes don't even appear in the written text

This chapter explains how to pronounce vowels and consonants in French, gives you the scoop on different accent marks (including the cedilla), introduces the concept of the **liaison** for pronunciation, and helps you understand French stress and syllables.

You have several wonderful tools at your disposal as you discover how to sound out French words, some of which you may not even know about! I'm talking of your own vocal organs. Every time you say *hi* or *good morning* to someone, you're moving your jaws, your tongue, your lips, and your vocal cords, all at the same time. Your jaws can open more or less depending on the sounds you want to produce; your lips can shape different sounds when puckered, rounded, or stretched out; your tongue helps direct air flow by going up or down against your palate; and your throat releases more or less air to produce various sounds. As you work on sounding out words, I suggest you use a mirror so you can look at the articulation of your mouth and your lips. Also, you can check out numerous websites where you can hear French words (such as www.frenchlanguageguide.com/french/pronunciation/lettere.asp or www.forvo.com/languages-pronunciations/fr), as well as books on French phonetics (the official term for the rules of pronunciation).

Starting with Vowels

French vowels are all pure and short. (French doesn't have *diphthongs,* which are modulations of sounds, kind of like a wave, as in the English words *face* and *mule.*) In fact, French has no long sounds at all like you hear in the English words *beach* and *freeze.* The following sections review the pronunciation of each vowel and then move on to combining vowels to create new sounds. I even throw in the nasal sounds — I think you can handle them.

Pronouncing individual vowels

Each of the vowels in French has one or more sounds, as you find out in the following sections.

The vowel a

The French **a** has the sound *ah,* as in *father,* with the jaws slightly tenser but the mouth very open (your jaw should go lower than when you say the *a* in *father*). It never sounds like the diphthongued (modulated) *a* of the word *face.* French words that feature this sound include **machine** (mah-sheen) (*machine*), **madame** (mah-dahm) (*Mrs.*), and **façade** (fah-sahd) (*facade*).

The vowel e

The letter **e** has several sounds in French, To pronounce it by itself, bring your lips almost together and slightly forward, with the tip of your tongue inside your lower front teeth, like for the *e* of *the* (not *thee*). It's used in two main ways in French:

- **e** is mostly silent when it ends a singular or plural word, like **la table** or **les tables** (*the table; the tables*), and all the **-er** verb endings of the present tense, like **je parle** (*I speak*), **tu manges** (*you eat*), **il joue** (*he plays*), and **elles écoutent** (*they listen*). You stop your voice just before the **e** when you say these words. So for instance, the word **table** is pronounced tah-bl in French. (Flip to Chapter 6 for more about **-er** verbs in the present tense.)

- **e** is pronounced as *uh,* like *the,* in two situations:

    - At the end of eight short French words: **de** (*of*), **le** (*the*), **je** (*I*), **me** (*me*), **se** (*oneself*), **que** (*that*), **ce** (*this*), and **ne** (*not*).

    - In the middle of words. Examples of words that feature this sound include: **venir** (vuh-neer) (*to come*), **jeter** (zhuh-tey) (*to throw away*), and **leçon** (luh-soh) (*lesson*).

- **e** is pronounced as *eh,* like in the word *get,* when it precedes a double consonant. Examples of words that feature this sound include: **belle** (behl) (*beautiful*), **cette** (seht) (*this*), and **chaussette** (shoh-seht) (*sock*).

The vowel i

The French **i** has the sound *ee,* like in *ski or sea* but very brief and with the lips stretched way out to the side. It never sounds like the diphthongued *i* in *cries.* Examples of French words that include this sound are **petit** (puh-tee) (*small*) and **assis** (ah-see) (*seated*).

To make the **i** sound, place the tip of your tongue inside your lower front teeth and stretch your lips sideways, as in a giant fake smile!

The vowel o

The French **o** has two sounds:

- ✔ The vowel **o** is pronounced as *ohh* (like in *gl**o**ve*), with the lips somewhat rounded, like the first **o** in in *October* (which is short) but without any diphthong. Here are some examples of words that feature this sound: **octobre** (ohhk-tohh-br) (*October*), **comme** (kohhm) (*like*), and **bonne** (bohhn) (*good*).

- ✔ **O** can also sound like the **o** in *Halloween*. Just don't linger on it like you would in *hello*. The shape of your lips is more rounded than for the other **o** sound; it's pronounced *oh* (as in *go*). Here are some examples of words that feature this sound: **mot** (moh) (*word*), **gros** (groh) (*fat*), **moto** (moh-toh) (*motorcycle*), and **chose** (shohz) (*thing*).

The vowel u

The sound of the **u** is pretty unique to French; the closest sound you can get in English is *ew*, but without the diphthong. But maybe kissing a *mutant* can help? If you pronounce the English word *mutant* without the diphthong, you get close to the French **u**. You can hear this sound in French words like **fume** (fewm) (*smoke*) and **musique** (mew-zeek) (*music*).

If kissing a mutant is not your thing, you can pronounce **u** by putting the tip of your tongue just inside your lower front teeth, and pucker up, as in kissing from a distance! If you are having trouble, try to say the French letter **i** (which sounds like *ee*) but with the lips rounded.

Try to say the following pairs several times in a row, to practice the position of the tongue (the difference being the lips from stretched to the sides to puckered): **si-su**; **ti-tu**; **pi-pu**.

Combining vowels

Now that you've got individual vowels under control, you're ready to combine them to create new sounds. Several combinations are possible, as you find out in the following sections: two or three vowels together or a vowel and a consonant. But each time the sound produced is a vowel sound, even when a consonant is included. (Check out the later section "Considering Consonants" for full details.)

Combinations with a

The combination of **a** + **i** sounds like the first vowel sound (*eh*) in *pleasure*. Examples include **mais** (meh) (*but*), **faire** (fehr) (*to do*), and **jamais** (jah-meh) (*never*).

The combinations **a** + **u** and **e** + **a** + **u** have the sound *oh,* like the **o** in *Halloween*. Examples include, **cadeau** (kah-doh) (*gift*) and **l'eau** (loh) (*the water*).

Combinations with e

The combination **e** + **t** sounds like the first **e** in the English word *ceremony*. It is equivalent to the French **é** (**e** with an acute accent; I talk about this accent later in this chapter). Example words with this sound include **bonnet** (bohh-ney) (*wool cap*), **sonnet** (soh-ney) (*sonnet*), and **cadet** (kah-dey) (*youngest son*).

The combination **e** + **u** has the sound *uh*, like the **e** of *the*. Examples include: **jeu** (juh) (*game*), **peu** (puh) (*a little*), **deux** (duh) (*two*), and all adjectives ending in **eux**, such as **heureux** (uh-ruh) (*happy*).

The combination **e** + **z** also sounds like the first **e** in the English word *ceremony*. It is equivalent to the French **é**. Examples include: **nez** (ney) (*nose*), **chez** (shey) (*at the house of*), and most verb endings for the **vous** form of the present tense, such as **jouez** (zhooh-ey) (*you play*). (See Chapter 6 for details on the present tense.)

Combinations with o

The combination of **o** + **i** and **o** + **y** sounds like *wah,* as in the word *watt*. Examples include words like **quoi** (kwah) (*what*), **foire** (fwahr) (*fair*), and **moi** (mwah) (*me*) and also words with a **y**, like **voyager** (vwah-yah-zhey) (*to travel*).

The combination **o** + **u** has the sound *ooh*, like the **u** of *sushi*, but not at all like the **ou** of *you*, which is modulated! In fact, this difference is what you need to be aware of when pronouncing this sound: Do not modulate it. Examples include **mousse** (moohs) (*foam*), **coude** (koohd) (*elbow*), and **chou** (shooh) (*cabbage*).

Handling nasal sounds

A funny thing happens to the letters **n** and **m** when they get cozy with a vowel. They disappear! And the pair formed by **n/m** and any vowel turns into a new vowel sound that doesn't exist in English, a nasal sound. Some of these sounds may be difficult for you to pronounce, and you should be patient, but no matter what, just know to drop the **n/m**, unless a vowel follows it immediately.

There are three major nasal sounds.

- ✔ The nasal sound **an** (ahN) is like the word *entourage*.

    Spelling: **an, am, en, em**

    Examples: **croissant** (krwah-sahN) (*croissant*), **enfant** (ahN-fahN) (*child*), **lampe** (lahNp) (*lamp*), and **argent** (ahr-zhahN) (*money*).

- ✔ The nasal sound **in** (aN) sounds like the an sound in the English word *anger*.

    Spelling: **in, im, ym, en, ein, ain, un, um, ien, aim, é, en**

    Examples: **vin** (vaN) (*wine*), **plein** (plaN) (*full*), **lundi** (laN-dee) (*Monday*), **parfum** (par-faN) (*perfume*), and **faim** (faN) (*hunger*).

- ✔ The nasal sound **on** (ohN) is like the **on** in the English words *tongue* and *song*, with the lips more rounded.

    Spelling: **on, om**

    Examples: **mouton** (mooh-tohN) (*sheep*), **non** (nohN) (*no*), and **nom** (nohN) (*name*).

One notable exception is the **on** in the word **monsieur** (muh-see-uh) (*mister*). Both **on** and **eu** sound like the **e** of *the* (an *uh* sound).

The words in the following practice questions have one or more combination sounds (underlined). Match the correct sound(s) from the words on the following list to the words in the questions, using the letter given to each sound. Check out the example before you begin.

A. sound like o in *Halloween*

B. sound like ey in *they*

C. sound like on in *tongue*

D. sound like an in ***anger***

E. sound like en in ***en**tourage*

F. sound like wa in ***watt***

G. sound like e in *the*

H. sound like u in *sushi*

0. chap<u>eau</u>

A. A

1. c<u>om</u>b<u>ien</u> _____

2. l<u>oi</u> _____

3. ch<u>am</u>bre _____

4. <u>Eu</u>rope _____

5. v<u>en</u>dredi _____

6. p<u>ain</u> _____

7. m<u>an</u>teau _____

8. parl<u>ez</u> _____

9. p<u>ou</u>ssette _____

10. tr<u>oi</u>s _____

Considering Consonants

Pronouncing French consonants requires more tension of the jaws than English does, because the consonants take shape closer to the front of your mouth than you may be used to. Say *don't eat your soup* in English, and then say **ne mange pas ta soupe** in French. How many consonants do you truly hear in the English sentence? Compared to the French version, the consonants are quieter and less distinct.

The following sections give you the scoop on how to pronounce a variety of French consonants, no matter where they appear in a word.

Conquering a few individual consonants

In general, French consonants have less "color" than their English counterparts in the way they are articulated. For instance, when you say *p* in English, a lot of air passes out of your mouth, and if you put a piece of tissue paper in front of you it would be sent flying. Not so when you say a French **p**. Your tissue paper would pretty much stay put. The *g* also has a lot of punch in English (especially when you add a *d* in front of it), whereas the French g is very quiet. This section gives you the lowdown on French consonants, starting with the infamous **r**.

The infamous French r

You've heard it before: Simply stated, pronouncing the French **r** is not easy. For one thing, it is not a hard and spiteful sound. The French **r** is rather soft, smooth, and suave, to the point that sometimes an English ear doesn't hear it.

To form the French **r**, put the tip of your tongue inside your lower teeth. (It may be unnatural to you because to say the English *r*, you curl your tongue back.) Follow these steps to practice:

1. **Try to say the following sounds:**

   iri-ere-oro-ara, ga-ra-gra, go-ro-gro, gou-rou-grou, gan-gran-grande, gon-gron-gronde, gain-grin-graine

2. **Now that your mouth may be a little used to the French r, try these words, where the r rolls a little. Just don't over roll it!**

   garage, carafe, parade, coraux, peureux

3. **The words of this next set contain a very soft r. Be gentle.**

   père, mère, hiver, misère, légère, meilleur, rivière

Other tricky consonants

Other than the **r**, a few other French consonants present interesting pronunciation traits.

- The French **c** sounds like an **s** in front of **e** and **i** and like a **k** before **a**, **o**, and **u**. (Sometimes you have to break this rule, though; see the later section "Adding the cedilla" for details.)

  Examples of words that feature the **s** sound include: **cigale** (see-gahl) (*cicada*), **pouce** (poohs) (*thumb*), and **face** (fahs) (*face*).

  Examples of words that feature the **k** sound include: **cuisine** (kew-ee-zeen) (*kitchen*), **haricot** (ah-ree-koh) (*bean*), and **curé** (kew-rey) (*curate*).

- The French **g** has the sound *zh* (like the *s* in the word *leisure*) when it's in front of **e** and **i/y**, and it has a hard **g** sound (like *gut*) before **a**, **o**, and **u**.

  Examples of words that feature the *zh* sound include: **gymnase** (zheem-nahz) (*gym*), **original** (oh-ree-zhee-nahl) (*original*), and **végétal** (vey-zhey-tahl) (*vegetal*).

Examples of words that feature the hard sound include: **baguette** (bah-geht) (*baguette*), **garçon** (gahr-sohN) (*boy*), and **frigo** (free-goh) (*fridge*).

✔ The French **j** has the sound *zh*, like the **s** in the words *leisure*. It never sounds like the j in *jam*, except in the word **jean**, which is directly imported from English! Some words that feature this sound include **janvier** (jahN-vee-ey) (*January*), **ajoute** (ah-zhooht) (*add*), and **Jean** (jahN) (*John*).

✔ The French **h** has kind of a sad story: It's ignored by most French words. In a case of a determiner + word that begins with **h**, don't do the liaison that I describe later in this chapter; it's called the *aspirate h*.

Here are some examples of the aspirate h: **des haricots** (dey ah-ree-koh) (*some beans*), **en haut** (ahN oh) (*upstairs*), and **la Hollande** (lah ohh-lahNd) (*Holland*; instead of **l'Hollande**).

✔ In French, **s** sounds like a **z** (as in **z**oo) when it sits alone between two vowels, like in the words: **rose** (rohz) (*rose*) and **fraise** (frehz) (*strawberry*). It sounds like an **s** (as in **s**oft) in all other situations.

✔ The French **t** sounds like an **s** (as in **s**oft) in words that end in -**tion** and -**tie**. These words are generally feminine. The examples I give you have a very close English equivalent, but be sure to pronounce the French -**tion** or -**tie** ending differently from the equivalent English word.

Examples: **aristocratie** (ah-rees-tohh-krah-see) (*aristocracy*), **tradition** (trah-dee-see-ohN) (*tradition*), and **mention** (mahN-see-ohN) (*mention*).

Mixing consonants

Now that you have mastered the individual consonants, how about throwing them into words and observing how they react to other letters?

✔ The French **gn** sounds like the **ny** in the word *canyon*. The examples I give you have a very close English equivalent; be sure to pronounce the French **gn** differently from the equivalent English word.

Examples: **signal** (see-gnahl) (*signal*), **poignant** (pwah-gnahN) (*poignant*), **indigne** (aN-deegn) (*indignant*).

✔ The French **qu** almost always sounds like a **k**, as in the word *burlesque*. In the following examples, be sure to pronounce the French **qu** differently from the equivalent English word.

Examples: **banquet** (bahN-key) (*banquet*), **sequin** (suh-kaN) (*sequin*), **équivalent** (ey-kee-vah-lahN) (*equivalent*).

✔ In French, **th** sounds just a **t**, as in the word *to*. Keep that pronunciation in mind even when the French word is very similar to its English equivalent.

Examples: **thé** (tey) (*tea*), **théâtre** (tey-ahtr) (*theater*), **mythe** (meet) (*myth*).

Focusing on final consonants

You already know that sometimes French doesn't pronounce the final consonant(s) of a word. Need proof? Pronounce the English words that come from French, like *ballet*, *coup*, and *debris*. Don't pronounce a final consonant when:

- ✔ It's an **s** that marks a plural word, as in **amis** (ah-mee) (*friends*) or **voitures** (vwah-tur) (*cars*).

- ✔ It is the final consonant of a word, as in **petit** (puh-tee) (*small*), **parent** (pah-rahN) (*parent*), and **Paris** (pah-ree) (*Paris*).

- ✔ It's the **r** from the **-er** verbs infinitive, as in **parler** (par-ley) (*talk*), **jouer** (zhooh-ey) (*to play*), and **manger** (mahN-zhey) (*eat*).

Of course, this rule has exceptions. If the final consonant is C R F L (the four consonants of the word *careful*, incidentally), then you pronounce it. Here are some examples of these pronounced final consonants:

- ✔ **C: parc** (pahrk) (*park*), **chic** (sheek) (*chic*), **avec** (ah-vehk) (*with*)

- ✔ **R: l'amour** (lah-moohr) (*love*), **pour** (poohr) (*for*)

- ✔ **F: chef** (shehf) (*chief*), **bref** (brehf) (*brief*)

- ✔ **L: sel** (sehl) (*salt*), **idéal** (ee-dey-ahl) (*ideal*), **Noël** (noh-ehl) (*Christmas*)

Just sit tight; you're not done yet. The "careful" exceptions have exceptions of their own!

- ✔ Don't pronounce the final **r** in **-er** verb infinitives. For example, you don't prounounce the final letters of **parler** (pahrl-ey) (*to talk*) and **manger** (mahN-zhey) (*to eat*).

- ✔ Don't pronounce the final consonant of the following words, even though they end in C R F L:

banc (bahN) (*bench*)	**léger** (ley-zhey) (*light*)
blanc (blahN) (*white*)	**nerf** (nehr) (*nerve*)
boulanger (booh-lahN-zhey) (*baker*)	**outil** (ooh-tee) (*tool*)
dernier (dehr-nee-ey) (*last*)	**papier** (pah-pee-ey) (*paper*)
escalier (es-kah-lee-ey) (*stairs*)	**porc** (pohhr) (*pork*)
estomac (ehs-toh-mah) (*stomach*)	**premier** (pruh-mee-ey) (*first*)
franc (frahN) (*frank*)	**tabac** (tah-bah) (*tobacco*)
gentil (zhahN-tee) (*kind*)	

- ✔ Do pronounce the final consonant of the following words, even though they don't end in C R F L:

abrupt (ah-bruhpt) (*abrupt*)	**contact** (kohN-tahkt) (*contact*)
as (ahss) (*ace*)	**coq** (kohhk) (*rooster*)
autobus (oh-toh-bews) (*city bus*)	**direct** (dee-rehkt) (*direct*)
cap (kahp) (*cap*)	**est** (ehst) (*east*)
concept (kohN-sehpt) (*concept*)	**fils** (fees) (*son*)

gas (gahz) (*gaze*)

hélas (hey-lahs) (*unfortunately*)

index (aN-dehks) (*index*)

maïs (mah-ees) (*corn*)

net (neht) (*clear*)

ouest (wehst) (*west*)

script (skreept) (*script*)

sens (sahNs) (*direction*)

sud (sewd) (*south*)

✔ Do pronounce the final consonant of words of foreign origin, like **tennis**, **parking**, **sandwich**, and **jean**.

Working with Accents and the Cedilla

French uses accents on certain vowels for various reasons, and emphasis has nothing to do with it. An accent can change the sound of a vowel or help distinguish between two different words that would otherwise be spelled the same, like **sur** (*on*) and **sûr** (*certain*). The cedilla is a funny-looking mark that always changes the sound of the letter **c** it gets attached to, from a **k** sound to a soft sound like the **s** in *sea*. The following sections explain accents and the cedilla in more detail.

Checking out different types of accent marks

On the letter **e**, a different accent means a different sound. On other vowels, an accent mark does not modify the sound of that vowel, just its appearance, except for the diaeresis. French uses four accents:

✔ The acute, which only goes on the **e**: **é**

✔ The grave, which goes over **e**, **a**, or **u** like this: **è**, **à**, **ù**

✔ The circumflex, which typically goes over the **e** (like this: **ê**), and occasionally over **a** (**â**), **o** (**ô**), and **u** (**û**)

✔ The least-common accent, the diaeresis, which is only used in combinations of vowels like **oë**

The acute

The acute can only sit over the **e**, and it changes its sound from *uh*, like the **e** of *the*, to the first **e** in the English word *ceremony*.

É is the accent of the past tense. All **-er** verbs form their past participle with an **-é** like this: **il a mangé** (*he has eaten*). (See Chapter 15 for the lowdown on the present perfect, also known as the **passé composé**.)

Examples of words ending in **é** are: **liberté** (lee-behr-tey) (*freedom*), **égalité** (ey-gah-lee-tey) (*equality*), and **fraternité** (frah-tehr-nee-tey) (*brotherhood*).

The grave

The grave accent sits over the **a** when it is the prepostion **à**. It distinguishes it from its homonym **a**, which is the third person singular form of the verb **avoir** in present tense. For instance, **Il a une belle voiture** (*He has a nice car*) isn't the same as **Elle habite à Nice** (*She lives in Nice*). The accent doesn't change the pronunciation of the **a**. Other words with **à** are **déjà** (*already*) and **voilà** (*here is*).

The same is true for **ù**. The accent helps distinguish between homonyms like **ou** and **où** (*or* and *where*), for example.

The grave accent does change the pronunciation of the **e**. Say the English word *bet,* which has an *eh* sound, and you'll be close to the French **è** sound.

To get a good grip on the difference between the sounds of the **é** (the acute accent) and the **è** (the grave accent), practice saying the following pairs that end in **é** and **è**:

> **cuisinier-cuisinière** (kew-ee-zee-nee-ey – kew-zee-nee-ehr) (*cook – female cook*)
>
> **berger-bergère** (behr-zhey – behr-gehr) (*shepherd – shepherdess*)
>
> **boulanger-boulangère** (booh-lahN-zhey – booh-lahN-zhehr) (*baker – female baker*)

The circumflex

The circumflex accent is definitely a shy one. It doesn't come out very often, and when it does, it is to mimic the sound of its brother the grave over the letter **e** (see the preceding section). Here are some examples: **bête** (beht) (*beast*), **forêt** (fohh-reh) (*forest*), **fête** (feht) (*party*), **même** (mehm) (*same*).

Over **a**, **o**, and **u**, the circumflex has no sound effect! Here are some examples: **mâle** (mahl) (*male*), **pâle** (pahl) (*pale*), **théâtre** (tey-ah-tr) (*theatre*), **sûr** (sur) (*certain*), and **tôt** (toht) (*early*).

However, the circumflex comes in handy when distinguishing between nearly identical words! It makes the difference between **du** and **dû** (dew) (*some* and *due*), **jeune** and **jeûne** (zhuhn) (*young* and *fast*), and **mur** and **mûr** (mewr) (*wall* and *ripe*).

The diaeresis

The diaeresis (called the **tréma** in French) is only a cousin of the three accents in the preceding sections because it affects the sound of a pair of vowels, not just one. When it sits above the second one of a pair, the diaeresis indicates that each vowel must be pronounced alone. For instance in the word **mais** (meh) (*but*), the pair **a** + **i** make one single sound. Put the diaeresis over the **i** and you get a different word: **maïs** (mah-ees) (*corn*), where the **a** and the **i** are pronounced separately.

Adding the cedilla

Once upon a time, sweet little **c**, which was on hard **k** sound duty, developed a soft spot for the letters **e** and **i**. Each time it saw them, **c** would curl up into a soft **ç** and whistle *sssss* (it couldn't whistle very well). And so now **c** had two different sounds: a hard **k** as in the English word *cod* in front of **a**, **o**, and **u**; and a soft **s** as in *sofa* in front of **e** and **i**!

If you want that soft **s** sound in front of **a**, **o**, and **u**, then you use a **c** with a cedilla. **Garçon** (gahr-sohN) (*boy*) and **reçu** (ruh-sew) (*received*) are examples of the **ç** in use. In these instances, the **c** sound isn't hard like usual; it's soft.

Correct the spelling of the following words by adding the cedilla when necessary, and write a 0 when no action is needed.

O. **ca** (*that*)

A. ça

11. **Francais** (*French*) _____

12. **facon** (*manner*) _____

13. **cet** (*this*) _____

14. **facade** (*facade*) _____

15. **foncé** (*dark*) _____

16. **garcon** (*boy*) _____

17. **glace** (*ice*) _____

18. **commencer** (*to begin*) _____

19. **fiancailles** (*engagement*) _____

20. **saucisse** (*sausage*) _____

Making Your French Sound Polished with the Liaison

When you listen to French being spoken, do you ever try to pick out single words that you may recognize? And find yourself often unable to do so? That's because French speakers like to link everything together! The **liaison** is the main culprit in this affair because it links words together by adding sounds to the sentence. You have to be careful because this rule of French pronunciation is invisible (does not appear in writing).

The most common sounds added by the **liaison** are:

- The sound **z** that occurs between **s** or **x** and a vowel, as in **les amis** (ley-zah-mee) (*the friends*) and **beaux oiseaux** (boh-zwah-zoh) (*beautiful birds*).

- The sound **t** between **t** or **d** and a vowel, as in **petit enfant** (puh-tee-tan-fahN) (*little kid*) and **grand arbre** (grahN-tahr-br) (*big tree*).

- The sound **n** between **n** and a vowel, as in **un étudiant** (aN-ney-tew-dee-ahN) (*a student*) and **on aime** (ohN-nehm) (*we like*).

These liaisons occur less frequently:

✓ The sound **p** between **p** and a vowel, as in **beaucoup aimé** (boh-kooh-peh-mey) (*loved a lot*).

✓ The sound **v** between **f** and the words **an** (*year*) and **heure** (*hour*), as in **neuf heures** (nuh-vuhr) (*nine o'clock*) and **neuf ans** (nuh-vahN) (*nine years*).

Be careful, because you can't use the **liaison** every time you find a word ending in one of those consonants followed by a vowel! As you find out in the following sections, sometimes you have to use it, and sometimes you must not use it.

The **liaison** has a sidekick, called the *linking* (**l'enchaînement**). It consists of using a pronounced final consonant (at the end of a word) to bridge over the first vowel of the following word, making the two words sound as one. Here is an example: **Paul est arrivé** (*Paul has arrived*) sounds like this when you do the **enchaînement** and the **liaison:** poh-leh-tah-ree-vey, with the **l** of **Paul** now grouped with the next word. See the later section "Breaking words and sentences into syllables" for more information.

Knowing when you have to use the liaison

When you know a little bit of French and you read the sentence **elle est ici** (eh-ley-tee-see) (*she's here*), you may think of the last-consonant rules I explain in the earlier section "Focusing on final consonants" and think the **t** should be silent. And yet, when you hear this phrase aloud, you definitely hear a **t**. What gives? You hear it because of the **liaison** between **est** and **ici;** there's a *t* sound between the **t** of **est** and the **i** of **ici.** And you always hear this one, because it's a mandatory liaison. Other types of **liaison** are also mandatory.

You must do a **liaison** between two words in the following cases:

✓ The two words are a determiner and a noun that begins with a vowel, singular or plural.

For example: **un ami** (aN-nah-mee) (*a friend*), **des enfants** (deh-zahN-fahN) (*some kids*), **ces étudiants** (sey-zey-tew-dee-anN) (*these students*).

A determiner is a little word used to determine a noun. Determiners match the noun in gender and number and are required 99 percent of the time. They are: articles, possessives, demonstratives, and interrogatives like **quel** (*which/what*) (see Chapter 3 for more on determiners).

✓ The two words are an adjective and a noun, plural or singular, that begins with a vowel.

For example: **petit éléphant** (puh-tee-tey-ley-fahN) (*small elephant*), **beaux arbres** (boh-zahr-br) (*beautiful trees*).

The opposite is not true: Usually you don't use a liaison between a noun followed by its adjective, as in **enfants ° intelligents** (*intelligent kids*). (The ° symbol means that there is no liaison between these two words.)

✔ The two words are a short preposition or some short adverbs and a word that begins with a vowel.

For example: **en acier** (ahN-nahs-ee-ey) (*in steel*)

✔ The two words are a subject pronoun and a verb that begins with a vowel.

For example: **ils arrivent** (eel-zah-reev) (*they're arriving*), **nous aimons** (nooh-zey-mohN) (*we like*)

✔ The two words are an object pronoun and a verb that begins with a vowel.

For example: **tu en as** (tew ahN-nah) (*you have some*)

✔ The two words are a verb and an object or subject pronoun that begins with a vowel (**il**, **elle**, **on**, **ils**, and **elles**) or an object pronoun: **en** and **y**.

For example: **Vas-y!** (vah-zee) (*Go there!*)

✔ The two words are the third person singular and plural (**ils/elles**; **il/elle/on**) of the verb **être** in any tense and a word that begins with a vowel:

For example: **c'est affreux** (sey-tah-fruh) (*it's awful*), **c'était inévitable** (sey-teh-tehn-hey-vee-tahbl) (*it was unavoidable*)

Figuring out when you shouldn't use the liaison

Other times, even though you may be in the presence of a pair where the first word ends in a consonant and the second one begins with a vowel, you should not use the **liaison**. Don't do **liaison** between two words when they are:

✔ The word **et** (*and*) and any word that begins with a vowel: **toi et ° elle** (twah-ey-ehl) (*you and her*).

✔ A name and a word that begins with a vowel: **Robert ° arrive** (roh-behr-ah-reev) (*Robert is arriving*),

✔ A singular noun and an adjective that begins with a vowel: **avocat ° attentif** (ah-voh-kah-ah-tahN-teef) (*focused lawyer*)

✔ A plural noun and a verb that begins with a vowel: **les filles ° aiment danser** (ley-fee-ehm-dahn-sey) (*girls like to dance*)

✔ **ils**, **elles**, or **on** and a past participle that begins with a vowel, in an inversion: **Ont-ils ° aimé le film?** (OhN-teel-eh-mey-luh-feelm) (*Did they like the movie?*)

✔ The question words **comment** (*how*), **combien** (*how many/much*), and **quand** (*when*), and a word that begins with a vowel: **Quand ° irez-vous** (kahN-ee-rey-vooh) (*When will you go*), **Combien ° avez-vous** (kohn-bee-ahN-ahv-ey-vooh) (*How many do you have?*), **Comment ° ont-ils fait ça?** (koh-mahN-onh-teel-feh-sa) (*How did they manage that?*)

 Two fixed phrases are exceptions to this final rule: **Comment allez-vous?** (koh-mahn-tah-ley-vooh) (*How are you?*) and questions beginning with **quand est-ce que . . .** (kahN-tehs-kuh) (*When . . .*)

Surveying Stress and Syllables

No doubt it takes a while to master French pronunciation. On top of letters that sound different, there's also the "music" of a sentence that is different from English. In music what's important is the beat, the rhythm. And the music of the language has a rhythm, too! To help you get into the right one, you have to think of two things: syllables (sound units) and stress, or rather, absence thereof in French.

Keeping stress out of French words

Ever heard a French person say the word *Mississippi*? It sounds nothing like the original! And yet it's a very simple word. The hiccup for a French person is the stress that English puts on the second **-ssi** (third syllable).

In French, all syllables of a word are created equal. The flip side of this is that, when you say that word in French, you should drop the stress, or risk not being well understood by a French person. The only stress French may add is more like an emotional one, and it is put on a whole word (as opposed to a syllable in English) in a sentence, as in **Tu as vu ça?!** (Tew-ah-vuh-sah) (*Did you see that?!*) with a big emphasis on **ça**.

Try pronouncing the following French words (that look just like their English counterparts), putting the stress on the very last syllable, and then do a second pass without any stress at all. What a difference, right? I detach that last syllable from the rest of the word by a hyphen.

- **constitu-tion** (kohNs-tee-tew-seeohN)
- **démocra-tique** (dey-moh-krah-teek)
- **élec-trique** (ey-lehk-treek)
- **élé-phant** (ey-ley-fahN)
- **i-diot** (ee-deeoh)
- **médi-cal** (mey-dee-kahl)
- **ré-flexe** (rey-flehks)
- **républi-cain** (rey-puh-blee-kaN)
- **restau-rant** (rehs-toh-rahN)
- **Virgi-nie** (veer-zhee-nee)

Breaking words and sentences into syllables

Understanding syllables and what they do for you gets you one step closer to mastering French pronunciation. A *syllable* is a unit of pronunciation, and each sentence you utter can be broken into a number of syllables. For instance, the sentence *The students are happy* has six syllables: the-stu-dents-are-ha-ppy. Note that syllables do their own thing, regardless of word boundaries! They are just sounds, without meaning of their own.

To syllabize words, simply say them out loud and count how many sounds you hear:

- ✔ The word **bonjour** (*hello*) has two syllables: **bon-jour**
- ✔ **Déjeuner** has three syllables: **dé-jeu-ner**
- ✔ **Provençal** has three syllables: **pro-ven-çal**

Syllabizing a sentence takes into account the added sounds of the **liaison** and the linking of words (I discuss the liaison earlier in this chapter). Consider this example:

> **Paul est arrivé.** (*Paul has arrived.*)

When you say this sentence, you break it down into five syllables, regardless of individual word boundaries and of spelling: pah-leh-tah-ree-vey. The second syllable, leh, comes from the linking of **Paul** and **est**. Notice the third syllable (tah). I add a **t** sound that wasn't there originally because of the **liaison** between the words **est** and **arrivé**.

Here's another example that also includes a **liaison** and a linking. **C'est pour un ami.** (*It is for a friend.*) I can break it down into five syllables, like so: **sey-poh-ruhN-ah-mee**. Did you notice the extra **na** sound? It's due to the liaison again, between the words **un** and **ami**.

If you try to say these sentences word by word, you'll get by and you will be understood. However, if you try to pronounce them the way I just showed you, your ear will get used to that rhythm, and it will really help your understanding of spoken French.

Write how many syllables these words and sentences have. Here's an example:

0. matin

A. 2

21. Virginie _____

22. constitution _____

23. il déjeune à midi _____

24. elle est belle _____

25. c'est un ami _____

26. petit à petit _____

27. bonjour maman _____

28. la ratatouille est un plat provençal _____

29. écoutez le professeur _____

30. je n'ai pas compris _____

Answer Key

1 C and D

2 F

3 E

4 G

5 E

6 D

7 E and A

8 B

9 H and G

10 F

11 **Français**

12 **façon**

13 0

14 **façade**

15 0

16 **garçon**

17 0

18 0

19 **fiançailles**

20 0

21 3: veer-gee-nee

22 4: kohn-stee-tew-shohn

`23` 6: eel-dey-zhuh-nah-mee-dee

`24` 5: ehl-eh-behl

`25` 4: sey-taN-na-mee

`26` 5: puh-tee-ta-puh-tee

`27` 4: bohn-zhoohr-mah-mahN

`28` 10: lah-rah-tah-tooh-yey-taN-plah-proh-vahN-sahl

`29` 7: ey-kooh-tey-luh-prohh-feh-suhr

`30` 5: zhuh-ney-pah-kohN-pree

Chapter 3

Using Nouns and Determiners

*I*n French, like in English, a noun names beings and things. The big difference though is that French refers to all beings and things as masculine and feminine! Everything has a gender, from spiders to saints.

You can go about finding out if a noun is masculine (a *he*) or feminine (a *she*) in several ways. First, you can look up the noun in a French-English dictionary and check out whether the word is indicated **n.m.** (masculine noun) or **n.f.** (feminine noun). But you can also consider a set of characteristics that help you tell masculine and feminine nouns apart, including the articles, possessives, and demonstratives that accompany nouns, and this chapter details them all for you.

Finding the Gender of Nouns

When a noun describes a live being, its gender often reflects the gender of the being in question. For example: The word **cheval** (*horse*) is masculine, whereas **jument** (*mare*) is feminine, because they both reflect the gender of the animal. Makes sense? Good. But determining gender isn't always that logical, especially with inanimate objects, like things and ideas.

For nouns that describe things and concepts, logic has nothing to do with the gender. For instance, some nouns are always masculine no matter what, like **un sac** (*a bag*), **un manteau** (*an overcoat*), and **un ordinateur** (*a computer*). Others are always feminine, like **une voiture** (*a car*), **une maison** (*a house*), and **une école** (*a school*). And some words are the tricksters of the bunch, taking on different meanings with different genders, like **livre**, which is a *book* when masculine but a *pound* when feminine!

The following sections help you identify a number of masculine and feminine nouns; they also discuss nouns of fixed gender and feminine nouns derived from masculine nouns.

I recommend always checking the gender of an unfamiliar noun in a French-English dictionary.

Identifying masculine nouns

The following sections cover a number of patterns you can use to recognize inanimate masculine nouns. Just keep in mind that as helpful as these patterns are, you always have to be prepared to deal with nouns that don't fall into categories. Listing them all would be way too long and beyond the scope of this book.

Picking out masculine nouns by their endings

You can recognize many masculine nouns by the type of ending they have. Table 3-1 presents some of the most common examples of the masculine endings.

Table 3-1	Typical Masculine Noun Endings
Noun Ending	**Examples**
-acle	**miracle** (*miracle*), **spectacle** (*show*), **obstacle** (*obstacle*)
-age	**fromage** (*cheese*), **voyage** (*trip*), **bagage** (*luggage*)
-aire	**frigidaire** (*fridge*), **anniversaire** (*birthday*), **commentaire** (*commentary*)
-é (but not -té)	**degré** (*degree*), **marché** (*market*), **congé** (*holiday*)
-eau	**drapeau** (*flag*), **chapeau** (*hat*), **cadeau** (*gift*)
-er and -ier	**dîner** (*dinner*), **panier** (*basket*), **cahier** (*notebook*)
-isme	**tourisme** (*tourism*), **absolutisme** (*absolutism*), **capitalisme** (*capitalism*)
-ment	**gouvernement** (*government*), **ornement** (*ornament*), **divertissement** (*entertainment*)

Noting masculine nouns by category

Besides just memorizing noun endings (in the preceding section), you can also spot masculine nouns by certain categories. For the most part, nouns included in the following categories are masculine:

✔ Names of trees: **chêne** (*oak tree*), **olivier** (*olive tree*), **pommier** (*apple tree*)

✔ Names of metals: **or** (*gold*), **acier** (*steel*), **fer** (*iron*)

✔ Names of metric units: **mètre** (*a meter*), **kilo** (*a kilo*), **centimètre** (*centimeter*)

✔ Names of colors: **le rouge** (*red*), **le vert** (*green*), **le bleu** (*blue*)

✔ Names of languages: **le chinois** (*chinese*), **l'allemand** (*german*), **le français** (*French*)

✔ Nouns of English origin: **tennis** (*tennis*), **parking** (*parking lot*), **football** (*soccer*)

I note the articles (**le** and **l'**) in front of colors and languages above, because without them, the French words would be adjectives instead of nouns. You can find out more about articles in the later section "Using Articles to Help You with Nouns' Gender."

Recognizing feminine nouns

In the following sections, I give you some helpful tips to spot a feminine noun, based on its ending or category.

Picking out feminine nouns by their endings

Table 3-2 gives you the noun endings that typically designate female gender and some common examples.

Table 3-2	Typical Feminine Noun Endings
Noun Ending	**Examples**
-ade	**façade** (*facade*), **promenade** (*a walk*), **limonade** (*lemon drink*)
-ance	**enfance** (*childhood*), **naissance** (*birth*), **assurance** (*insurance*)
-ée	**idée** (*idea*), **journée** (*day*), **mosquée** (*mosque*)
-ence	**différence** (*difference*), **innocence** (*innocence*), **influence** (*influence*)
-ette	**crevette** (*shrimp*), **chaussette** (*sock*), **baguette** (*baguette*)
-ie	**comédie** (*comedy*), **industrie** (*industry*), **démographie** (*demography*)
-sion	**prévision** (*forecast*), **compréhension** (*understanding*), **révision** (*revision*)
-té	**société** (*society*), **publicité** (*advertising*), **charité** (*charity*)
-tié	**amitié** (*friendship*), **moitié** (*half*), **pitié** (*pity*)
-tion	**information** (*information*), **éducation** (*education*), **question** (*question*)
-ure	**voiture** (*car*), **couverture** (*blanket*), **confiture** (*jelly/jam*)

Noting feminine nouns by category

A number of more logical categories also help you spot those feminine nouns. For the most part, nouns included in the following categories are feminine:

- Names of sciences and school subjects: For example, **chimie** (*chemistry*), **histoire** (*history*), and **médecine** (*medical sciences*). In particular, sciences and subjects ending in **-graphie** — like **photographie** (*photography*), **géographie** (*geography*), and **chorégraphie** (*choreography*) — are feminine.

- Names of automobiles: **une Renault** (*a Renault*), **une Porsche** (*a Porsche*), **une Fiat** (*a Fiat*).

- Names of businesses: **boulangerie** (*bread shop*), **parfumerie** (*perfume shop*), **charcuterie** (*deli*).

Determine whether the following nouns are masculine (write M) or feminine (write F), based on their ending. Here's an example:

Q. boucherie

A. F

1. littérature ____

2. isolement ____

3. épicerie ____

4. rouge ____

5. cadeau ____

6. modération ____

7. anniversaire ____

8. baguette ____

9. fer ____

10. publicité ____

Fixing on nouns with fixed gender

Some nouns referring to beings are either always masculine or always feminine, regardless of the gender of the being described. For example, **professeur** (*professor*) is always masculine in French, even though the person being described can be a man or a woman. Here are examples of nouns with a fixed gender:

- ✔ **une personne** (*a person*, male or female)
- ✔ **une connaissance** (*an acquaintance*, male or female)
- ✔ **une mouche** (*a fly*, male or female)
- ✔ **une victime** (*a casualty*, male or female)
- ✔ **un bébé** (*a baby*, male or female)

If a woman's profession is named with a masculine word, like **un peintre** (*a painter*), you just add the word **femme** (*woman*) in front of the masculine noun, like this: **une femme peintre**. Other examples are **une femme soldat** (a female soldier) and **une femme médecin** (a female doctor).

The noun **médecine** exists, but it is not the feminine form of **médecin** (*doctor*). It means *medical science* and is used with a definite article: **la médecine**.

Deriving feminine nouns from their masculine counterparts

Some masculine nouns describing males have feminine equivalents to describe their female counterparts. These feminine nouns are often derived from the masculine form, the same way the adjectives go from masculine to feminine (see Chapter 4).

Here are some examples:

Masculine	*Feminine*
président (*male president*)	**présidente** (*female president*)
infirmier (*male nurse*)	**infirmière** (*female nurse*)
acteur (*actor*)	**actrice** (*actress*)
boulanger (*male baker*)	**boulangère** (*female baker*)
veuf (*widower*)	**veuve** (*widow*)

But the feminine noun is not always derived from the masculine, and that's when a French-English dictionary comes in handy! Here are examples of such pairs:

Masculine	*Feminine*
roi (*king*)	**reine** (*queen*)
homme (*man*)	**femme** (*woman*)
garçon (*boy*)	**fille** (*girl*)
oncle (*uncle*)	**tante** (*aunt*)

Still other nouns share the same form in masculine and feminine, and the only way to tell them apart is their article, like **un camarade** (masculine for *comrade*) and **une camarade** (feminine for *comrade*). Similar nouns include the following (see the later section "Using Articles to Help You with Nouns' Gender" for more about articles):

Masculine	*Feminine*
un enfant (*a male child*)	**une enfant** (*a female child*)
un malade (*a sick male*)	**une malade** (*a sick female*)
un athlète (*a male athlete*)	**une athlète** (*a female athlete*)
un touriste (*a male tourist*)	**une touriste** (*a female tourist*)
un artiste (*a male artist*)	**une artiste** (*a female artist*)

Making Nouns Plural

When you need to talk about more than one thing in French, you need the plural of a noun, just like in English. The following sections show you how to go from the singular of a noun to its plural.

Applying a simple rule

The most common form of plural is to add **-s** or **-x** to a masculine or feminine noun. Most nouns take **-s** in the plural. Here are some examples:

Singular	Plural
résultat (*result*)	**résultats** (*results*)
ville (*city*)	**villes** (*cities*)
fou (*madman*)	**fous** (*madmen*)
fleur (*flower*)	**fleurs** (*flowers*)

Adding **-s** to a noun to make it plural does not change its pronunciation. Flip to Chapter 2 for more about sounding out French words.

Nouns that end in **-au** take **-x** in the plural. Here are some examples:

Singular	Plural
manteau (*overcoat*)	**manteaux** (*overcoats*)
bateau (*boat*)	**bateaux** (*boats*)
traineau (*sleigh*)	**traineaux** (*sleighs*)

Examining a few oddballs

Some nouns become a little odd when they're plural. For example, most nouns that end in **-ou** take **-s** in the plural, but some take **-x**. They include:

Singular	Plural
chou (*cabbage*)	**choux** (*cabbages*)
bijou (*jewel*)	**bijoux** (*jewels*)
genou (*knee*)	**genoux** (*knees*)
caillou (*pebble*)	**cailloux** (*pebbles*)

Nouns that end in **-al** drop that ending for an **-aux** ending in the plural. They include:

Singular	*Plural*
cheval (*horse*)	**chevaux** (*horses*)
hôpital (*hospital*)	**hôpitaux** (*hospitals*)
journal (*newspaper*)	**journaux** (*newspapers*)
signal (*signal*)	**signaux** (*signals*)
animal (*animal*)	**animaux** (*animals*)

Nouns that end in **-s**, **-x**, or **-z** don't change at all in the plural; you just change the article, like so:

Singular	*Plural*
une fois (*one time*)	**des fois** (*several times*)
un virus (*a virus*)	**des virus** (*viruses*)
un Français (*a Frenchman*)	**des Français** (*Frenchmen*)
un prix (*a price*)	**des prix** (*prices*)
un nez (*a nose*)	**des nez** (*noses*)

Family names are not pluralized in French. For example, *the Martins* loses the **-s** in French: **Les Martin**.

As you know, some English nouns are always singular, such as *fruit* and *shrimp*. Their French equivalents don't necessarily have that irregularity; some on the contrary are always plural. For example, two common non-matching plurals words between French and in English are *hair* and *vacation*. In French they are the plural nouns **vacances** (*vacation*) and **cheveux** (*hair*).

If you're not sure about a word, look it up in an English-French dictionary.

Give the plural of the following masculine and feminine nouns.

0. **fois**

A. **fois**

11. **animal** (*animal*) _____

12. **quartier** (*neighborhood*) _____

13. **eau** (*water*) _____

14. **bijou** (*jewel*) _____

15. **fille** (*girl*) _____

16. **Français** (*Frenchman*) _____

17. fruit (*fruit*) _____

18. cadeau (*gift*) _____

19. roi (*king*) _____

20. cou (*neck*) _____

Using Articles to Help You with Nouns' Gender

A sure way to know the gender of a noun is to look at its article — when it's available, of course! Like English, French has definite articles, indefinite articles, and partitive articles. Obviously, French has more articles than English because of the gender issue. You have a lot to choose from, and you have to choose often because in French, a noun is used with an article 99 percent of the time. The following sections go over the different types of articles and tell you how to choose among them.

Delving into definite articles

The French definite article is the equivalent of *the*. But French has four forms of **article défini**. Table 3-3 details these forms and their usage.

Table 3-3	French Definite Articles	
French Article	**Usage in French**	**Example**
le	Before masculine singular nouns	**le matin** (*the morning*)
la	Before feminine singular nouns	**la vie** (*life*)
l'	Before masculine or feminine singular nouns beginning with a vowel or a mute -**h**	**l'amour** (*love*)
les	Before masculine or feminine plural nouns	**les bonbons** (*candies*)

Le and **les** disappear completely when they are preceded by the prepositions **à** (*at*) and **de** (*of/from*). This omission is called a contraction, and here's what happens:

- ✔ **à** + **le** changes to **au**
- ✔ **de** + **le** changes to **du**
- ✔ **à** + **les** changes to **aux**
- ✔ **de** + **les** changes to **des**

Here are some examples:

Il va au (à + le) travail. (*He goes to work.*)

Nous rentrons des (de + les) îles. (*We're returning from the islands.*)

So when can you use definite articles?

✔ Use a definite article to accompany a noun when you're expressing a preference, using a verb like **aimer** (*to like/to love*), **préférer** (*to prefer*), or **détester** (*to detest*). Here are some examples:

> **J'aime le chocolat.** (*I like chocolate.*)
>
> **Il déteste les huîtres.** (*He hates oysters.*)

Negative preferences still count as preferences (see Chapter 8 for more about negative words and phrases). Here's what I mean:

> **Elle n'aime pas les bananes.** (*She does not like bananas.*)
>
> **Tu n'aimes pas le froid.** (*You don't like the cold.*)

✔ Use a definite article to name a category in general, like **les hommes** (*men*) or **le pain** (*bread*), or a concept, like **la vie** (*life*) or **l'amour** (*love*). Note that in English, the article is often skipped in such instances. Here are some examples:

> **C'est la vie.** (*That's life.*)
>
> **Le prix de l'essence a encore augmenté.** (*The price of gas went up again.*)

✔ Use a definite article to refer to something known to the listeners because it is unique (there's only one). For example:

> **Le président va faire un discours.** (*The president is going to make a speech.*)
>
> **Le Pape est allé au Mexique.** (*The pope went to Mexico.*)

✔ Use a definite article to refer to something made specific by what follows it. For example:

> **Le chat des voisins est un siamois.** (*The neighbors' cat is a Siamese.*)
>
> **Le livre que tu m'as prêté est formidable.** (*The book you lent me is great.*)

✔ Use a definite article to name a geographical place.

> **la France** (*France*)
>
> **les États-Unis** (*the United States*)

✔ Use a definite article before a day of the week to indicate *every*.

> **le lundi** (*every Monday* or *on Mondays*)
>
> **le dimanche** (*every Sunday* or *on Sundays*)

✔ Use a definite article (instead of a possessive adjective like in English) before a part of the body, with a reflexive verb (for more on reflexive verbs, see Chapter 7). Here are a few examples:

> **Tu te brosses les dents.** (*You're brushing your teeth.*)
>
> **Nous nous lavons les mains.** (*We wash our hands.*)

✔ Use a definite article to name languages. For example:

> **Il apprend l'italien.** (*He's learning Italian.*)
>
> **J'étudie le français.** (*I study French.*)

Give the appropriate definite article for each noun. To figure out the gender, follow guidance from the earlier section "Finding the Gender of Nouns."

0. _____ États-Unis

A. les

21. _____ amour

22. _____ médecin

23. _____ couverture

24. _____ fromage

25. _____ céréales

Discovering indefinite articles

Do you ask about *one* thing, describe *a couple of* things that happened, and make plans for *an* outing that hasn't yet been defined? If so, you're an indefinite article kind of person, like the French! And as such, you should treat the **article indéfini** as the default article in French. The French indefinite article is the equivalent to *a/an* and *some* (but English often skips it). Table 3-4 details French indefinite articles.

Table 3-4	French Indefinite Articles		
French Article	*Usage in French*	*English Equivalent*	*Example*
un	Before masculine singular nouns	*a/an*	**un chat** (*a cat*)
une	Before feminine singular nouns	*a/an*	**une maison** (*a house*)
des	Before masculine or feminine plural nouns	*some*	**des enfants** (*some children*)
de, or **d'** before nouns beginning with a vowel or a mute -**h**	Instead of any indefinite article, after a negative verb	*no* or *not any*	**pas d'ordinateur** (*no computer*)

Use the indefinite article when you talk about one or several individual things that you can count, as opposed to an entire category of things.

Il y a un livre sur la table. (*There is a book on the table.*)

Tu as mangé une banane. (*You ate a/one banana.*)

Il a vu des lions au zoo. (*He saw (some) lions at the zoo.*)

You also can use the indefinite articles **un** and **une** before an expression of quantity, like **une tranche de** (*a slice of*), **un morceau de** (*a piece of*), and **un peu de** (*a little bit of*). For more on those, see Chapter 5.

In a sentence with a negative verb, **un**, **une**, and **des** are replaced by **de**, even if the noun it introduces is plural. Here are some examples.

> **Il n'y a pas de souris dans notre garage.** (*There is not a mouse in our garage.*)

> **Elle ne veut pas d'enfants.** (*She doesn't want any children.*)

 This rule has one exception. Don't use **de** when the negative verb is **être** (*to be*). Just use the indefinite article as if the sentence was affirmative. Here are some examples:

> **Cet animal n'est pas un chien. C'est un renard.** (*This animal is not a dog. It's a fox.*)

> **—C'est une voiture rouge, n'est-ce pas? —Non ce n'est pas une voiture rouge! C'est une voiture noire.** (*—It's a red car, right? —No, it's not a red car! It's a black car.*)

 Choose between the definite article (**le**, **la**, **l'**, **les**) and the indefinite article (**un**, **une**, **des**, and **de**) to complete the sentences. Check a French-English dictionary if you need help with the vocabulary. Here's an example.

Q. **Nous avons mangé _____ tarte.**

A. **une**

26. _____ France est magnifique.

27. Vous étudiez _____ français.

28. Il n'aime pas _____ chocolat.

29. As-tu déja mangé _____ escargots?

30. Ce n'est pas _____ avion. C'est un nuage.

31. As-tu _____ enfants?

32. Il y a _____ oiseaux sur la branche.

33. C'est _____ livre du prof.

34. Nous avons visité _____ Canada récemment.

35. Il n'y a pas _____ pommes sur l'arbre.

Assessing partitive articles

Last night, did you eat *a whole chicken* (**un poulet**)? Or just *some* of it (**du poulet**)? In the morning, do you drink *all the coffee in the world* (**le café**), or more reasonably *some coffee* (**du café**)? Partitive articles are just what you need to express those reasonable quantities of things that can't be handled as a whole but can't be counted as one, two, or three either. French has four partitives, and Table 3-5 presents them with their English equivalents.

Table 3-5	French Partitive Articles		
French Article	*Usage in French*	*English Equivalent*	*Example*
du	Before masculine singular nouns	*some*	**du pain** (*some bread*)
de la	Before feminine singular nouns	*some*	**de la soupe** (*some soupe*)
de l'	Before masculine or feminine singular nouns beginning with a vowel or a mute **-h**	*some*	**de l'eau** (*some water*)
des	Before masculine or feminine plural nouns	*some/any*	**des petits pois** (*peas*)
de	Instead of any partitive article, after a negative verb	*no* or *not any*	**pas de café** (*no coffee*)

You put partitive articles to good use in the following ways:

✔ Use the partitive before a noun that describes a partial category. For example:

Elle met du sucre dans son café. (*She puts (some) sugar in her coffee.*)

À table nous buvons de l'eau minérale. (*At the table, we drink some bottled water.*)

✔ Use **d'** instead of **des** before the plural adjective **autres** (*others*). For example:

Avez-vous d'autres idées? (*Do you have other ideas?*)

✔ Use the partitive after **faire** (*to do/to make* or *to practice*) + a sport, a musical instrument, or a school subject. Each category is named using the definite article, so **de** + some definite articles are contracted: **de** + **le** forms **du**; **de** + **les** forms **des**. For example:

Paul fait de l'escrime. (*Paul fences.*)

Je fais du violon. (*I play the violin.*)

Ce semestre elle fait de la chimie. (*This semester, she studies chemistry.*)

✔ Use the partitive after **jouer** (*to play*) + a musical instrument. (**Jouer** is more common than **faire** in this expression.) The contracted forms of **de** + definite article apply here as well. For example:

Nous jouons du piano et nous chantons. (*We play piano and we sing.*)

In a negative sentence, **du**, **de la**, **de l'**, and **des** are replaced by **de**, whether the noun is singular or plural. Here are some examples:

> **Cet homme n'a pas de chance.** (*This man has no luck.*)
>
> **Nous ne mettons pas de glaçons dans notre eau.** (*We don't put ice cubes in our water.*)

This rule has one exception. Don't use **de** when the negative verb is **être** (*to be*), like for the indefinite articles in the preceding section. Just use the partitive as if the sentence was affirmative. Here are some examples:

> **Ne bois pas ça. Ce n'est pas de l'eau, c'est de la vodka!** (*Don't drink that. It's not water, it's vodka!*)
>
> **Ce ne sont pas des haricots verts, ce sont des fèves.** (*These are not green beans, they are fava beans.*)

Choose the correct partitive to complete each sentence. Choose between **du**, **de la**, **de l'**, **des**, and **de**.

Q. **Il faut gagner _____ argent.**

A. **de l'**

36. **Le vendredi, mangez _____ poisson.**

37. **Paul fait _____ gym.**

38. **Je mets _____ sucre dans mon café.**

39. **Vous buvez _____ eau.**

40. **Tu n'as pas _____ chance!**

Selecting the correct article

Un pain? Du pain? Le pain? Still not sure? Here I compare some articles to give you a few more tips on how to pick the right one.

✔ **Partitive or definite?** The difference between partitive and definite articles is the difference between partial category and whole category. For instance, you drink *(some)* water (partial category, requiring a partitive article) but not all the water in the world (whole category, requiring a definite article). Here's another example that contrasts the two:

> **Quand on travaille, on gagne de l'argent.** (*When you work, you make money.*) But not all the money in the world.
>
> **L'argent est nécessaire.** (*Money is necessary.*) Refers to *money* in a general way.

✔ **Partitive or indefinite?** The difference between partitive and indefinite articles is the difference between something you can't really count, like *water* (**de l'eau**), *spinach* (**des épinards**), and *coffee* (**du café**), all requiring a partitive article, and something you can actually count, like *a cat* (**un chat**) and an apple (**une pomme**), all requiring an indefinite article. Here are examples that contrast the two:

Uncountable: **Nous mangeons du poisson.** (*We eat fish.*)

Countable: **Tu as acheté des baguettes.** (*You bought some baguettes.*)

Expressing Possession

Is it *Paul's book?* Or is it *your book?* In English, you have two ways of being possessive, and French also has two ways — but they are a bit different, and of course you have to take care to use the correct gender. The following sections show you how to say something like *his book* and also how to turn things around to say *Paul's book.*

Considering common possessives

The word *possession* implies an owner and an object owned. In English, the possessive is only concerned with the owner. You say *his books* and *his car. His* reflects only the *he* owner, not the *books* (which are masculine, plural) or the *car* (which is feminine, singular). French takes everything into consideration: who the owner is (yourself, him, them), like in English, and also the gender and number of the object owned. Table 3-6 shows you how for a single English possessive adjective, French has two or three equivalents.

Table 3-6	French Possessive Adjectives		
Owner	*Gender and Number of Object Owned*	*French Possessive*	*Example*
je (*I*)	masculine singular	**mon** (*my*)	**mon sac** (*my bag*)
	feminine singular	**ma** (*my*)	**ma voiture** (*my car*)
	masculine and feminine plural	**mes** (*my*)	**mes amis** (*my friends*)
tu (*you* [singular informal])	masculine singular	**ton** (*your*)	**ton sac** (*your bag*)
	feminine singular	**ta** (*your*)	**ta voiture** (*your car*)
	masculine and feminine plural	**tes** (*your*)	**tes amis** (*your friends*)
il and **elle** (*he* and *she*)	masculine singular	**son** (*his/her*)	**son sac** (*his/her bag*)
	feminine singular	**sa** (*his/her*)	**sa voiture** (*his/her car*)
	masculine and feminine plural	**ses** (*his/her*)	**ses amis** (*his/her friends*)

Owner	Gender and Number of Object Owned	French Possessive	Example
nous (*we*)	masculine and feminine singular	**notre** (*our*)	**notre sac** (*our bag*) **notre voiture** (*our car*)
	masculine and feminine plural	**nos** (*our*)	**nos amis** (*our friends*)
vous (*you* [singular formal or plural formal and informal])	masculine and feminine singular	**votre** (*your*)	**votre sac** (*your bag*) **votre voiture** (*your car*)
	masculine and feminine plural	**vos** (*your*)	**vos amis** (*your friends*)
ils and elles (*they*)	masculine and feminine singular	**leur** (*their*)	**leur sac** (*their bag*) **leur voiture** (*their car*)
	masculine and feminine plural	**leurs** (*their*)	**leurs amis** (*their friends*)

When **ma**, **ta**, and **sa** precede a noun starting with a vowel or a mute **-h**, they change to **mon**, **ton**, and **son** for pronunciation's sake. Here are some examples:

> **Ma amie** (*my* [female] *friend*) must change to **mon amie**.

> **Ta éducation** (*your education* [which is always feminine]) must change to **ton éducation**.

> **Sa humeur** (*his/her mood*) changes to **son humeur**.

Use the correct possessive adjective, based on the subject in parentheses and the number and gender of the noun. Check out a French-English dictionary if you need help with the vocabulary. Here's an example.

Q. (ils) _____ amis

A. leurs

41. (je) _____ amies

42. (vous) _____ maison

43. (Paul) _____ amie

44. (tu) _____ voiture

45. (nous) _____ livres

Discovering other ways to express possession

Sometimes you need to name the owner of an object and you can't use just the possessive adjective like this: **son chien** (*his dog*). If you need to say whose dog it is specifically, you use a different sentence structure in French: **Le chien de Paul** (*Paul's dog*). Now it's clear! The English formula [owner + '*s* + object owned] is actually flipped around in French: [definite article + object owned + **de** (*of*) + owner]. Here are some examples:

> **l'ami de ma fille** (*my daughter's friend*)
>
> **les enfants des Dupont** (*the Duponts' children*)

Sometimes you need to use a definite article when you're naming an object's owner, such as **le chien de la voisine** (*the dog of the (female) neighbor*). Keep in mind that **de + le** (*of the*) contracts into **du**, and **de + les** (*of the*) contracts into **des**. (See the earlier section "Delving into definite articles" for more information.)

Express possession using the correct French translation (possessive adjectives or construction with **de**). Here's an example:

Q. Julie's car

A. **la voiture de Julie**

46. the teacher's book _____

47. his wife _____

48. our house _____

49. my dad's car _____

50. their children _____

Pointing at Things with Demonstratives

Do you prefer *this* thing here or *that* thing there? *This, that, these,* and *those* are English demonstrative adjectives. You use them to show more precisely what you want of two things. French has also a set of demonstrative adjectives, but they work differently. French has three demonstratives in singular and one in plural. I put them in Table 3-7 for quick reference.

If you're trying to decide between *this color* and *that color*, the French demonstrative alone won't help you! It would be like comparing *this color* and . . . *this color!* Enter the compound demonstratives:

- ✔ **ce** [noun]-**ci**
- ✔ **cet** [noun]-**ci**
- ✔ **cette** [noun]-**ci**
- ✔ **ces** [noun]-**ci**

- ✔ **ce** [noun]-**là**
- ✔ **cet** [noun]-**là**
- ✔ **cette** [noun]-**là**
- ✔ **ces** [noun]-**là**

That invariable little tag, **-ci** or **-là**, is hyphenated to the noun; **-ci** indicates the object or person closest to you, and **-là**, the other one.

Table 3-7	French Demonstratives	
French Demonstrative	**Usage in French**	**Examples**
ce (*this/that*)	Before masculine singular nouns	**ce matin-ci** (*this morning*)
		ce matin-là (*that morning*)
cet (*this/that*)	Before masculine singular nouns beginning with a vowel or a mute **-h**	**cet homme-ci** (*this man*)
		cet homme-là (*that man*)
cette (*this/that*)	Before feminine singular nouns	**cette maison-ci** (*this house*)
		cette maison-là (*that house*)
ces (*these/those*)	Before masculine and feminine plural nouns	**ces enfants-ci** (*these children*)
		ces enfants-là (*those children*)

Here are some examples of demonstratives in action:

> **J'aime ce gâteau-ci, mais pas ce gâteau-là.** (*I like this cake but not that cake.*)

> **Tu préfères ces lunettes-ci ou ces lunettes-là?** (*Do you prefer these glasses or those glasses?*)

Fill in the blanks with the correct demonstrative adjective. To determine the gender of these nouns, flip to the earlier section "Finding the Gender of Nouns." Here's an example.

Q. ____ **livre est intéressant.**

A. Ce

51. ____ **obstacle est incontournable!**

52. **Regarde** ____ **choses!**

53. **Est-ce que tu connais** ____ **fille?**

54. ____ **chapeau est ridicule.**

55. ____ **panier est plein.**

Introducing Things and People

Sometimes, an English *she* does not translate to **elle** in French. For example, to say *She is my friend*, you'd say **c'est mon amie**. What happened to *she*? Find out when to use these in the following sections.

Using c'est and ce sont

If someone asks you, "Who is that woman?", you'd probably answer with *"She's . . ."*. To answer this type of question, French uses **c'est** in singular (masculine and feminine) and **ce sont** in plural instead of **il/elle est** and **ils/elles sont**. **C'est** is the demonstrative adjective **ce** (abbreviated to **c'** before **est**) + the third person singular of the verb **être** (*to be*), and **ce sont** is the demonstrative adjective **ce** + the third person plural of **être**. Here are more examples:

> **C'est un chien.** (*It's/this is a dog.*)
>
> **Ce sont mes enfants.** (*They're my children.*)

Use **ce** in the negative (singular and plural) before **ne** (see Chapter 8 for more about negative words and phrases).

> **Ce n'est pas mon sac.** (*It's not my bag.*)
>
> **Ce ne sont pas des diamants!** (*These are not diamonds.*)

So why do you want to use **c'est** to express *she's my friend*? It's because, for once, the gender doesn't matter as much as the act of presenting the person or thing. Here's when you should use **c'est** or **ce sont** intead of **elle/il est** or **ils/elles sont**.

> ✔ Use **c'est** or **ce sont** before a noun, a name, or a stress pronoun (see Chapter 13) to name a person or answer the question **qui** (*who*). For example:
>
>> **C'est ma mère.** (*That's my mother.*)
>>
>> **Ce sont Julie et Anne.** (*They are Julie and Anne.*)
>
> ✔ Use **c'est** or **ce sont** before a noun, to name a thing, or answer the question **qu'est-ce que c'est?** (*what is it?*). For example:
>
>> **Cette machine? C'est une agrafeuse.** (*That machine? It's a stapler.*)
>>
>> **C'est le Grand Canyon.** (*That's the Grand Canyon.*)

C'est can also express your own reaction to a situation, or an object, when it's followed by a masculine singular adjective instead of a noun. For example, you see the sunset and you exclaim **C'est beau!** (*It's beautiful!*)

Knowing what to do with il/elle est

If you use **c'est** to introduce people, you may wonder when can you use **il/elle est**. The answer is kind of simple and kind of not. **Il/elle est** is followed by an adjective; **c'est** is followed by a noun, like this:

> Use **il/elle est** or **ils/elles sont** + matching adjective
>
> Use **c'est/ce sont** + article + noun

That part is fairly clear, right? The problem is with the names of nationalities, religions, and professions that can be used as nouns (used with an article) *or* as adjectives (used without an article)! In other words, you choose. Now I give you some examples to illustrate the difference between the two types of sentences:

✔ If you describe a woman who is French, use the adjective to say: **Elle est française.**

If you introduce a Frenchwoman, you say: **C'est une Française.**

When a nationality such as **français** (*French*) is used as an adjective, it is not capitalized (**il est français**). When it is used as a noun (*Frenchman*), it is capitalized and used with an article: **un Français** (*a Frenchman*).

✔ If you describe a man who is Catholic, use the adjective to say: **Il est catholique.**

If you introduce a man as a Catholic, you say: **C'est un catholique.**

✔ If you describe a person who is a professor, use the adjective to say: **Il/elle est professeur.**

If you introduce a person as a professor, you say: **C'est un professeur.**

Complete the sentences using **c'est** or **il/elle est**. Here's an example:

Q. _____ ma meilleure amie.

A. C'est

56. _____ un professeur.

57. _____ brésilienne.

58. _____ ma mère.

59. _____ moi.

60. _____ américaines.

Answer Key

1	F	*22*	le	*43*	son	
2	M	*23*	la	*44*	ta	
3	F	*24*	le	*45*	nos	
4	M	*25*	les	*46*	le livre du prof	
5	M	*26*	La	*47*	sa femme	
6	F	*27*	le	*48*	notre maison	
7	M	*28*	le	*49*	la voiture de mon père	
8	F	*29*	des	*50*	leurs enfants	
9	M	*30*	un	*51*	Cet	
10	F	*31*	des	*52*	ces	
11	animaux	*32*	des	*53*	cette	
12	quartiers	*33*	le	*54*	Ce	
13	eaux	*34*	le	*55*	Ce	
14	bijoux	*35*	de	*56*	C'est	
15	filles	*36*	du	*57*	Elle est	
16	Français	*37*	de la	*58*	C'est	
17	fruits	*38*	du	*59*	C'est	
18	cadeaux	*39*	de l'	*60*	Elles sont	
19	rois	*40*	de			
20	cous	*41*	mes			
21	l'	*42*	votre			

Chapter 4

Describing Nouns with Adjectives

In This Chapter
- ▶ Making adjectives agree with nouns
- ▶ Using irregular adjectives
- ▶ Positioning adjectives properly

In French, like in English, nouns and verbs are the primary building blocks of a sentence. For example, **l'enfant dort** (*the child sleeps*) and **l'opération a réussi** (*the sugery succeeded*) are perfectly clear sentences. But the child could be small and feverish, and the surgery could be delicate. You change the context by including adjectives, which are words such as *small*, *feverish*, and *delicate* that indicate size, color, shape, taste, or other characteristics to the nouns. French and English have quite a few differences when using adjectives, so in this chapter I detail and explain the proper way to include them in French sentences.

The Agreement: Matching Adjectives to the Nouns They Describe

As you find out in Chapter 3, French nouns have a number and gender (yes, French has she-things and he-things), so any word that describes a noun, particularly an adjective, has to reflect that. In other words, adjectives must match the gender (masculine or feminine) and number (singular or plural) of the nouns they describe. Because a noun can be masculine singular, feminine singular, masculine plural, or feminine plural, an adjective has potentially four forms: masculine singular (MS), feminine singular (FS), masculine plural (MP), and feminine plural (FP).

In the following sections, I give you details on the regular forms of adjectives; I move on to irregular forms in the later section "Examining Irregular Adjectives."

Forming the feminine singular from the masculine singular

In a French-English dictionary, you find adjectives under their masculine singular form. Depending on the noun you want to modify, you may have to change that adjective form to feminine. The regular way of marking the feminine singular of an adjective is by adding an **-e** to the default form of the adjective (the masculine singular). If you want to say that a dress (**une robe**) is green, for example, you need to make **vert** (*green*) feminine singular to match **une robe** (a feminine singular noun), so you add an **-e** to the default form of **vert**: **une robe verte** (*a green dress*). Table 4-1 notes a few more examples.

Table 4-1	Masculine Singular and Feminine Singular Adjectives	
Masculine Form	*Feminine Form*	*English Translation*
bleu	bleue	*blue*
content	contente	*satisfied*
dur	dure	*hard*
fatigué	fatiguée	*tired*
mauvais	mauvaise	*bad*
préféré	préférée	*favorite*
ravi	ravie	*delighted*
supérieur	supérieure	*superior*
vrai	vraie	*true*

In many cases, adding **-e** to form the feminine singular can change the pronunciation of adjectives like **mauvais** (*bad*) and **petit** (*small*), which end in a silent consonant in the masculine. With the addition of the **-e**, the consonant that was silent must now be pronounced. For example, you pronounce **mauvaise** with a **z** sound at the end, and you pronounce **petite** with a **t** sound at the end. (See Chapter 2 for more about sounding out French words.)

Some masculine singular adjectives already end in **-e**. For those, do not add an extra **-e** to form the feminine singular. They remain as is. For instance, **aimable** (*nice*), **bête** (*stupid*), **calme** (*calm*), **énorme** (*enormous*), **facile** (*easy*), **jeune** (*young*), **moderne** (*modern*), **timide** (*shy*), **riche** (*rich*), **triste** (*sad*), and **utile** (*useful*) have the same form in masculine singular and in feminine singular. And in plural, they also have the same form for masculine and feminine: **aimables**, **bêtes**, **calmes**, **énormes**, **faciles**, **jeunes**, **modernes**, **timides**, **riches**, **tristes**, and **utiles**. In other words, these adjectives have only two forms, one for both MS and FS and one for both MP and FP, instead of the regular four. (See the following section for more about plural adjectives.)

Give the feminine form of the following adjectives. Here's an example:

O. **petit** (*small*)

A. petite

1. **occupé** (*busy*) _____

2. **sincère** (*sincere*) _____

3. **anglais** (*English*) _____

4. **parfait** (*perfect*) _____

5. **court** (*short*) _____

6. **noir** (*black*) _____

7. **final** (*final*) _____

8. **haut** (*high*) _____

9. **américain** (*American*) _____

10. **gris** (*gray*) _____

Forming the plural from the singular

The regular way of making an adjective plural is by adding an **-s** to the masculine singular form or the feminine singular form. That additional **-s** does not change the pronunciation — it is silent. Table 4-2 lists a few examples.

Table 4-2	Singular and Plural Adjectives		
Masculine Singular	*Masculine Plural*	*Feminine Singular*	*Feminine Plural*
bleu	bleus	bleue	bleues
content	contents	contente	contentes
dur	durs	dure	dures
fatigué	fatigués	fatiguée	fatiguées
mauvais	mauvais	mauvaise	mauvaises
préféré	préférés	préférée	préférées
ravi	ravis	ravie	ravies
supérieur	supérieurs	supérieure	supérieures
vrai	vrais	vraie	vraies

If the adjective already ends in an **-s** or an **-x** in masculine singular, like **mauvais** (*bad*) in Table 4-2, it does not take another **-s** to form the plural. It remains as is and has the same form in masculine singular and plural. A few more adjectives of this type are **épais** (*thick*), **anglais** (*English*), **gris** (*gray*), **gros** (*fat*), **frais** (*fresh*), **bas** (*low*), **chinois** (*Chinese*), **curieux** (*curious*), **amoureux** (*in love*), **honteux** (*shameful*), **jaloux** (*jealous*), and **heureux** (*happy*).

Give the plural form of the following masculine and feminine adjectives. Here's an example:

0. **carré** (*square*)

A. **carrés**

11. **gris** (*gray*) _____

12. **gentil** (*kind*) _____

13. **anxieux** (*nervous*) _____

14. **intelligente** (*clever*) _____

15. **jeune** (*young*) _____

16. **bonne** (*good*) _____

17. **bref** (*brief*) _____

18. **blanc** (*white*) _____

19. **jolie** (*pretty*) _____

20. **américaine** (*American*) _____

Examining Irregular Adjectives

In a perfect world, this chapter would stop here. Unfortunately, some adjectives don't follow the rules of the majority. Some have a slight irregularity, and others are downright wicked! But the following sections sort them out for you so you can master the full array of adjectival twists and turns.

Dealing with irregular feminine singular endings

To form the feminine singular form, some masculine singular adjectives require a little more than just adding **-e** (as I describe in the earlier section "Forming the feminine singular from the masculine singular"). In this section I put the irregular feminine adjectives in nine categories based on verb ending so they're easier for you to spot.

> ✔ **Ending in vowel + consonant:** For adjectives that end in a vowel + consonant, you form the FS adjective by doubling that consonant before adding the **-e** of the feminine singular. Some examples include **ancien** (*old/former*) to **ancienne**, **exceptionnel** (*exceptional*) to **exceptionnelle**, and **net** (*clear*) to **nette**.

This rule has exceptions, and not all adjectives ending in vowel + consonant double that consonant before the **-e** of the feminine. Here are a few examples: **féminin** (*feminine*) to **feminine**, **fin** (*fine*) to **fine**, **normal** (*normal*) to **normale**, **brun** (*dark-haired*) to **brune**, and **gris** (*gray*) to **grise**.

✔ **Ending in -eur or -eux:** For adjectives that end in **-eur** or **-eux**, replace the masculine singular ending with **-euse** to form the feminine singular. Some examples include **fumeur** (*smoking*) to **fumeuse** and **luxueux** (*luxurious*) to **luxueuse**.

This rule also has exceptions, and not all adjectives in **-eur** turn to **-euse** in the feminine. For some, just add **-e** to the masculine **-eur** form: **inférieur** (*inferior*) becomes **inférieure**, **supérieur** (*superior*) becomes **supérieure**, **intérieur** (*interior*) becomes **intérieure**, and **meilleur** (*better*) changes to **meilleure**.

✔ **Ending in -teur:** For adjectives that end in **-teur**, replace **-teur** with **-trice** to form the feminine singular, like **protecteur** (*protective*) to **protectrice**, **conservateur** (*conservative*) to **conservatrice**, and **indicateur** (*indicative*) to **indicatrice**.

✔ **Ending in -er:** For adjectives that end in **-er**, replace **-er** with **-ère** to form the feminine singular, like **dernier** (*last*) to **dernière**, **premier** (*first*) to **première**, and **cher** (*expensive*) to **chère**.

✔ **Ending in -et:** For adjectives that end in **-et**, replace **-et** with **-ète** to form the feminine singular, like **discret/discrète** (*discreet*), **complet/complète** (*complete*), and **secret/secrète** (*secret*).

✔ **Ending in -f:** For adjectives that end in **-f**, replace **-f** with **-ve** to form the feminine singular, like **neuf** to **neuve** (*new*), **naïf** to **naïve** (*naive*), **négatif** to **négative** (*negative*), and **sportif** to **sportive** (*athletic*).

✔ **Ending in -on or -ien:** For adjectives that end in **-on** or **-ien**, double the **-n** before adding the **-e** to form the feminine singular, like **mignon** to **mignonne** (*cute*).

Many adjectives of nationality and regionality are in this category, like **canadien/canadienne** (*Canadian*), **parisien/parisienne** (*Parisian*), and **italien/italienne** (*Italian*). However, adjectives of nationality that end in **-ain**, like **américain/américaine** (*American*), **mexicain/mexicaine** (*Mexican*), and **marocain/marocaine** (*Moroccan*) don't double the **-n**. (Note that English capitalizes adjectives refering to nationalities and religions, but French doesn't.)

✔ Some adjectives have a completely irregular form that doesn't follow any pattern. I put the most common ones in Table 4-3 so you can easily find them.

Table 4-3	Common Adjectives That Change Completely in Feminine Singular	
Masculine Singular	*Feminine Singular*	*English Translation*
beau	belle	*handsome, beautiful*
blanc	blanche	*white*
bref	brève	*brief*
doux	douce	*soft*

(continued)

Table 4-3 *(continued)*

Masculine Singular	Feminine Singular	English Translation
faux	fausse	untrue
favori	favorite	favorite
fou	folle	crazy
frais	fraîche	fresh
franc	franche	honest
grec	grecque	greek
long	longue	long
mou	molle	soft
nouveau	nouvelle	new
public	publique	public
rigolo	rigolote	funny
roux	rousse	red haired
sec	sèche	dry
vieux	vieille	old

Give the irregular feminine singular form of the following masculine singular adjectives.

Q. sec

A. sèche

21. long _____

22. bon _____

23. américain _____

24. premier _____

25. luxueux _____

26. conservateur _____

27. complet _____

28. sportif _____

29. mignon _____

30. parisien _____

31. **beau** _____

32. **blanc** _____

33. **favori** _____

34. **mauvais** _____

35. **fin** _____

Getting a handle on irregular plural endings

As you find out earlier in this chapter, to form the plural of an adjective, you usually add an **-s** to its masculine singular form (if the noun you're describing is masculine) or to its feminine singular form (if it's feminine). However, some adjectives require different steps to form their plural. For some, you only need to make a minor tweak, whereas others look very different in plural.

Irregular masculine plural endings fall into one of three categories:

✔ For masculine singular adjectives that end in **-al**, drop the **-al** and replace it with **-aux** to form the plural. For example: **normal** becomes **normaux**, and **global** becomes **globaux**.

However, a handful of adjectives ending in **-al** don't follow this rule. Instead, they form their plural regularly, by just adding **-s** to the singular form. They are **banal/banals** (*banal*), **fatal/fatals** (*fatal*), **final/finals** (*final*), **glacial/glacials** (*icy*), and **naval/navals** (*naval*).

✔ Masculine singular adjectives that end in **-eau** form their plural by adding **-x** instead of an **-s**. For instance, **beau** becomes **beaux** in the plural, and **nouveau** becomes **nouveaux**.

✔ The masculine singular adjective **tout** (*all*) becomes **tous** in the masculine plural. Easy enough!

Good news! Irregular feminine plural endings don't exist. All you need to do is add **-s** to the feminine singular form, whether it's regular or irregular. For example: The feminine singular form of **vert** (*green*) is **verte**, so the feminine plural is **vertes**. The feminine singular form of **beau** (*handsome*) is **belle**, so the feminine plural is **belles**.

Form the plural of the following irregular masculine adjectives.

Q. **petit**

A. **petits**

36. **fatal** _____

37. **nouveau** _____

38. tout _____

39. final _____

40. normal _____

Knowing the Proper Place of Adjectives

Most adjectives that describe the characteristics of a noun are placed after that noun. Some adjectives, however, must be placed before the noun they describe, and still others can go either before or after, depending on their meaning. You get the scoop in the following sections.

Adjectives that go after the nouns they describe

In general, and unlike English, adjectives are placed after the noun they describe. Here are a few adjectives that illustrate this difference with English.

> **une maison blanche** (*a white house*)
>
> **un visage intéressant** (*an interesting face*)
>
> **des gâteaux délicieux** (*delicious cakes*)

In these examples, the adjectives are **blanche** (*white*), **intéressant** (*interesting*), and **délicieux** (*delicious*). Simple to remember, right?

Adjectives that go before the nouns they describe

Not all French adjectives go after nouns; the following sections break down these adjectives into a few categories.

Beginning with BAGS

Adjectives that refer to some specific qualities must precede the noun they describe instead of following it. The qualities they describe can be summarized by the acronym BAGS:

- ✔ B for beauty: **beau** (*beautiful*), **joli** (*pretty*)
- ✔ A for age: **jeune** (*young*), **vieux** (*old*), **nouveau** (*new*)
- ✔ G for goodness: **bon** (*good*), **meilleur** (*better*), **mauvais** (*bad*), **gentil** (*kind*)
- ✔ S for size: **petit** (*small*), **haut** (*high*), **gros** (*fat*)

A handful of adjectives that refer to the qualities contained in the BAGS are not placed before the noun. In the category of beauty, exceptions are **laid** (*ugly*) and **affreux** (*atrocious*); in age, **âgé** (*old*); and in the category of goodness, **méchant** (*mean*). Watch that difference in action:

> **une maison laide** (*an ugly house*)
>
> **des personnes âgées** (*old people*)
>
> **un chien méchant** (*a mean dog*)

More adjectives that go before nouns

Ordinal adjectives — that is, adjectives that describe the order in which things come, like first, second, last — appear before nouns. Here are some examples:

> **Le premier jour de la semaine est lundi.** (*The first day of the week is Monday.*)
>
> **Nous vivons au vingt-et-unième siècle.** (*We live in the twenty-first century.*)
>
> **C'est la deuxième fois qu'il fait une erreur.** (*It is the second time that he makes a mistake.*)

The adjective **tout** (*all*, *every*) precedes not just the noun but also the article + noun. Here are examples for all four forms of **tout** (masculine singular, feminine singular, masculine plural, and feminine plural):

> **Elle mange tout le temps.** (*She eats all the time.*)
>
> **Il a plu toute la journée.** (*It rained all day.*)
>
> **Tu travailles tous les jours.** (*You work every day.*)
>
> **Toutes les filles de la classe sont blondes.** (*All the girls of the class are blond.*)

The adjectives **autre** (*other*), **même** (*same*), **tel** (*such*), and **faux** (*false, untrue*) also go before nouns. Here are a couple of examples:

> **Je voudrais voir un autre film.** (*I'd like to see another movie.*)
>
> **une fausse sortie** (*a false exit*)

Changing the meaning of an adjective by changing its place

Some adjectives can go before or after the noun, depending what they mean. For a literal meaning, place the adjective after the noun; for a more figurative meaning, you place it before. See Table 4-4 for some common adjective with meaning changes.

Table 4-4	Adjectives with Meaning Changes	
Adjective	*English Translation before Noun*	*English Translation after Noun*
ancien	former	antique, old
certain	some	sure
cher	dear	expensive
dernier	final	previous/last (in expressions of time)
grand (for people)	great	tall
pauvre	wretched, miserable	poor, broke
prochain	next (in a sequence)	next/following
propre	(my) own	clean
seul	only	alone
simple	mere	simple

Check out some of these adjectives in action:

Le dernier jour de la semaine est dimanche. (*Sunday is the final day of the week.*)

Dimanche dernier, il a fait des crêpes. (*Last Sunday, he made crêpes.*)

Ces pauvres animaux ont faim. (*Those miserable animals are hungry.*)

Paul est un homme pauvre. (*Paul is a poor man.*)

Leur ancienne voiture était une Fiat. (*Their former car was a Fiat.*)

Il a acheté une armoire ancienne. (*He bought an antique armoire.*)

Translate the following sentences into French; you can check a French-English dictionary if you need help. Be sure to place the adjective in the correct spot (before or after the noun) based on its meaning. Don't forget to make it agree with the noun as well.

Q. *This is a sure thing.*

A. **C'est une chose certaine.**

41. *His only friend is a dog.*

_____

42. *My daughter has her own car now.*

_____

43. *Charles De Gaulle was a great man.*

_____

44. *She wears an expensive dress.*

_____

45. *December 31st is the last day of the year.*

_____

46. *We propose a simple solution.*

_____

47. *Last Saturday, we went out.*

_____

48. *Some students got 100 on the exam!*

_____

49. *He adored his former car.*

_____

50. *Dear friends, how are you?*

_____

Answer Key

1	**occupée**
2	**sincère** (no change)
3	**anglaise**
4	**parfaite**
5	**courte**
6	**noire**
7	**finale**
8	**haute**
9	**américaine**
10	**grise**
11	**gris** (no change)
12	**gentils**
13	**anxieux** (no change)
14	**intelligentes**
15	**jeunes**
16	**bonnes**
17	**brefs**
18	**blancs**
19	**jolies**
20	**américaines**
21	**longue**
22	**bonne**
23	**américaine**
24	**première**

25 luxueuse

26 conservatrice

27 complète

28 sportive

29 mignonne

30 parisienne

31 belle

32 blanche

33 favorite

34 mauvaise

35 fine

36 fatals

37 nouveaux

38 tous

39 finals

40 normaux

41 Son seul ami est un chien.

42 Ma fille a sa propre voiture maintenant.

43 Charles De Gaulle était un grand homme.

44 Elle porte une robe chère.

45 Le 31 décembre est le dernier jour de l'année.

46 Nous proposons une solution simple.

47 Samedi dernier, nous sommes sortis.

48 Certains étudiants ont eu 100 à l'examen!

49 Il adorait son ancienne voiture.

50 Chers amis, comment allez-vous?

Chapter 5

Dealing with Numbers, Dates, and Times

Numbers are necessary in just about everything you do. In addition to just counting, you need them to talk about specific dates, tell time, and more. This chapter is all about numbers, quantities, dates, and times of all types.

Counting from Zero to a Billion: Cardinal Numbers

Les nombres cardinaux (*cardinal numbers*) are for counting. In the following sections, I list cardinal numbers from 0 to 100 and beyond, and I provide some tips for using cardinal numbers in French.

From 0 to 16

Starting off easy with French cardinal numbers is a good idea. In Table 5-1, I present the numbers 0 to 16.

Table 5-1		Counting from 0 to 16	
Number	*French*	*Number*	*French*
0	zéro	9	neuf
1	un	10	dix
2	deux	11	onze
3	trois	12	douze
4	quatre	13	treize
5	cinq	14	quatorze
6	six	15	quinze
7	sept	16	seize
8	huit		

From 17 to 69

After 16 (**seize**), you change things up and start reusing some of the smaller cardinal numbers. You write the tens number (10, 20, 30, 40, 50, or 60) and the ones number (1 to 9) with a hyphen in between. In Table 5-2, I give you the numbers 17 through 29 and then the tens numbers for 30, 40, 50, and 60.

Table 5-2	Counting from 17 to 69
Number	*French*
17	dix-sept
18	dix-huit
19	dix-neuf
20	vingt
21	vingt-et-un
22	vingt-deux
23	vingt-trois
24	vingt-quatre
25	vingt-cinq
26	vingt-six
27	vingt-sept
28	vingt-huit
29	vingt-neuf
30	trente
40	quarante
50	cinquante
60	soixante

Note that for 21, 31, 41, 51, and 61, you have to add **et** (*and*) before **un**, like this:

  number + hyphen + **et** + hyphen + number

From 70 to 99

The numbers change again when you get out of the 60s. To say 70 in French, you say **soix-ante-dix**; literally you're saying **60-10**! You follow the same pattern for the other numbers in the seventies: Start with **soixante**, and then add the appropriate number in the tens. For 71, say **soixante-et-onze** (or **60 + 11**); for 72, you say **soixante-douze** (60 + 12); and so on. (Note that you add **et** before **onze** for 71.)

To say 80, say **quatre-vingts**, which is literally **4-20s**, so this time, you're multiplying 4 by 20! For 81 and the rest of the 80 numbers, just add the ones numbers after **quatre-vingts**, drop-ping the **-s** like this: **quatre-vingt-un** (81), **quatre-vingt-deux** (82), **quatre-vingt-trois** (83), **quatre-vingt-quatre** (84), **quatre-vingt-cinq** (85), and so on.

The number 21 is **vingt-et-un** (as you find out in the preceding section), but the **et** is dropped for 81. It's just **quatre-vingt-un**.

To say 90, you have to add numbers again. You say **quatre-vingt-dix**, which means **80-10**, so you're adding 10 to 80. For the rest of the 90 numbers, attach the tens numbers to **quatre-vingt** like this: **quatre-vingt-onze** (91), **quatre-vingt-douze** (92), **quatre-vingt-treize** (93), and so on.

You're ready to do some counting. For each number listed, give the number that comes before and after it. Here's an example.

Q. **vingt-deux**

A. **vingt-et-un** and **vingt-trois**

1. **dix** _____

2. **dix-neuf** _____

3. **quatre-vingt-dix-sept** _____

4. **trente-deux** _____

5. **soixante-dix** _____

6. **soixante-dix-neuf** _____

7. **quarante-neuf** _____

8. **neuf** _____

9. **quatre-vingt-deux** _____

10. **un** _____

The big leagues: 100 and beyond

French numbers starting at 100 and above have some noteworthy characteristics that I detail here.

- ✔ To say 100 in French, say **cent** (don't pronounce the final -**t**). The hundreds don't use **et** or a hyphen between **cent** and the number that follows. 101 is **cent un**, 102 is **cent deux**, and so on, using all the numbers from 1 to 99 in the preceding sections.

- ✔ To say numbers by the hundreds, like 200, 300, and so on up to 900, say **deux cents**, **trois cents**, and so on, using the cardinal numbers for two through nine before **cents**. You use the -**s** when no other number follows, but you don't use it with another number, like this: **deux cent un** (201), **deux cent cinquante** (250), and so on.

- ✔ The word for *thousand* in French is **mille**. 1,000 in French is spelled without a comma, like this: **1000**. Numbers in the thousands don't use **et** or a hyphen between **mille** and the number that follows. 1001 is **mille un**, 1002 is **mille deux**, and so on. Repeat the same process for numbers by the thousands as for numbers by the hundreds. For example, for 2,000 and 3,000 you say **deux mille** and **trois mille**.

    Note: In French numbers, a comma indicates a decimal number! See the following section for more information.

- ✔ *100* (**cent**) and *1,000* (**mille**) are never preceded by an article. For example:

    Il a fait le tour cent fois. (*He went around 100 times.*)

    Un chèque de mille dollars. (*A check for 1,000 dollars.*)

- ✔ All the big numbers starting at 1,000 (except numbers by the thousands from 2,000 to 9,000) take an -**s** if they're plural, as in **trois millions** (*3 million*); **deux milliards** (*2 billion*). Here are some significant ones here:

    - **mille** (*1,000*)

    - **dix mille** (*10,000*)

    - **cent mille** (*100,000*)

    - **un million** (*1 million*)

    - **dix millions** (*10 million*)

    - **cent millions** (*100 million*)

    - **un milliard** (*1 billion*)

Spell out the following cardinal numbers in French. (Note that the numerals are presented the English way, with a comma indicating thousands.) Here's an example:

Q. 4,367

A. **quatre mille trois-cent-soixante-sept**

11. 201 _____

12. 3,000 _____

13. 150 _____

14. 1,000 _____

15. 2,999 _____

A few guidelines for using cardinal numbers

Cardinal numbers in French and English have a few differences. Here are some guidelines for using French cardinal numbers:

✔ The number 7 is written with a little bar across the vertical bar in French like this: 7̵.

✔ The French symbol for # is **n°**. For example:

Il habite au n° 34 rue des Lilas. (*He lives at #34 Lilas Street.*)

✔ French decimals are written with a comma, not a period. The word for *comma* is **virgule**. For example:

You read **40,001** as **quarante virgule zéro, zéro un** (*forty*-comma-*zero zero one*, or *40.001*).

✔ **un** (*one* in masculine form) changes to **une** (*one* in feminine form) before a feminine noun (see Chapter 3 for details about noun gender). For example:

vingt-et-une heures (*21 hours*)

quarante-et-une pages (*41 pages*)

✔ When a cardinal number and the words **premier** (*first*) or **dernier** (*last*) appear side by side, the number comes first. Also, **premier** and **dernier** are adjectives, so they become **première** and **dernière** in the feminine, and both masculine and feminine forms take an **-s** in the plural. It's the opposite in English. For example:

les dix premiers pas (*the first ten steps*)

les vingt derniers jours (*the last 20 days*)

Putting Things in Order: Ordinal Numbers

Ordinal numbers help you put things in order with words like **premier** (*first*), **deuxième** (*second*), and so on. To form an ordinal number in French, you simply add **-ième** to the cardinal number. For example, **sept** (*seven*) becomes **septième** (*seventh*). A few numbers need extra steps before adding **-ième**, though:

✔ All numbers ending with an **-e** drop the **-e** before **-ième**. For example:

quatre → **quatrième** (*fourth*)

onze → **onzième** (*eleventh*)

mille → **millième** (*thousandth*)

✔ For numbers ending with **cinq**, add a **-u** before **-ième**, like this: **cinquième** (*fifth*)

✔ For numbers ending with **neuf**, change **-f** to **-v** before **-ième**, like this: **neuvième** (*ninth*)

To abbreviate a French ordinal number like the English *7th*, write the cardinal number followed by the letter **-e** in superscript, like this: **7**^{e}. This symbol works for all numbers except **un**. To say *first* in French, say **premier** (or **première** before a feminine noun; you also add an **-s** for plural forms). To abbreviate it, use **-er** or **-ère** in superscript, like this: **1**^{er} or **1**^{ère}.

Here are some examples of ordinal numbers in a sentence:

Mon bureau est au cinquième étage. (*My office is on the fifth floor.*)

C'est la millième fois que je te le dis! (*It's the thousandth time I tell you this!*)

Practice forming ordinal numbers from the cardinal numbers given here. Check out the example first.

Q. 6 (**six**)

A. sixième

16. 100 (**cent**) _____

17. 30 (**trente**) _____

18. 45 (**quarante-cinq**) _____

19. 99 (**quatre-vingt-dix-neuf**) _____

20. 207 (**deux cent sept**) _____

Discussing Quantities

If you'd like *a little bit* of sugar in your coffee, obviously you can't use numbers. Expressions of quantity (including those related to food) are just what you need. I detail the most common ones in the following sections.

Specific expressions of quantities

You use an expression of quantity to express a quantity that's less specific than a number and yet a bit more specific than a partitive article like **du** (*some*) (see Chapter 3 for details on these articles). Most expressions of quantity end with **de** (*of*), but **quelques** (*several/a few*), **plusieurs** (*several*), and **aucun/aucune** (*none*) don't. Here's a list of common expressions of quantity:

✔ **assez de** (*enough of*)

✔ **beaucoup de** (*a lot of/many*)

✔ **combien de** (*how much/how many*)

- ✔ **la plupart de** (*most of*)
- ✔ **moins de** (*more/less of*)
- ✔ **ne . . . plus de** (*not any more of*)
- ✔ **peu de** (*little of*)
- ✔ **plus de** (*more of*)
- ✔ **plusieurs** (*several*)
- ✔ **quelques** (*several/some/a few*)
- ✔ **trop de** (*too much of*)
- ✔ **un peu de** (*a little bit of*)

Here are some examples of these expressions in action:

> **Il y a beaucoup d'emissions intéressantes ce soir.** (*There are many interesting programs on tonight.*)

> **Dépêche-toi! Nous avons peu de temps.** (*Hurry! We have little time.*)

> **Ils ont plusieurs enfants.** (*They have several children.*)

Food-related expressions of quantities

Would you like *a slice of pie*? Or *a platter of oysters, with a glass of wine*? The following list gives you all the words you need for ordering in a French restaurant, making a list of groceries, or even reading a French recipe.

- ✔ **une bouteille de** (*a bottle of*)
- ✔ **un verre de** (*a glass of*)
- ✔ **un litre de** (*a liter of*; liquids only)
- ✔ **un quart de** (*a quarter liter of*)
- ✔ **une tasse de** (*a cup of*)
- ✔ **une douzaine de** (*a dozen of*)
- ✔ **une boîte de** (*a box/can of*)
- ✔ **un paquet de** (*a bag of/packet of*)
- ✔ **un pot de** (*a jar of*)
- ✔ **un morceau de** (*a piece of*)
- ✔ **une tranche de** (*a slice of*)
- ✔ **une cannette de** (*a can*; drinks only)
- ✔ **un kilo de** (*a kilo of*)
- ✔ **une assiette de** (*a plate of*)
- ✔ **une tablette de chocolat** (*a bar of chocolate*)
- ✔ **un plat de** (*a dish/platter of*)

Complete the following sentences with the appropriate expression of quantity. Be sure to check a French-English dictionary if you need help with the vocabulary. Multiple answers may be possible, even though I only provide one answer. Here's an example:

O. un _____ pommes

A. kilo de

21. une _____ petits pois

22. une _____ jambon

23. un _____ fromage

24. une_____ thé

25. une _____ oeufs

26. un _____ vin

27. une _____ coca

28. une _____ chocolat

29. un _____ lait

30. un _____ riz

Talking about Days, Months, Seasons, and Dates

To talk about dates, you need numbers (which I cover earlier in this chapter) and also the names of the days and of the months. The following sections tell you what you need to know (including the seasons of the year).

Days of the week

The French week (**la semaine**) starts on Monday (**lundi**), and the days of the week are not capitalized. Here are the days of the week (**les jours de la semaine**), starting with Monday.

- ✔ **lundi** (*Monday*)
- ✔ **mardi** (*Tuesday*)
- ✔ **mercredi** (*Wednesday*)
- ✔ **jeudi** (*Thursday*)

✔ **vendredi** (*Friday*)

✔ **samedi** (*Saturday*)

✔ **dimanche** (*Sunday*)

Using the definite article **le** (*the*) + a day of the week indicates *every* + day of the week. For example: **Le jeudi j'allais chez ma grand-mère** (*Every Thursday, I used to go to my grandmother's house*). See Chapter 3 for more about definite articles.

Months and seasons

The names of the months (**mois**) are not capitalized in French, and they are never preceded by an article. Here are the 12 months with their English translations:

✔ **janvier** (*January*)

✔ **février** (*February*)

✔ **mars** (*March*)

✔ **avril** (*April*)

✔ **mai** (*May*)

✔ **juin** (*June*)

✔ **juillet** (*July*)

✔ **août** (*August*)

✔ **septembre** (*September*)

✔ **octobre** (*October*)

✔ **novembre** (*November*)

✔ **décembre** (*December*)

To say *in + month*, say **en** + month, like this:

> **En août, tout ferme en France.** (*In August, everything closes down in France.*)
>
> **Noël est toujours en décembre.** (*Christmas is always in December.*)

In French, all four seasons (**saisons**) are masculine:

✔ **le printemps** (*spring*)

> To say *in the spring*, say **au printemps**.

✔ **l'été** (*summer*)

> To say *in the summer*, say **en été**.

✔ **l'automne** (*fall*)

> To say *in the fall*, say **en automne**.

✔ **l'hiver** (*winter*)

> To say *in the winter*, say **en hiver**.

Specific dates

It's easy to say a date (**la date**) in French if you follow this simple formula:

> Day + le + cardinal number + month + year

For example: **mercredi le 12 septembre 2012** (*Wednesday, September 12, 2012*).

When abbreviating dates in French, the order of day and month is the reverse from English. So if you want to say *December 25th*, you write **25/12**.

If you don't name the day, you can simply say the cardinal number and the month, like **le 12 septembre** (*September 12th*), using the definite article **le** before the cardinal number. For example:

> **Ils sont partis le 4 janvier.** (*They left on January 4th.*)
>
> **La date de son anniversaire est le 5 avril.** (*His birthday is on April 5th.*)

Never use ordinal numbers, like *25th*, to express a date in French. Just say **le 25** (literally *the 25*). An exception is the first of the month: **le 1er janvier** (*January 1st*).

Here are a few expressions that are useful when you're saying dates in French:

- ✔ **aujourd'hui** (*today*)
- ✔ **demain** (*tomorrow*)
- ✔ **hier** (*yesterday*)
- ✔ **avant-hier** (*the day before yesterday*)
- ✔ **après-demain** (*the day after tomorrow*)
- ✔ **quelle est la date?** (*what's the date?*)
- ✔ **quel jour sommes-nous?** (*what day is it?*)
- ✔ **quel jour?** (*what day?*)
- ✔ **en quel mois?** (*in what month?*)
- ✔ **en quelle année?** (*in what year?*)
- ✔ **début** + [month] (*at the beginning of*)
- ✔ **mi-**[month] (*in the middle of*)
- ✔ **fin** + [month] (*at the end of*)
- ✔ **aujourd'hui c'est** + [day of the week] (*today is*)
- ✔ **demain ce sera** + [day of the week] (*tomorrow will be*)
- ✔ **hier c'était** + [day of the week] (*yesterday was*)

Express the following dates in French. Note that the dates are presented the way they're used in the United States — month/day/year. Here's an example:

Q. 8/5/12

A. **le 5 août 2012** (5/8/12)

31. 1/31/07 _____

32. 6/1/13 _____

33. 12/12/01 _____

34. 7/14/05 _____

35. 11/2/10 _____

Telling Time

As you discuss days, months, and specific dates (covered earlier in this chapter), you're going to need tell time (**l'heure**). The following sections tell you how to do so on both the 12-hour and 24-hour clocks.

Using the 12-hour clock

Time is typically expressed on a 12-hour clock. In French, you say the hour then the minutes, and it's a little different from the way it's done in English. But this section explains it all.

On the hour

To tell a time on the hour in French, use **il est** + [number] + **heure(s)**. For example: **il est deux heures** (*it is two o'clock*). *Note:* When it is *one o'clock*, say: **il est une heure** (*it is one o'clock*), using the feminine singular **une** instead of **un** because the word **heure** (*hour*) is feminine.

Always say the word **heure(s)** (*hour[s]*) when telling time. Even if familiar language often skips **il est**, it never skips **heure(s)**. For example: **quelle heure est-il?** (*what time is it?*) **Huit heures** (*eight o'clock*).

So many minutes

French minutes (**minutes**) have a few twists and turns that you may not expect. I detail them here:

✔ To say 1 to 30 minutes past the hour, simply say the number of minutes after the hour, like this:

Il est deux heures dix. (Literally *It is two hours ten*; which is to say *It is 2:10.*)

Il est sept heures vingt-cinq. (*It is 7:25.*)

✔ For 15 minutes past the hour say, **et quart** (*and a quarter*). For example: **Il est une heure et quart.** (*It's a quarter past one.*)

✔ For 30 minutes past the hour, say **et demie** (*and a half*). For example: **Il est une heure et demie.** (*It's half past one.*)

✔ For 31 to 59 minutes past the hour, say the next hour **moins** (*minus*) the number of minutes, like this:

Il est quatre heures moins dix. (Literally *4 hours minus 10,* or *3:50.*)

Il est huit heures moins vingt. (Literally *8 hours minus 20,* meaning *7:40.*)

✔ For a quarter until the hour, say **moins le quart** (*minus the quarter*). For example: **Il est trois heures moins le quart.** (*It is a quarter until 3;* meaning *2:45.*)

✔ To abbreviate a time in French, don't use a colon between the hour and minutes like in English. Instead, use the letter **h** (for **heure**), like this: **8h10** (*8:10*).

✔ French has specific words for noon and midnight: **midi** (*noon*) and **minuit** (*midnight*). Those two words are used without saying **heures**. For example: **Il est minuit. Tout le monde au lit!** (*It's midnight. Everybody to bed!*)

✔ With the 12-hour clock, you may need to clarify if it's *8 a.m* or *8 p.m.* Could make a big difference! French uses phrases to express the difference between *morning* (**le matin**), *afternoon* (**l'après-midi**), and *evening/night* (**le soir**).

- **du matin** (*in the morning* or *a.m.*)

  For example: **Il part à six heures et demie du matin.** (*He leaves at 6:30 a.m.*)

- **de l'après-midi** (*in the afternoon* or *p.m.*)

  For example: **En hiver il fait nuit à cinq heures de l'après-midi.** (*In the winter, it's dark at 5 p.m.*)

- **du soir** (*in the evening/at night* or *p.m.*)

  For example: **Ils dînent à sept heures du soir.** (*They eat dinner at 7 p.m.*)

The line between afternoon and evening is not a very fixed one. It varies with the perception of the speaker, the seasons, even the weather.

Here are a few expressions that can come in handy when telling time in French.

✔ **pile** (*on the dot*). For example: **Il mange à midi pile.** (*He eats at noon on the dot.*)

✔ **à** (*at*). For example: **Viens à trois heures.** (*Come at 3.*)

✔ **C'est à quelle heure?** (*At what time is it?*)

✔ **vers** (*around*). For example: **Je passerai vers 9 heures.** (*I will stop by around 9.*)

In French, tell what the time is, using the 12-hour clock. Don't forget to mention the French equivalent of *a.m.* and *p.m.* each time. Here's an example.

Q. 8:10 a.m.

A. **Il est huit heures dix du matin.**

36. 9:30 p.m. _____

37. 1:15 p.m. _____

38. 11:25 a.m. _____

39. 6:45 p.m. _____

40. 12 a.m. _____

Using the 24-hour clock

If you travel in France, this section may mean the difference between making your train or missing it! Using the 24-hour clock is really quite simple, because all you do is add. No more **moins le quart** or **et demie** and the like. All you need is keep in mind that the 24-hour clock begins at **zéro heure** (*12 a.m.*) and ends at **23.59** (*11:59 p.m.*), and you write a period between the two parts of the time instead of abbreviating **h**. For example, **13.00** (**treize heures**) is *1 p.m.*; **14.00** (**quatorze heures**) is *2 p.m.*, **15.00** (**quinze heures**) is *3 p.m.*, and so on. And because it's clear that all times after 12 (noon) are p.m., you have no need for **du matin**, **de l'après-midi**, or **du soir** any more.

Here are some examples:

> **Le film commence à 20.40 (vingt heures quarante).** (*The movie begins at 8:40 p.m.*)
>
> **Le bureau est ouvert de 8.00 (huit heures) à 17.30 (dix-sept heures trente).** (*The office is open from 8 a.m. to 5:30 p.m.*)
>
> **Le déjeuner est servi à 12.15 (douze heures quinze) et le diner à 19.45 (dix-neuf-heures quarante-cinq).** (*Lunch is served at 12:15, and dinner at 7:45.*)

Convert the following times on the 24-hour clock to times on the 12-hour clock, in French. Be sure to include a.m. and p.m. Here's an example.

Q. 13.45

A. deux heures moins le quart de l'après-midi

41. 21.40 _____

42. 18.30 _____

43. 12.15 _____

44. 0.10 _____

45. 14.40 _____

Answer Key

1 neuf and onze

2 dix-huit and vingt

3 quatre-vingt-seize and quatre-vingt-dix-huit

4 trente-et-un and trente-trois

5 soixante-neuf and soixante-et-onze

6 soixante-dix-huit and quatre-vingts

7 quarante-huit and cinquante

8 huit and dix

9 quatre-vingt-un and quatre-vingt-trois

10 zéro and deux

11 deux cent un

12 trois mille

13 cent cinquante

14 mille

15 deux mille neuf cent quatre-vingt-dix-neuf

16 centième

17 trentième

18 quarante-cinquième

19 quatre-vingt-dix-neuvième

20 deux cent septième

21 boîte de

22 tranche de

23 morceau de

24 tasse de

25 douzaine d'

26 verre de

27 cannette de

28 tablette de

29 litre de

30 paquet de

31 le 31 janvier 2007 (31/1/07)

32 le 1er juin 2013 (1/6/13)

33 le 12 décembre 2001 (12/12/01)

34 le 14 juillet 2005 (14/7/05)

35 le 2 novembre 2010 (2/11/10)

36 Il est neuf heures et demie du soir.

37 Il est une heure et quart de l'après-midi.

38 Il est onze heures vingt-cinq du matin.

39 Il est sept heures moins le quart du soir.

40 Il est minuit.

41 dix heures moins vingt du soir

42 six heures et demie du soir

43 midi et quart

44 minuit dix

45 trois heures moins vingt de l'après-midi

Part II
Constructing Sentences, Saying No, and Asking Questions

Common Negative Words and Phrases in French

French Negative Word	English Equivalent
aucun/aucune (+ noun)	none
jamais	never
même pas	not even
ni . . . ni	neither . . . nor
nulle part	nowhere
pas	not
pas encore	not yet
pas grand-chose (informal)	not much
pas non plus	either/neither
personne	no one, nobody
plus	not any more/no longer
rien	nothing

Get the scoop on building negative French sentences in an article at www.dummies.com/extras/frenchgrammar.

In this part . . .

✔ Find out how to construct a basic subject-verb sentence in the present tense.

✔ Discover how to use pronominal verbs, which are conjugated with extra pronouns.

✔ Express that you aren't doing something with the help of negative words and phrases.

✔ Build yes-no questions and information questions, and react enthusiastically with exclamations.

Chapter 6

Acquainting Yourself with the Present Tense

In This Chapter

▶ Grasping the basics of French verbs

▶ Conjugating regular, not-quite-regular, and irregular verbs in the present tense

● ●

The present tense is the tense of the here and now. A verb in the present tense (**le présent**) describes an action that is happening at the moment you speak, is habitual, or is general. For example:

> **Il mange une pomme.** (*He eats/is eating an apple.*)
>
> **Nous dînons toujours vers huit heures.** (*We always have dinner around 8 p.m.*)
>
> **Les enfants aiment les bonbons.** (*Children like sweets.*)

The present tense can tell about your current surroundings and your thoughts of the moment, as in **Il pleut; je n'aime pas ça** (*It's raining; I don't like it*). The present is also the tense of ordinary communication, such as common questions like "What do you need?" or "What are you doing?"

As these examples show, English has several ways of expressing the present tense: You can say *she reads*, *she's reading*, or *she does read*. French has only one present tense, though. In this chapter you get well acquainted with it, because it's the most important tense of all. First, I give you a brief overview of subject pronouns and infinitives. Then you take on regular, moody, and irregular conjugations before you start writing your first sentence!

A dictionary doesn't tell you outright if a verb is regular or irregular. The only way to find out is to use a verb book or read the French examples given in the dictionary.

Understanding French Verb Fundamentals

In any language, a verb is the pulse of a sentence because it conveys the action that's taking place and indicates whether it is occurring now (in the present), it was occurring (in the past), or it will occur (in the future). The verb also indicates who performs that action through the use of a subject, like **je** (*I*), **tu** (*you*), **il** (*he*), and so on, and its form changes with each different subject. In the following sections, I talk about subject pronouns and how they help in conjugating verbs from the infinitive.

Starting with subject pronouns

In order to put a verb in motion, you need to know who performs the action: the subject. French has nine possible subjects, and the following sections detail all you need to know about them. Here is the list of French subject pronouns with their English equivalents.

- **je** (**j'** before a vowel) (*I*)
- **tu** (*you* [singular informal])
- **il** (*he* or *it*)
- **elle** (*she* or *it*)
- **on** (*one*)
- **nous** (*we*)
- **vous** (*you* [singular formal or plural informal and formal])
- **ils** (*they* [masculine])
- **elles** (*they* [feminine])

The pronoun je

Je means *I*. In front of a vowel, **je** becomes **j'**. It is the only subject pronoun that gets *elided* (that is, the **-e** gets dropped before a vowel or a mute **-h**; see Chapter 3 for details on elision), as the following examples illustrate.

> **J'aime les bonbons.** (*I like candy.*)

> **J'ai un chat.** (*I have a cat.*)

The pronoun tu

Tu expresses *you* in familiar speech, when you're addressing a single person you know well, such as a family member, a classmate, or a child. Don't say **tu** to a person you've never met before, to someone you should show respect to, or to a business relation such as a doctor or a clerk in a store. (When talking to one unfamiliar person or a group of people, you use **vous**, the formal/plural *you*. I discuss **vous** later in this chapter.)

The pronouns il, elle, and on

Il means *he* or *it* and can refer to a masculine person or a masculine thing like **un livre** (*a book*). As a matter of fact, you have to use **il** when talking about a masculine thing, as in this example (see Chapter 3 for more about the gender of nouns):

> **Où est ton livre? Il est sur mon bureau.** (*Where is your book? It is on my desk.*)

Il can also express an impersonal subject. It's used in phrases that only exist in an impersonal mode, such as **il faut** (*it's necessary*), **il fait beau** (*the weather is nice*), **il pleut** (*it's raining*), **il est midi** (*it is noon*), and all expressions about time and weather.

Unlike English, the **il** form of a French verb never ends in **-s**. Depending on the conjugation group, the **-s** is for **je** and **tu**.

The pronoun **elle** can refer to a feminine person or a feminine thing, like **une maison** (*a house*). Use **elle** when talking about a feminine thing, as in this example:

> **Regarde cette maison! Elle est vraiment belle.** (*Look at this house. It's really beautiful.*)

The pronoun **on** has a few different uses.

- ✔ It can mean *one/someone*, as in **Écoute! On ouvre la porte!** (*Listen! Someone is opening the door!*)

- ✔ It is also used to speak about people in general, as in **On ne se parle plus; on envoie des textos.** (*People don't talk any more; they text.*)

- ✔ Finally, it is the informal equivalent of **nous** (*we*), as in **On se voit demain.** (*We see each other tomorrow.*) Even when **on** means *we* (a plural subject), the verb is conjugated as a third person singular. Only the context reveals which **on** you're dealing with.

On is not the equivalent of the English *it* to refer to a thing. In fact, **on** never refers to a thing.

The pronoun nous

Nous means *we*. When you use **nous**, you're including yourself in the group. All verb endings triggered by the subject **nous** end in **-ons** in all tenses, except **être** (*to be*) in present, which is conjugated as **nous sommes**. (I discuss the verb **être** in more detail later in this chapter.) Here are some examples: **nous aimons** (*we like*), **nous finissons** (*we finish*), and **nous avons** (*we have*).

The pronoun vous

The pronoun **vous** expresses the singular formal *you* and also the plural for *you*, both formal and informal. A group of children or several family members would be addressed as **vous**, but so would a group of professors. Even when it expresses a singular formal *you*, **vous** still commands a plural verb form and it always ends in **-ez**, except for the verbs **dire** (*to tell*), **faire** (*to do, to make*), and **être** (*to be*). I cover these verbs in more detail later in this chapter.

The pronouns ils and elles

Ils is the plural equivalent of **il** singular. It means *they*, when *they* refers to all masculine subjects, or a mix of feminine and masculine subjects. A group of mostly feminine subjects and one masculine subject is described with **ils**. See what I mean in this example:

> **Ton fils et tes trois filles, comment vont-ils?** (*Your son and three daughters, how are they doing?*)

Elles is the plural equivalent of **elle** singular. It means *they*, only when *they* are all feminine, as when talking about a group of female students: **Elles sont intelligentes.** (*They are smart.*)

All **ils/elles** forms in the present tense end in **-ent**, with the exception of **être** (to be), **avoir** (*to have*), **aller** (*to go*), and **faire** (*to do, to make*). Those exceptions end in **-ont**. (You can find out more about these verbs later in this chapter.)

Complete the following sentences with the correct subject pronoun, based on the English translation of each sentence. Here's an example:

0. _____ **aime le chocolat.** (*I like chocolate.*)

A. **J'**

1. _____ **va au cinéma.** (*We* [informal] *go to the movies.*)

2. _____ **danse bien.** (*She dances well.*)

3. **Voulez-**_____ **du café?** (*Do you* [formal singular] *want some coffee?*)

4. _____ **suis fatigué aujourd'hui.** (*I am tired today.*)

5. **Est-ce que** _____ **peux m'aider?** (*Can you* [informal singular] *help me?*)

6. _____ **sortons ce soir.** (*We're going out tonight.*)

7. **Où est ton livre?** _____ **est sur la table.** (*Where is your book? It is on the table.*)

8. **Jules et ses soeurs vont en France.** _____ **ont de la chance!** (*Jules and his sisters are going to France. They are lucky.*)

9. **"Salut mes amis!** _____ **voulez venir au ciné avec moi?"** (*"Hey friends! Do you want to come to the movies with me?"*)

10. **Ces boissons** [f.] **fument!** _____ **sont trop chaudes!** (*These beverages are smoking. They are too hot!*)

Introducing infinitives and conjugations

An *infinitive* is a verb form in which no one is performing the action. In English, the word *to* always precedes the infinitive; for example, *to speak* and *to dance* are infinitives. In French, an infinitive has one of three endings: **-er**, **-ir**, or **-re**. For example **parler** (*to speak*), **finir** (*to finish*), and **vendre** (*to sell*).

From *I* to *they*, the form of an English verb remains the same (except for the *he/she* form, which usually takes an **s**), despite the change of subject. Here are the present tense forms for the verb *to speak:*

I speak	*we speak*
you (singular) *speak*	*you* (plural) *speak*
he/she/it speaks	*they speak*

In French, each verb form corresponds to a different subject. Using the appropriate version of a verb for a particular subject is called the *conjugation* of a verb. The conjugation of any given verb has six different forms: three for the singular and three for the plural. Here's the present tense conjugation for the verb **parler** (*to speak*) so you can compare it with its English equivalent:

parler (to speak)	
je **parle**	nous **parlons**
tu **parles**	vous **parlez**
il/elle/on **parle**	ils/elles **parlent**

Sometimes the **je** and **tu** forms look alike, and sometimes the **je** and **il/elle/on** forms look alike, but other than that, all the forms are different from one another.

Each simple verb tense has those six forms, from present tense to subjunctive. The essential simple tenses are the present, the imperfect (see Chapter 16), the future (see Chapter 17), the conditional (see Chapter 18), and the subjunctive (see Chapter 19). It's a lot of verb conjugations to digest, right? But wait! Each tense has its own pattern, a way to help you conjugate the verb, that's shared by most verbs.

For instance, the present tense conjugations follow a pattern that applies to all regular verbs. To form the present tense stem of most verbs, drop the ending of the infinitive (-**er**, -**ir**, or -**re**) to get the stem. When you have the stem, you can proceed to attach the endings to it. Endings are different for each one of the three groups. (See the next section for details.)

Conjugating Regular Verbs

Think of all the things you can possibly do in one day. Yes, that's a lot! And that's also a lot of verbs to conjugate. To simplify things, French has classified regular verbs into three types, based on the ending of their infinitives.

- ✔ The largest group is the verbs whose infinitive ends in -**er** (the -**er** verbs), like **parler** (to speak).

- ✔ The second largest group is made up of the verbs whose infinitive ends in -**ir** (the -**ir** verbs), like **finir** (to finish).

- ✔ The third group consists of the -**re** ending verbs (the -**re** verbs), like **vendre** (to sell).

Each type follows a pattern of conjugation for every tense. In the following sections, you discover the pattern for the present tense for each group and start conjugating.

Think of the infinitive as the family name of a verb: A family shares a common last name, but each individual has his or her own characteristics, right. Use the infinitive to recognize the verb type (-**er**, -**ir**, or -**re**) that allows you to find its conjugation pattern and also look up the verb in the dictionary.

Taking on -er verbs

More than 80 percent of French verbs are -**er** verbs. It's great for you, because after you know their pattern of conjugation in the present tense, you can pretty much conjugate 80 percent of French verbs. Doesn't that sound great?

To conjugate a regular -**er** verb, drop the -**er** of the infinitive to get the stem. Then add the six present tense endings specific to -**er** verbs: -**e**, -**es**, -**e**, -**ons**, -**ez**, -**ent**, and you're done. Easy! The following table conjugates a regular -**er** verb: **aimer** (*to like*).

aimer (*to like*)	
j'**aime**	nous **aimons**
tu **aimes**	vous **aimez**
il/elle/on **aime**	ils/elles **aiment**

Aller (*to go*) is a very common verb, and it looks like a regular -**er** verb. However, it is not. **Aller** is a very irregular verb; check out its conjugation in the later section "Conquering the fatal four: **être**, **avoir**, **aller**, and **faire**."

Investigating -ir verbs

The -**ir** verb group is the second most common verb type. To form the present tense of a regular -**ir** verb, drop the -**ir** of the infinitive to get the stem for the present tense conjugation. Then add the present tense endings specific to -**ir** verbs: -**is**, -**is**, -**it**, -**issons**, -**issez**, -**issent**. The following table conjugates a regular -**ir** verb: **finir** (*to finish*).

finir (*to finish*)	
je **finis**	nous **finissons**
tu **finis**	vous **finissez**
il/elle/on **finit**	ils/elles **finissent**

Not all -**ir** verbs follow this pattern. In the later section "Revealing oddball -**ir** verbs," you get acquainted with some -**ir** verbs that follow a different pattern. So just use a little more caution when dealing with -**ir** ending verbs.

Working with -re verbs

Verbs that end in -**re** are the third conjugation type. To form the present tense of an -**re** verb, drop the -**re** of the infinitive, like you do for -**er** and -**ir** verbs. When you do that, you're left with the stem for the conjugation of the present tense, and you can add the present tense endings specific to -**re** verbs: -**s**, -**s**, nothing, -**ons**, -**ez**, -**ent**. The following table conjugates a regular -**re** verb: **vendre** (*to sell*).

vendre (*to sell*)	
je **vends**	nous **vendons**
tu **vends**	vous **vendez**
il/elle/on **vend**	ils/elles **vendent**

Give the present tense of the following regular -**er**, -**ir**, and -**re** verbs, using the subject pronoun in parentheses. Here's an example:

Q. **aimer (je)**

A. **j'aime**

11. **choisir (il)** _____

12. **entendre (vous)** _____

13. **réagir (nous)** _____

14. **travailler (tu)** _____

15. **grandir (ils)** _____

16. **donner (ils)** _____

17. **répondre (je)** _____

18. **réussir (elle)** _____

19. **descendre (elles)** _____

20. **jouer (on)** _____

Dealing with a Few Moody Regular -er Verbs

With so many French verbs being -**er** verbs, you can imagine that they don't all follow the pattern with the same level of obedience. This section sorts out misbehaving -**er** verbs in several groups that make them easier for you to spot. The good news is that they all *mostly* follow the conjugation pattern of a regular -**er** verb: They drop the -**er** of the infinitive to get the stem, and they have the same present tense endings. That's why these moody verbs are still considered regular. They only misbehave within the stem, before the ending.

Verbs that end in -cer and -ger

Sometimes, for pronunciation's sake, a verb needs just a little tweak to maintain a consistent sound in all its forms. (I'm not talking of the endings, of course.) Those verbs end in -**cer** and -**ger.** The following sections show you how to tweak them.

Verbs that end in -cer

In French, **c** has two sounds: one is soft, as in the English word *soft*, and the other is hard, as in the English word *cod*. The French **c** follows these pronunciation rules:

✔ **c** is soft when it precedes -**e** or -**i**

✔ **c** is hard when it precedes -**a**, -**o**, or -**u**.

Verbs that end in **-cer** have the soft sound in the infinitive and want to maintain it throughout their present tense conjugation. As long as the ending begins with **-e** or **-i**, everything's good, because most endings in the present are **c** + **e**, a soft sound. For example, some present tense forms for the verb **prononcer** (*to pronounce*) are **je prononce**, **tu prononces**, **il/elle/on prononce**, **vous prononcez**, and **ils/elles prononcent**.

The problem arises when the **-ons** ending of the **nous** form is added after the stem, because **c** + **o** produces a hard sound. To return to the soft sound of the infinitive, you have to modify the **c** itself by putting a cedilla on it, like this: **ç**. (For more on the cedilla and French pronunciation, see Chapter 2.) You wind up with **nous prononçons**.

Other verbs that follow this pattern include **commencer** (*to begin*), **annoncer** (*to announce*), and **remplacer** (*to replace*).

Verbs that end in -ger

In French, the letter **g** can have two sounds: a soft *j* or *zh* sound, as in the English word *leisure*, and a hard sound, as in the English word *guitar*. The French **g** follows these pronunciation rules:

- ✔ **g** is soft when it precedes **-e** or **-i**
- ✔ **g** is hard when it precedes **-a**, **-o**, or **-u**

Verbs that end in **-ger** have a soft sound in the infinitive and want to maintain it throughout their conjugation. As long as the ending begins with **-e** or **-i**, you're good because most endings in the present are **g** + **e**, a soft sound. For example, some present tense forms for the verb **manger** (*to eat*) are **je mange**, **tu manges**, **il/elle/on mange**, **vouz mangez**, and **ils/elles mangent**.

The problem arises when the **-ons** ending of the **nous** form is added after the stem, because **g** + **o** produces a hard sound! To return to the soft sound, you add an **-e** before the **-ons**, because the soft sound is so happy with the **-e** endings. The tweaked form is **nous mangeons**. Note: the added **-e** is not pronounced.

Other verbs that follow this pattern include **changer** (*to change*), **voyager** (*to travel*), **nager** (*to swim*), and **ranger** (*to tidy up*).

Verbs that end in -yer

Verbs that end in **-yer** — like **payer** (*to pay*) — alternate between **-y** + ending and **-i** + ending. These verbs

- ✔ Maintain the **-y** of the infinitive in front of the **nous** and **vous** endings: for example, **nous payons** (*we pay*) and **vous payez** (*you pay*).
- ✔ Replace the **-y** of the infinitive with **-i** in front of all the other endings: for example, **je paie** (*I pay*), **tu paies** (*you* [singular] *pay*), **il/elle/on paie** (*he/she/one pays*), and **ils/elles paient** (*they pay*).

Other verbs that follow this pattern include **s'ennuyer** (*to be bored*), **envoyer** (*to send*), and **nettoyer** (*to clean*).

Verbs that double their final consonant

Very few verbs follow the **appeler** (*to call*) and **jeter** (*to throw away*) pattern of conjugation. On both of them, the last consonant, the **-l** and the **-t**, respectively, get doubled for all forms of the conjugation, except for the **vous** and **nous** forms. I put them in tables for easy reference.

appeler (*to call*)	
j'**appelle**	nous **appelons**
tu **appelles**	vous **appelez**
il/elle/on **appelle**	ils/elles **appellent**

jeter (*to throw away*)	
je **jette**	nous **jetons**
tu **jettes**	vous **jetez**
il/elle/on **jette**	ils/elles **jettent**

Other verbs that follow this pattern include **épeler** (*to spell out*), **étinceler** (*to sparkle*), **renouveler** (*to renew*), and **feuilleter** (*to leaf through a book*).

Here are some examples.

> **Il feuillette toujours un livre avant de l'acheter.** (*He always leafs through a book before buying it.*)

> **Épelez votre nom, s'il vous plait.** (*Spell out your name, please.*)

Verbs that end in e/é + consonant + -er

Verbs that end in **e/é** + consonant + **-er** have stems that alternate between **e/é** and **è**. These verbs

- ✔ Maintain the **e/é** before the **nous** and **vous** endings: for example, **nous achetons** (*we buy*).
- ✔ Substitute the **e/é** for an **è** before all other endings: for example, **ils achètent** (*they buy*).

The following table gives you the complete conjugation of **acheter** (*to buy*).

acheter (*to buy*)	
j'**achète**	nous **achetons**
tu **achètes**	vous **achetez**
il/elle **achète**	ils/elles **achètent**

Other verbs in this category include **amener** (*to bring*), **enlever** (*to take off*), **geler** (*to freeze*), **se lever** (*to get up*), **se promener** (*to take a stroll*), **espérer** (*to hope*), **posséder** (*to own*), **préférer** (*to prefer*), **répéter** (*to repeat*), and **suggérer** (*to suggest*).

Conjugate the moody **-er** verbs in parentheses into the correct form of the present tense. Here's an example:

Q. Elle _____ un papier sale. (jeter)

A. jette

21. Elle _____ Julie. (s'appeler)

22. Nous _____ en train. (voyager)

23. Vous _____ le français ou les maths? (préférer)

24. Il _____ la facture. (payer)

25. Nous _____ le chapitre. (commencer)

26. Le professeur _____ la conjugaison. (répéter)

27. Les étoiles _____ dans le ciel. (étinceler)

28. J' _____ que tu viendras me voir. (espère)

29. Tu _____ des emails souvent. (envoyer)

30. Ses parents _____ ses études. (payer)

Tackling Irregular Verbs

Some verbs don't follow the regular patterns in the earlier section "Conjugating Regular Verbs" or even the moody patterns in the earlier section "Dealing with a Few Moody Regular -er Verbs" to form the present tense. They are irregular, and many of them actually don't follow much of a pattern at all! But you can still hold onto a few characteristics that are common to all verbs, regular or irregular: You still need to find the stem to which endings get added; and the **nous**, **vous**, and **ils/elles** endings are still respectively **-ons**, **-ez**, and **-ent**.

Some of the following irregular verbs share similar irregularities. I put them into several distinct groups so they're easier for you to recognize in the future. Get ready to discover the twists and turns of irregular verbs!

Revealing oddball -ir verbs

Many verbs have an **-ir** ending, but not all of them play nice! The **-ir** verbs I present in this section follow their own offbeat patterns.

Short -ir verbs

About 30 -**ir** verbs don't follow the regular -**ir** conjugation pattern of **finir** that I share in the earlier section "Investigating -**ir** verbs." I call them *short* verbs because they lack the -**iss** part of the plural endings that regular -**ir** verbs have. To conjugate such -**ir** verbs, the easiest way is to separate the singular forms (**je**, **tu**, **il/elle/on**) from the plural (**nous**, **vous**, **ils/elles**).

Here's how to conjugate the present tense of short -**ir** verbs for the **je**, **tu**, and **il/elle/on** forms:

1. **Drop the -ir ending as well as the final consonant before it.**

   For example, for the verb **partir** (*to leave*), you take off -**tir**, so you're left with **par-**.

2. **Now add the ending that fits your subject: -s, -s, or -t.**

   In the example, you wind up with this: **je pars**, **tu pars**, **il/elle/on part**.

Here's how to conjugate the present tense of short -**ir** verbs for the **nous**, **vous**, and **ils/elles** forms:

1. **Drop only the -ir of the infinitive to get the stem.**

   For example, for the verb **partir**, you take off -**ir**, so you're left with **part-**.

2. **Now add the ending -ons, -ez, or -ent.**

   You wind up with this: **nous partons**, **vous partez**, **ils/elles partent**.

The following tables give you an example of the short -**ir** conjugation, next to a regular -**ir** verb conjugation so you can clearly see the missing -**iss** in the plural . The short -**ir** verb is **partir**, and the long one **grandir**.

partir (*to leave*)	
je **pars**	nous **partons**
tu **pars**	vous **partez**
il/elle/on **part**	ils/elles **partent**

grandir (*to grow*)	
je **grandis**	nous **grandissons**
tu **grandis**	vous **grandissez**
il/elle/on **grandit**	ils/elles **grandissent**

Other examples of short -**ir** verbs include **dormir** (*to sleep*), **se sentir** (*to feel*), **sortir** (*to go out*), and **servir** (*to serve*).

-ir verbs that behave like -er verbs

Some -**ir** verbs behave like -**er** verbs. To conjugate them, you drop the -**ir** ending, like you would with a regular verb like **finir**. Then you add, well, the regular -**er** verb endings that I note earlier in this chapter: -**e**, -**es**, -**e**, -**ons**, -**ez**, and -**ent**! Here's the complete conjugation of one such verb, **ouvrir** (*to open*).

ouvrir (*to open*)	
j'ouvre	nous ouvrons
tu ouvres	vous ouvrez
il/elle/on ouvre	ils/elles ouvrent

Other verbs of this type include **découvrir** (*to discover*), **offrir** (*to offer*), and **souffrir** (*to suffer*).

The verbs venir and tenir

Finally, you meet a special group of verbs: **venir** (*to come*), **tenir** (*to hold*), and all their siblings (called *compound verbs* because they are formed with a prefix + **venir** or **tenir**). Such verbs include: **se souvenir** (*to remember*), **devenir** (*to become*), **revenir** (*to come back*), **appartenir** (*to belong*), and **soutenir** (*to support*).

To conjugate these irregular **-ir** verbs, drop the **-enir** of the infinitive and replace it with **-iens**, **-iens**, **-ient**, **-enons**, **-enez**, or **-iennent**. The following tables give you the complete present tense conjugation of **venir** and **tenir**.

venir (*to come*)	
je **viens**	nous **venons**
tu **viens**	vous **venez**
il/elle/on **vient**	ils/elles **viennent**

tenir (*to hold*)	
je **tiens**	nous **tenons**
tu **tiens**	vous **tenez**
Il/elle/on **tient**	ils/elles **tiennent**

The **je**, **tu**, **il/elle/on**, and **ils/elles** forms have the same stem (**-ien** + ending), whereas the **nous** and **vous** forms have the same stem as the infinitive (**-en**).

Conjugate the following oddball **-ir** verbs in present tense. Check out the example before you get started:

Q. je _____ (partir)

A. pars

31. tu _____ (ouvrir)

32. il _____ (revenir)

33. nous _____ (se souvenir)

34. vous _____ (**dormir**)

35. ils _____ (**offrir**)

36. je _____ (**appartenir**)

37. elle _____ (**se sentir**)

38. on _____ (**devenir**)

39. elles _____ (**tenir**)

40. ils _____ (**servir**)

Conquering the fatal four: être, avoir, aller, and faire

In French and in English, the verbs **être** (*to be*), **avoir** (*to have*), **aller** (*to go*), and **faire** (*to do*) are probably the most used verbs of our repertoire, which is also why they have become so twisted. Like your favorite sneakers, the more you use them, the more worn out and deformed they become! But you can't do without them. The four tables that follow give you the present tense conjugations of these verbs.

être (*to be*)	
je **suis**	nous **sommes**
tu **es**	vous **êtes**
il/elle/on **est**	ils/elles **sont**

avoir (*to have*)	
j'**ai**	nous **avons**
tu **as**	vous **avez**
il/elle/on **a**	ils/elles **ont**

For pronounciation, be very careful with **ils sont** (*they are*) and **ils ont** (*they have*), because they have pretty similar sounds. The difference is between the soft sound of **ils sont** and the *z* sound created by the **liaison** (the verbal link between the final **-s** and the following vowel) in **ils ont** (for more on the **liaison**, see Chapter 2).

aller (*to go*)	
je **vais**	nous **allons**
tu **vas**	vous **allez**
il/elle/on **va**	ils/elles **vont**

faire (*to do/to make*)	
je **fais**	nous **faisons**
tu **fais**	vous **faites**
il/elle/on **fait**	ils/elles **font**

For each of the following forms of the four verbs, choose the appropriate subject. The possibilities are

je (j')	**nous**
je or **tu**	**vous**
tu	**ils/elles**
il/elle/on	

Q. faites

A. vous

41. ai _____

42. fais _____

43. êtes _____

44. va _____

45. as _____

46. allons _____

47. font _____

48. ont _____

49. est _____

50. avez _____

Handling even more irregular verbs

The last group of irregular verbs includes some very common verbs that you don't want to ignore. I'm sorry to tell you that you have to memorize irregular rules for some common verbs, including **comprendre** (*to understand*) and **dire** (*to say/tell*), as well as verbs that often help another verb, like **pouvoir** (*can, to be able to*), **vouloir** (*to want*), and **devoir** (*must, to have to*). Check out the following sections for the scoop.

Helper verbs (plus a similar friend)

The verbs **pouvoir** (*can/to be able to*), **vouloir** (*to want*), and **devoir** (*must/to have to*) are important because they function as helper verbs in combination with another verb. In that case, the helper verb is conjugated but the other verb is in the infinitive. Here are some examples:

> **La police veut parler avec le suspect.** (*The police want to talk to the suspect.*)

> **Tu peux me prêter ta voiture s'il te plait?** (*Can you lend me your car, please?*)

> **Ils doivent finir leur travail.** (*They have to finish their work.*)

Unless you're dealing with a past tense like the **passé composé** (*present perfect*; see Chapter 15), you can only have an infinitive after a conjugated verb.

These verbs are irregular because they have two completely different stems: one for the **je**, **tu**, **il/elle/on**, and **ils/elles** forms and another one for the **nous** and **vous** forms. For instance, **pouvoir** alternates between a **peu-** stem and a **pouv-** stem. To form the present for **pouvoir**, you start with the appropriate stem and add the specific ending for each subject: **-x**, **-x**, **-t**, **-ons**, **-ez**, or **-vent**.

See the complete conjugation of **pouvoir** in the following table.

pouvoir (*can, to be able to*)	
je **peux**	nous **pouvons**
tu **peux**	vous **pouvez**
il/elle/on **peut**	ils/elles **peuvent**

Vouloir alternates between a **veu-** stem for the **je**, **tu**, **il/elle/on**, and **ils/elles** forms and a **voul-** stem for the **nous** and **vous** forms, with the following endings: **-x**, **-x**, **-t**, **-ons**, **-ez**, and **-lent**. The following table shows the complete conjugation.

vouloir (*to want*)	
je **veux**	nous **voulons**
tu **veux**	vous **voulez**
il/elle/on **veut**	ils/elles **veulent**

Devoir alternates between a **doi-** stem for the **je**, **tu**, **il/elle/on**, and **ils/elles** forms and a **dev-** stem for the **nous** and **vous** forms, with the following endings: **-s**, **-s**, **-t**, **-ons**, **-ez**, and **-vent**. The following table shows the complete conjugation.

devoir (*must, to have to*)	
je **dois**	nous **devons**
tu **dois**	vous **devez**
il/elle/on **doit**	ils/elles **doivent**

The endings for the **ils/elles** forms include the same consonant as the infinitive: -v for **pouvoir**, -l for **vouloir**, and -v for **devoir**.

Although it's not a helper verb, **boire** (*to drink*) has a a similar double stem irregularity as **pouvoir, vouloir,** and **devoir** (it is formed much like **devoir**), so it makes sense to place it in the same group. To form the present tense of **boire**, first separate the **je, tu, il/elle,** and **ils/elles** forms from the **nous** and **vous** forms, like you did for the helper verbs **pouvoir, vouloir,** and **devoir.**

- ✔ For **je, tu, il/elle,** and **ils/elles,** drop -**re** to get the stem **boi-** and then add the endings you need: -**s**, -**s**, -**t**, or -**vent.**

- ✔ For **nous** and **vous,** the stem is **buv-.** Add the ending -**ons** or -**ez** to get the corresponding present tense forms.

Here the complete conjugation for **boire.**

boire (*to drink*)	
je **bois**	nous **buvons**
tu **bois**	vous **buvez**
il/elle/on **boit**	ils/elles **boivent**

To recall that **pouvoir, vouloir, devoir,** and **boire** share a similar irregularity, you can use this little phrase: **Je veux et je peux boire mais je ne dois pas** (*I want to drink, and I can drink, but I must not*).

The verbs lire, dire, and conduire

The meanings of the verbs **lire** (*to read*), **dire** (*to say/tell*), and **conduire** (*to drive*) have nothing in common. However, they have a similar irregularity, so if you group them together, you may have more luck remembering them. This is how you form their present tense:

1. **Drop the -re of the infinitive to get the stem.**

2. **Add the ending for the subject you need: -s, -s, -t, -sons, -sez, or -sent.**

    The one exception in this group of irregular verbs is the vous form of **dire.** It is **dites,** not **disez.** (I mark it with an asterisk in the verb table to help you remember.)

The following tables give you the present tense conjugation of **lire, dire,** and **conduire.**

lire (*to read*)	
je **lis**	nous **lisons**
tu **lis**	vous **lisez**
il/elle/on **lit**	ils/elles **lisent**

dire (*to tell*)	
je **dis**	nous **disons**
tu **dis**	vous **dites***
il/elle/on **dit**	ils/elles **disent**

conduire (*to drive*)	
je **conduis**	nous **conduisons**
tu **conduis**	vous **conduisez**
il/elle/on **conduit**	ils/elles **consduisent**

The verbs écrire and mettre

Two more verbs: **écrire** (*to write*) and **mettre** (*to put*) misbehave very much like **lire**, **dire**, and **conduire**, but for one small difference that sets them in a different group.

Proceed like this to conjugate **écrire** in present tense:

1. **Drop the -re of the infinitive to find the stem.**
2. **Add the ending for the correct subject: -s, -s, and -t for the singular and -vons, -vez, and -vent for the plural.**

Here is the complete present tense conjugation of **écrire**:

écrire (*to write*)	
j'**écris**	nous **écrivons**
tu **écris**	vous **écrivez**
il/elle/on **écrit**	ils/elles **écrivent**

For **mettre**, drop the **-tre** of the infinitive to find the stem. Then add these endings: **-s**, **-s**, and nothing for the singular and **-tons**, **-tez**, or **-tent** for the plural. Here is the complete present tense conjugation of **mettre**:

mettre (*to put*)	
je **mets**	nous **mettons**
tu **mets**	vous **mettez**
il/elle/on **met**	ils **mettent**

The verbs prendre, apprendre, and comprendre

The verbs **prendre** (*to take*), **apprendre** (*to learn*), and **comprendre** (*to understand*) may come in handy to you. How can you say that you don't understand if you can't conjugate **comprendre**? Both **apprendre** and **comprendre** are derived from **prendre** and have the same irregular pattern of conjugation. Here's how you conjugate **prendre** in present, and by extension the same way you conjugate **apprendre** and **comprendre**.

1. **Drop the -dre of the infinitive to get the stem pren-.**

2. **Add the appropriate ending for the subject: -ds, -ds, -d, -ons, -ez, or -nent.**

The stem **pren-** is pronounced in a nasal way as long as no vowel follows it (that is, for the **je**, **tu**, **il/elle**, and **ils/elles** forms). With the vowels of the **nous** and **vous** endings (**-ons** and **-ez**), **pren-** is not nasal any more. (See Chapter 2 for an introduction to pronunciation.)

The following tables give you the complete present tense conjugation of **prendre**, **apprendre**, and **comprendre**.

prendre (*to take*)	
je **prends**	nous **prenons**
tu **prends**	vous **prenez**
il/elle/on **prend**	ils/elles **prennent**

apprendre (*to learn*)	
j'**apprends**	nous **apprenons**
tu **apprends**	vous **apprenez**
il/elle/on **apprend**	ils/elles **apprennent**

comprendre (*to understand*)	
je **comprends**	nous **comprenons**
tu **comprends**	vous **comprenez**
il/elle/on **comprend**	ils/elles **comprennent**

The verbs voir and croire

The verbs **voir** (*to see*) and **croire** (*to believe*) are alone in their group, although the particularity of their conjugation makes them somewhat akin to regular but moody **-yer** verbs (which I describe earlier in this chapter). Like those verbs, they have regular endings, but their stem has a little twist: they replace the **-i** with a **-y** in the **nous** and **vous** forms. Here's how to conjugate these verbs:

✔ For **je**, **tu**, **il/elle**, and **ils/elles**, drop the ending of the infinitive to get the stem (either **voi-** or **croi-**). Then add the correct choice from the following endings: **-s**, **-s**, **-t** and **-ent**.

✔ For **nous** and **vous**, drop the ending of the infinitive to get the stem (either **voi-** or **croi-**) and change the **-i** in the stem to **-y**. Then add the ending: **-ons** for **nous** and **-ez** for **vous**, like this: **nous voyons** (*we see*) and **nous croyons** (*we believe*), and **vous voyez** (*you see*) and **vous croyez** (*you believe*).

The following tables present the complete conjugation for both **voir** and **croire**.

voir (*to see*)	
je **vois**	nous **voyons**
tu **vois**	vous **voyez**
il/elle/on **voit**	ils/elles **voient**

croire (*to believe*)	
je **crois**	nous **croyons**
tu **crois**	vous **croyez**
il/elle/on **croit**	ils/elles **croient**

Put the following irregular verbs into the correct present tense form.

Q. il _____ (**vouloir**)

A. veut

51. vous _____ (**voir**)

52. il _____ (**croire**)

53. je _____ (**pouvoir**)

54. ils _____ (**lire**)

55. nous _____ (**comprendre**)

56. tu _____ (**mettre**)

57. ils _____ (**écrire**)

58. vous _____ (**dire**)

59. elle _____ (**conduire**)

60. on _____ (**boire**)

Answer Key

1	On	22	voyageons	42	je or tu
2	Elle	23	préférez	43	vous
3	vous	24	paie	44	il/elle/on
4	Je	25	commençons	45	tu
5	tu	26	répète	46	nous
6	Nous	27	étincellent	47	ils/elles
7	Il	28	espère (J'espère)	48	ils/elles
8	Ils	29	envoies	49	il/elle/on
9	Vous	30	paient	50	vous
10	Elles	31	ouvres	51	voyez
11	il choisit	32	revient	52	croit
12	vous entendez	33	nous souvenons	53	peux
13	nous réagissons	34	dormez	54	lisent
14	tu travailles	35	offrent	55	comprenons
15	ils grandissent	36	appartiens (j'appartiens)	56	mets
16	ils donnent	37	se sent	57	écrivent
17	je réponds	38	devient	58	dites
18	elle réussit	39	tiennent	59	conduit
19	elles descendent	40	servent	60	boit
20	on joue	41	je (j')		
21	s'appelle				

Chapter 7

Acting on Oneself and on Each Other: Pronominal Verbs

• •

In This Chapter

▶ Understanding the basics of pronominal verbs

▶ Using reflexive verbs to talk about yourself

▶ Talking about each other with reciprocal verbs

▶ Getting the hang of idiomatic verbs

• •

*W*henever you look at yourself, talk to yourself — all the time, right? — or prepare yourself, you (the subject) are doing something to yourself (the object). In English, you add a form of *oneself* after a regular verb like this: *to look at oneself*. In French, you use what's called a pronominal verb. The term *pronominal* may help you grasp the particular form of these verbs better: They are conjugated with an extra pronoun. It means that, on top of the subject pronoun (**je**, **tu**, and so on) they require another type of pronoun called a *reflexive pronoun* (**me**, **te**, **se**, or whichever is appropriate).

Pronominal verbs can be divided into three categories, as you discover in this chapter:

✔ **Reflexive verbs:** Express an action done by the subject to itself, such as **Je me regarde** (*I look at myself*).

✔ **Reciprocal verbs:** Indicate that two subjects are doing something to one another, as in **Ils se parlent** (*They talk to each other*).

✔ **Idiomatic pronominal verbs:** The extra pronoun indicates neither *to oneself* nor *to one another*, like **Tu te souviens** (*You remember*).

Introducing Pronominal Verbs in the Present Tense

Before you can use any type of pronominal verb (reflexive, reciprocal, or idiomatic), you need to familiarize yourself with reflexive pronouns and know how to use them with verbs in the present tense (both regular verbs and stem-changing verbs). The following sections give you the scoop. (For details on how to use pronominal verbs in the past tense, check out Chapter 15.)

Discovering reflexive pronouns

As a general rule, reflexive pronouns go directly before the verb in the infinitive. For example, in **se laver** (*to wash oneself*), **laver** is the verb in the infinitive, and **se** is the reflexive pronoun that goes before the verb. When you conjugate the verb to indicate a different subject, the reflexive pronoun **se** must also be modified according to the subject of the verb. For instance, if the subject is **je** (*I*), **se** changes to **me**; for the subject **tu** (*you*), **se** changes to **te**; and so on. Table 7-1 gives you the list of the reflexive pronouns and their English equivalent.

Table 7-1	Reflexive Pronouns and Their English Equivalents	
Subject	*Reflexive Pronoun*	*English Translation*
je	me/m' (before a vowel or a mute -h)	*myself*
tu	te/t' (before a vowel or a mute -h)	*yourself*
il	se/s' (before a vowel or a mute -h)	*himself*
elle	se/s' (before a vowel or a mute -h)	*herself*
on	se/s' (before a vowel or a mute -h)	*oneself*
nous	nous	*ourselves*
vous	vous	*yourselves*
ils/elles	se/s' (before a vowel or a mute -h)	*themselves*

In the imperative (command form) of a pronominal verb, the pronoun is placed behind the verb and attached to it with a hyphen like so: **lavez-vous** (*wash yourselves*). The imperative has only three forms: **tu** (*you* [singular informal]), **nous** (*us*, as in *let's*), and **vous** (*you* [plural or singular formal]). Also keep in mind that the reflexive pronoun **te** becomes **toi** when placed after the verb in the imperative: **Lave-toi!** (*Wash yourself!*) See Chapter 20 for full details on the imperative.

Putting together a reflexive pronoun and a verb

To form the present tense of pronominal verbs, follow these easy steps.

1. **Conjugate the verb in the present tense to match your subject, without worrying about the reflexive pronoun se for now.**

   For example, you want to express that you're getting ready. The French verb is **se préparer**. Because you're talking about yourself, you conjugate **préparer** in the **je** form: **prépare**. Your subject-verb unit is ready!

2. **Change the reflexive pronoun to match your subject and place it immediately before the verb.**

   In the example, **se** needs to reflect the subject **je**, so use **me**. Now place **me** immediately before the verb, which puts it between the subject **je** and the verb **prépare**, like this: **je me prépare**.

For example, here is the complete present tense conjugation of **se laver** (*to wash oneself*). Note the place of the reflexive pronoun each time. (The verb **laver** is a regular **-er** verb; see Chapter 6 for more about these types of verbs.)

se laver (*to wash oneself*)	
je **me lave**	nous **nous lavons**
tu **te laves**	vous **vous lavez**
Il/elle/on **se lave**	ils/elles **se lavent**

To make any of these statements negative, just add **ne** between the subject and the reflexive pronoun; then add **pas** after the verb. For example, **je ne me lave pas** means *I don't wash*. See Chapter 8 for more about negative expressions.

Complete the following verb forms in present tense with the correct reflexive pronoun. Here's an example:

O. **Nous** _____ **lavons.**

A. **Nous nous lavons.**

1. Je _____ coiffe.

2. Tu _____ laves.

3. Il _____ couche.

4. Vous _____ maquillez.

5. Nous _____ réveillons.

Dealing with stem-changing pronominal verbs

Here's the good news. Most pronominal verbs are regular **-er** verbs, and conjugating them in the present tense is the same as conjugating any other verb (except for the pronoun, of course!). So in the present, drop the **-er** ending of the infinitive and add the ending **-e**, **-es**, **-e**, **-ons**, **-ez**, or **-ent**, based on what subject you have chosen (see Chapter 6 for details). Don't forget that the reflexive pronoun must match the subject of the verb (as I explain in the preceding section).

The bad news, however, is that some **-er** verbs go through a stem change in four forms of the conjugation: **je**, **tu**, **il/elle**, and **ils/elles**. The other two forms, **nous** and **vous**, have the same stem as the infinitive. (Of course you can flip to Chapter 6 for more about stem-changing conjugations in the present tense.)

Some stem-changing pronominal verbs double the consonant at the end of the stem. The following table shows how to conjugate the verb **s'appeler** (*to be called*), which you use to say what someone's name is.

s'appeler (*to be called*)	
je **m'appelle**	nous **nous appelons**
tu **t'appelles**	vous **vous appelez**
Il/elle/on **s'appelle**	ils/elles **s'appellent**

Some stem-changing pronominal verbs have a **y** at the end of the stem that changes to an **i**. The following table shows how to conjugate the verb **s'ennuyer** (*to be bored*).

s'ennuyer (*to be bored*)	
je **m'ennuie**	nous **nous ennuyons**
tu **t'ennuies**	vous **vous ennuyez**
il/elle/on **s'ennuie**	ils/elles **s'ennuient**

Se lever (*to get up*) and **se promener** (*to stroll/take a walk*) are **e/é** + consonant + **er** types of pronominal verbs that change their **e/é** to an **è** in the **je**, **tu**, **il/elle**, and **ils/elles** forms of the conjugation. The following table shows how to conjugate **se lever** in the present tense.

se lever (*to get up*)	
je **me lève**	nous **nous levons**
tu **te lèves**	vous **vous levez**
il/elle/on **se lève**	ils/elles **se lèvent**

If a sentence has two verbs (one conjugated and the other a pronominal verb in the infinitive), as in *You want to wash yourself*, place the correct form of the reflexive pronoun before the infinitive like so: **Tu veux te laver** (*You want to wash yourself*).

Mirror, Mirror: Acting on Oneself with Reflexive Verbs

When you look at yourself in a mirror, the mirror reflects your image back to you. When your brother looks at himself in the mirror, he sees himself reflected, not you. And when you want to express that reflection in French, you use a reflexive verb. The name says it all: A reflexive pronoun reflects the subject. When you want to indicate that you're doing a particular action on yourself, use a reflexive verb with a reflexive pronoun.

Note: Using a reflexive verb without its reflexive pronoun indicates that the subject does something to someone else. See the difference in these examples:

Je me réveille. (*I wake myself up.*)

Je réveille les enfants. (*I wake up the kids.*)

A lot of verbs that you use to describe things relating to yourself are reflexive, in particular those dealing with daily routines. Check out a few very common ones:

- **se brosser** (**les dents**; **les cheveux**) (*to brush [one's teeth/hair]*)
- **se casser** (**le bras**; **la jambe**) (*to break [one's arm/leg]*)
- **se coucher** (*to go to bed*)
- **se couper/se couper les cheveux** (*to cut oneself/to cut one's hair*)
- **se coiffer** (*to do one's hair*)
- **se doucher** (*to take a shower*)
- **se laver** (**les cheveux**; **les mains**) (*to wash up/to wash one's [hair; hands]*)
- **se lever** (*to get up*)
- **se mouiller** (*to get wet*)
- **se maquiller** (*to put on makeup*)
- **se préparer** (*to get ready*)
- **s'habiller** (*to get dressed*)
- **se regarder** (*to look at oneself*)
- **se réveiller** (*to wake up*)
- **se raser** (*to shave [oneself]*)

Here are some common reflexive verbs in action.

> **Je me brosse les dents trois fois par jour.** (*I brush my teeth three times a day.*)
>
> **Tu t'habilles vite.** (*You get dressed fast.*)
>
> **Elles se maquillent.** (*They put on makeup.*)

When verbs like **se brosser**, **se casser**, and **se laver** are followed by a body part, that body part comes with the definite article **le**, **la**, or **les**, as in **Je me brosse les dents** (*I brush my teeth*). Flip to Chapter 3 for an introduction to definite articles.

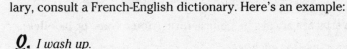

Translate the following sentences with a common reflexive verb. (These verbs are regular **-er** verbs; see Chapter 6 if you need help conjugating them.) If you need help with any vocabulary, consult a French-English dictionary. Here's an example:

0. *I wash up.*

A. Je me lave.

6. *You* [singular] *are doing your hair.*

_____

7. *She puts her makeup on.*

_____

8. *He takes a shower.*

_____

9. *We're getting dressed.*

_____

10. *I brush my hair.*

_____

11. *You [plural] go to bed.*

_____

12. *She looks at herself in a mirror.*

_____

13. *You [singular] are getting ready.*

_____

14. *They don't shave.*

_____

15. *She doesn't get wet.*

_____

Back and Forth: Expressing Reciprocal Actions

Pronominal verbs are also used to express reciprocity when two subjects are doing something to each other, as in **Ils se parlent** (*They talk to each other*). In reciprocal sentences, two grammatical rules always apply:

✔ The reciprocal verbs are always in a plural form (**nous**, **vous**, or **ils/elles**).

✔ The pronoun **se** means *(to) each other*.

The following sections discuss specific reciprocal verbs of communication and show you how to turn any verb into a reciprocal verb.

Not all plural reciprocal verbs actually express reciprocity. For instance, **ils se souviennent** means *they remember*, not *they remember each other*. Likewise, **ils s'ennuient** doesn't mean *they bore each other* but simply *they are bored*. See the later section "Idiomatic Verbs: Expressing Neither Oneself nor Each Other" for more details.

Talking about communication

Communication between two people is often expressed using a reciprocal verb. Here are some common reciprocal verbs of communication:

- ✔ **s'écrire** (*to write to each other*)
- ✔ **se dire** (*to tell each other*)
- ✔ **s'envoyer (des lettres/des emails/des textos)** (*to send to each other [letters/e-mails/texts]*)
- ✔ **se parler** (*to talk to each other*)
- ✔ **se téléphoner** (*to phone each other*)

Parler and **téléphoner** are regular **-er** verbs; **envoyer** alternates between **-y** and **-i** in the stem, and **écrire** and **dire** are irregular verbs. See Chapter 6 for detailed conjugations.

Here are some examples of these verbs in action:

Nous nous téléphonons chaque soir. (*We phone each other every evening.*)

Elles s'écrivent pendant les vacances. (*They write each other during the vacation.*)

In the **passé composé** (*present perfect*), past participles do not change to agree with the subject, as shown in these examples (see Chapter 15 for more about the **passé composé**):

Nous nous sommes téléphoné. (*We phoned each other.*)

Elles se sont écrit. (*They wrote to each other.*)

Put the following statements into French, using the proper reciprocal noun of communication. If you need help with any vocabulary, consult a French-English dictionary. Here's an example.

0. *They [feminine] send each other e-mails.*

A. **Elles s'envoient des e-mails.**

16. *You write to each other often.*

_____

17. *We call/phone each other every day.*

_____

18. *They [masculine] talk to each other often.*

_____

19. *They [feminine] tell the truth to each other.*

_____

20. *We text each other.*

_____

Making your own reciprocal verbs

French is very economical when it comes to mutual/reciprocal actions, and you can express *to each other* and *one another* just by using a plural verb with a reflexive pronoun. For instance, you can say *Pierre loves Julie* using a singular subject (Pierre), a singular verb (loves), and an object (Julie); or you can say *Pierre and Julie love each other* using a plural subject (Pierre and Julie) and a plural verb (love) and adding *each other* (denoted by a reflexive pronoun). This is the French version:

> With a regular verb: **Pierre aime Julie.**

> With a reciprocal verb: **Pierre et Julie s'aiment.**

Here are a few common verbs that function like this.

- ✔ **s'aimer** (*to love/like each other*)
- ✔ **s'embrasser** (*to kiss each other*)
- ✔ **se rencontrer** (*to meet each other for the first time*)
- ✔ **se tutoyer** (*say "tu" to each other*)
- ✔ **se voir** (*to see each other*)
- ✔ **se vouvoyer** (*say "vous" to each other*)

However, if the English verb is followed by *together* instead of *each other* or *one another*, don't use the pronominal form in French. You need to use **ensemble** (*together*). Look at the difference:

> **Les enfants jouent ensemble.** (*The kids play together.*)

Turn the following sentences into reciprocal statements, using a pronominal verb in the plural. To get you started, here's an example:

Q. **Pierre parle à Julie, et Julie parle à Pierre.**

A. **Pierre et Julie se parlent.**

21. **Grand-père écrit des lettres à grand-mère, et grand-mère écrit des lettres à grand-père.**

_____

22. **Anne envoie un texto à Jeanne, et Jeanne envoie un texto à Anne.**

_____

23. **Paul téléphone à Valérie, et Valérie téléphone à Paul.**

_____

24. Jeanne dit des blagues à Maurice, et Maurice dit des blagues à Jeanne.

_____

25. Caroline explique un problème à Sylvie, et Sylvie explique un problème à Caroline.

_____

Idiomatic Verbs: Expressing Neither Oneself nor Each Other

With idiomatic pronominal verbs, the reflexive pronoun **se** doesn't reflect the subject or subjects, and it doesn't mean *(to) oneself* or *(to) each other*. For example **s'ennuyer** means *to be bored*, not *to bore oneself* nor *to bore each other*. Likewise **il s'appelle** doesn't mean *he calls himself* but simply *his name is.* So what does the pronoun mean? Pretty much nothing, but it must stay! Without it, the verb would mean something else and sometimes wouldn't even exist, as shown in Table 7-2.

Table 7-2		Idiomatic Pronominal Verbs	
Idiomatic Pronominal Verb	*English Translation*	*Same Verb without Pronominal*	*English Translation*
s'amuser	to have fun	amuser	to amuse
s'appeler	to be named	appeler	to call
s'arrêter	to stop	arrêter	to stop
s'en aller	to leave	(None)	
s'ennuyer	to be/get bored	ennuyer	to bother/to bore
s'entendre	to get along	entendre	to hear
se débrouiller	to manage	débrouiller	to untangle
se demander	to wonder	demander	to ask
se dépêcher	to hurry	(None)	
se disputer	to argue	(None)	
s'occuper (de)	to take care of	occuper	to occupy
se rendre compte	to realize	rendre compte	to account for
se reposer	to rest	reposer	to put back
se sentir	to feel	sentir	to smell
se souvenir	to remember	(None)	
se taire	to be quiet	(None)	
se tromper	to make a mistake	tromper	to dupe
se trouver	to be located	trouver	to find

Here are a couple of these idiomatic verbs in action:

> **Elle s'occupe des enfants.** (*She takes care of the kids.*)

> **Les étudiants occupent l'université.** (*The students occupy the college.*)

Translate the following sentences into English. The practice questions include all three types of pronominal verbs: reflexive, reciprocal, and idiomatic. Here's an example.

0. Je m'ennuie.

A. *I am bored/I'm getting bored.*

26. Notre-Dame se trouve à Paris.

_____

27. Ils s'entendent bien.

_____

28. Le prof se dépêche.

_____

29. Le train s'arrête.

_____

30. Tu te demandes si tu as raison.

_____

31. Julie s'amuse avec son chat.

_____

32. Comment vous appelez-vous?

_____

33. Il s'occupe de ses enfants.

_____

34. Je me souviens de vous.

_____

35. Nous nous disputons.

_____

Answer Key

1 me

2 te

3 se

4 vous

5 nous

6 Tu te coiffes.

7 Elle se maquille.

8 Il se douche.

9 Nous nous habillons.

10 Je me brosse les cheveux.

11 Vous vous couchez.

12 Elle se regarde dans un miroir.

13 Tu te prépares.

14 Ils ne se rasent pas.

15 Elle ne se mouille pas.

16 Vous vous écrivez souvent.

17 Nous nous appelons/téléphonons tous les jours.

18 Ils se parlent souvent.

19 Elles se disent la vérité.

20 Nous nous envoyons des textos.

21 Ils s'écrivent des lettres.

22 Elles s'envoient des textos.

23 Ils se téléphonent.

24 Ils se disent des blagues.

25 **Elles s'expliquent des problèmes.**

26 *Notre-Dame is located in Paris.*

27 *They get along.*

28 *The professor hurries.*

29 *The train stops.*

30 *You wonder if you're right.*

31 *Julie plays with her cat.*

32 *What is your name?*

33 *He takes care of his children.*

34 *I remember you.*

35 *We argue/are arguing.*

Chapter 8

Just Say No: Negative Words and Phrases

In This Chapter

▶ Beginning with negative basics

▶ Applying some rules to negative sentences

▶ Just saying no with negative answers

When you *can't* do something, or you *don't want* to go anywhere, because you *don't have* any clothes to wear, you use a negative. French negative usage is very different from English, but this chapter guides you through those differences so you can master the art of the "no." You get the scoop on different words and phrases, figure out how to build negative sentences, and discover how to respond negatively to questions.

Discovering the Basics of Negative Words and Phrases

French always uses two negative words to form a negative sentence. A negative always starts with the word **ne**, which doesn't translate into anything really in English, and then you also have to use **pas** (*not*) and its brothers. Like in an English negative, in which you can have *not any more*, *never*, and *nowhere*, a French negative has all those options that can take the place of **pas**. The section below details them for you as well as where exactly to put them in the sentence.

Starting with a few common negative words and phrases

A French negative sentence is built on a different pattern than an English one (see the following section for details), but negative words like *nothing*, *never*, and *no one* all have French equivalents: **rien**, **jamais**, and **personne**, in this case. Here's a list of common French negative words and phrases with their English equivalents.

✔ **aucun/aucune** [+ noun] (*no/none/not any*)

✔ **jamais** (*never*)

✔ **même pas** (*not even*)

✔ **ni . . . ni** (*neither . . . nor*)

✔ **nulle part** (*nowhere*)

✔ **pas** (*not*)

✔ **pas encore** (*not yet*)

✔ **pas grand-chose** (*not much*) (informal)

✔ **pas non plus** (*either/neither*)

✔ **personne** (*no one, nobody*)

✔ **plus** (*not any more/no longer*)

✔ **rien** (*nothing*)

Making a double negative

In English, one negative word, like *never*, or one negative verb, like *don't*, suffice to make a sentence negative. For example you say *I don't play soccer*, or *I never play soccer*. To express the same thing in French, however, you need two negative words: **ne** and **pas** (which together mean *not*) around the conjugated verb, kind of like the two speakers on either side of your stereo.

To form a French negative sentence, follow these easy steps:

1. **Start with the subject + verb.**

   For example: **Tu joues.** (*You play.*)

2. **Insert ne between the subject and verb.**

   Like this: **Tu ne joues.**

3. **Put pas right after the verb.**

   You wind up with something like this: **Tu ne joues pas.** (*You don't play.*)

If a verb begins with a vowel, **ne** becomes **n'** — for example, **Ils n'ont pas de chien.** (*They don't have a dog.*) In addition, **pas** can be replaced by other negative words. (See the previous section for a list.) **Ne** always stays. Here are some examples:

Il n'a plus d'argent. (*He doesn't have any more money.*)

Elle ne boit jamais de vin. (*She never drinks wine.*)

Nous n'irons nulle part pour les vacances. (*We won't go anywhere for the holidays.*)

Ces gens n'aiment personne. (*These people don't like anyone.*)

Ils ne font pas grand-chose le dimanche. (*They don't do much on Sundays.*)

Turn the following affirmative sentences into the negative, using the negative word in parentheses. Here's an example:

0. **Tu parles. (pas)**

A. **Tu ne parles pas.**

1. **Il réfléchit. (jamais)**

_____

2. **Tu as besoin de ta voiture. (plus)**

_____

3. **Ils aiment les animaux. (pas)**

_____

4. **Vous sortez le dimanche, et le samedi. (ni/ni)**

_____

5. **J'apprends la leçon. (pas encore)**

_____

Building a triple negative

Sometimes, French can be *really* negative and add another negative word — or sometimes two or three — to the original pair of **ne/pas** that I talk about in the preceding section. Just place the additional negative after the first one. Here are some examples, with a number after each sentence to indicate how many negative words were added to the original two:

> **Elle ne fera plus jamais rien.** (*She will never do anything ever again.*) + 2 (**jamais/rien**)

> **Elle ne pose jamais de questions à personne.** (*She never asks any questions to anyone.*) + 1 (**jamais**)

> **Rien ne l'intéresse plus.** (*Nothing interests him/her anymore.*) + 1 (**plus**)

> **Nous n'allons jamais nulle part pour les vacances.** (*We never go anywhere for the holidays.*) + 1 (**jamais**)

But you can let your imagination loose as long as the word order is respected for each negative word, in particular with the compound tenses (such as the present perfect in Chapter 15). In a compound tense (made with **être** or **avoir** + past participle), **ne** precedes the auxiliary, and the second (or more) negative word follows it, with a few exceptions listed in the next section. Here's an example of multiple negatives in a sentence with a compound verb:

> **Ils n'ont jamais rien trouvé nulle part.** (*They've never found anything anywhere.*)

Using negative expressions by themselves

Sometimes in conversation, you don't need to make a complete sentence to get your point across. Here are some useful negative expressions that you can use by themselves, without **ne** as in a regular negative sentence. Just be aware that these expressions are for verbal communication and carry a note of informality.

- **jamais plus** (*never again*)
- **moi non plus** (*me neither*)
- **pas du tout** (*not at all*)
- **pas grand-chose** (*not much*)
- **pas maintenant** (*not now*)
- **pas moi** (*not me*)
- **pas question** (*no way*)
- **personne** (*nobody*)
- **presque pas** (*almost not*)
- **rien** (*nothing*)

Here they are in action:

—**Tu veux sortir?** (*Do you want to go out?*)
—**Pas maintenant!** (*Not now.*)

—**Est-ce que tu retourneras là-bas?** (*Will you go back?*)
—**Jamais plus!** (*Never again!*)

—**Je n'ai pas faim maintenant, et toi?** (*I'm not hungry right now. And you?*)
—**Moi non plus.** (*Me neither.*)

—**Qui va faire la vaisselle?** (*Who's going to do the dishes?*)
—**Pas moi!** (*Not me!*)

—**Qu'est-ce qu'il y a?** (*What's the matter?*)
—**Rien.** (*Nothing.*)

Keeping a Few Handy Guidelines for Negatives in Mind

You need a few guidelines when you use negative words and phrases with a simple verb tense like the present, the imperfect (see Chapter 16), and the future (see Chapter 17). And unfortunately, negatives don't always fall neatly before and after the verb. Sometimes they move around! The following sections explain what you need to know about correctly using negatives in a variety of situations.

Talking about quantities in negative ways

Do you have *some money* (**de l'argent**) in your pocket? Or do you have *no money* (**pas d'argent**)? Maybe you have *a couple of ideas* (**des idées**), but maybe you have *no idea* (**aucune idée**)! To negate a quantity, or go from some/any to zero, French has a few options:

✔ Use **de** to negate **un** (*a* [masculine]), **une** (*a* [feminine]), **des** (*some*), **du** (*some* [masculine singular]), **de la** (*some* [feminine singular]), or **de l'** (*some* [used before a vowel]) in a negative sentence. For example:

—**Est-ce que tu as de la chance?** (*Do you have luck?*)
—**Non, je n'ai pas de chance.** (*No, I don't have any luck.*)

—**Est-ce qu'ils ont des chiens?** (*Do they have dogs?*)
—**Non, ils n'ont pas de chien.** (*No, they don't have dogs.*)

✔ Use **aucun/aucune** (*absolutely no/none whatsoever*) to replace **un**, **une**, **des**, **du**, **de la**, or **de l'** in a negative sentence to insist on the zero quantity. The trick is to remember that **aucun** is an adjective. As such, it matches the gender of the noun it accompanies, so it has a feminine form (**aucune**) and a masculine one (**aucun**), but no plural, because it means the quantity zero. For example:

Je n'ai aucune idée. (*I have absolutely no idea.*)

Cet "artiste" n'a aucun talent. (*This "artist" has no talent whatsoever.*)

✔ To say *none of the* + noun, use **aucun** (if the noun that follows is masculine) **des** + plural noun. For example:

Je n'ai trouvé aucun des livres que je voulais. (*I found none of the books I wanted.*)

Use **aucune** (if the noun that follows is feminine) **des** + plural noun. For example:

Il n'a choisi aucune des solutions proposées. (*He chose none of the proposed solutions.*)

Check out Chapter 5 for an introduction to talking about quantities.

Answer each question negatively. Don't forget that indefinite and partitive articles must change to **de** in a negative sentence. Here's an example:

Q. **Est-ce qu'il y a un portefeuille** (*a wallet*) **dans son sac?**

A. **Il n'y a pas de portefeuille dans son sac.**

6. **Est-ce que vous avez des cigarettes** (*cigarettes*)?

_____

7. **Est-ce qu'ils ont une voiture** (*a car*)?

_____

8. **Est-ce que vous utilisez un portable** (*a cellphone*)?

_____

9. **Est-ce que tu bois du café?**

_____

10. **Est-ce qu'il a de la monnaie** (*some change*)?

_____

Negating an infinitive

If a verb is in the infinitive form, the two negative words stick together, in front of the verb, instead of surrounding it as they do with conjugated verbs. Here are some examples:

> **Je préfère ne pas sortir ce soir.** (*I prefer not to go out tonight.*)

> **Ils aiment ne rien faire.** (*They like to do nothing.*)

See Chapter 6 for an introduction to infinitives.

Dealing with a verb plus a preposition

When you *talk to no one* or you *play with no one*, you use prepositions (like *to* and *with*), and you make negative words happy because they like prepositions. In fact, they like them so much that the second negative deserts the verb to follow the preposition! The order of words is like this:

> subject + **ne** + verb + preposition + second negative

Here are some examples:

> **Je n'ai besoin de rien.** (*I don't need anything.*)

> **Il ne joue avec personne.** (*He plays with no one.*)

See Chapter 11 for more about prepositions.

Handling object pronouns

In a negative sentence with an object pronoun, like **le/la** (*it*), **le/lui** (*him*), or **la/lui** (*her*), the order of words changes a little. With any object pronouns except **y** (the pronoun for places) and **en** (the pronoun for quantities), proceed like this:

> subject + **ne** + pronoun + verb + **pas** (or other negative word)

Here are some examples of a negative sentence with this structure:

> **Ils ne la veulent pas.** (*They don't want it* [feminine].)
>
> **Je ne le vois jamais.** (*I never see him.*)

With **y** and **en** in a negative sentence, proceed the same way, but use **n'** instead of **ne**, like this:

> **Nous n'y allons pas souvent.** (*We don't go there very often.*)
>
> **Tu n'en prends jamais.** (*You never take any.*)

Flip to Chapter 13 for full details about using object pronouns.

Rewrite each (currently incomplete) negative sentence to include the pronoun in parentheses. Here's an example:

Q. **Ils ne parlent pas. (lui)**

A. **Ils ne lui parlent pas.**

11. **Elle n'écoute jamais. (les)**

_____

12. **Vous n'allez pas. (y)**

_____

13. **Je ne veux pas. (en)**

_____

14. **Tu ne regardes pas. (la)**

_____

15. **Nous ne finissons pas. (le)**

_____

Using negative words as subjects

Rien (*nothing*) and **personne** (*no one, nobody*) can sometimes be the subject of the verb instead of playing second (negative) fiddle. When you want to express that *nothing is important* in French, start the sentence with **rien**, like in English, and proceed regularly, with **ne** followed by the verb.

Here are some examples:

> **Rien n'est important.** (*Nothing is important.*)
>
> **Personne ne fait la vaisselle.** (*Nobody does the dishes.*)

When **rien** and **personne** are subjects, the verb is always in third person singular. The following example shows you the passage from a plural verb in the question to a singular verb in the answer with **personne**:

Est-ce que les enfants regardent la télé? (*Are the children watching TV?*)

Non, personne ne regarde la télé. (*Nobody is watching TV.*)

Knowing rules for neither/nor

To say *neither . . . nor*, French uses **ne . . . ni . . . ni**. For example, **Il n'aime ni les chiens, ni les chats** (*He likes neither dogs nor cats*). Easy enough, right? But the tricky part is what to do with the rest of the sentence, because **ni** can negate nouns, prepositional phrases, adjectives, infinitives, and pronouns.

Nouns

Nouns always come with articles in French. With **ni** in the sentence, several things can happen, depending on the article that accompanies the noun (check out Chapter 3 for the full scoop on articles). Here's what you need to know:

- ✔ For nouns introduced by the definite article, keep the article and add **ni** in front of it, like this:

    —**Tu aimes les pommes, les bananes et les oranges?** (*You like apples, bananas, and oranges?*)
    —**Non, je n'aime ni les pommes, ni les bananes ni les oranges.** (*No, I like neither apples nor bananas, nor oranges.*)

    Like in English, if the list you're about to negate has **et** (*and*), drop it from the negative sentence.

- ✔ For nouns introduced by a possessive or demonstrative adjective, keep the adjective and add **ni** in front of it, like this:

    Nous ne verrons ni mon frère, ni mes oncles. (*We will see neither my brother nor my uncles.*)

- ✔ For nouns introduced by indefinite or partitive articles, replace each article by **ni** like this:

    —**Vous avez des chiens et des chats?** (*Do you have dogs and cats?*)
    —**Non, nous n'avons ni chiens ni chats.** (*No, we have neither dogs nor cats.*)

Prepositional phrases

When you negate prepositional phrases like **à la maison** (*at home*) or **au bureau** (*at work*) with **ni**, keep the entire phrase and add **ni** in front of it like this:

Mon sac n'est ni à la maison, ni au bureau, ni dans la voiture! (*My bag is neither at home nor at work nor in my car!*)

Elle ne parle ni à Jules, ni à Jacques. (*She speaks neither to Jules nor to Jacques.*)

Adjectives, infinitives, and pronouns

You're going to like how easy it is to negate adjectives, infinitives, and pronouns with **ni**!

✔ With adjectives, put **ne** before the conjugated verb and add **ni** in front of each adjective, like this:

> **Paul n'est ni beau, ni riche, mais il est très drole.** (*Paul is neither handsome nor rich, but he's very funny.*)

✔ With infinitives, put **ne** before the conjugated verb and add **ni** in front of each following infinitive, like this:

> **Elle n'aime ni courir, ni marcher.** (*She likes neither running nor walking.*)

✔ With stress pronouns, put **ne** before the conjugated verb and add **ni** in front of each pronoun, like this:

> **Ce n'est ni lui, ni elle.** (*It's neither he nor she.*)

Answer the following questions with the negative **ni**; consult a French-English dictionary if you need help with any vocabulary. Be particularly careful with the articles. Here's an example:

Q. Tu aimes les oranges et les bananes?

A. Non, je n'aime ni les oranges ni les bananes.

16. Tu aimes chanter et danser?

_____

17. Est-ce que tes amis sont ennuyeux et bêtes?

_____

18. Est-ce que vous avez des oiseaux et des chiens à la maison?

_____

19. Est-ce que tu manges au bureau ou à la maison le lundi?

_____

20. C'est toi ou eux?

_____

Responding Negatively

In order to give an accurate negative response to a question, you need to know some key words in the question. For example, if I ask you, **Est-ce que quelqu'un est malade?**

(*Is someone sick?*) but you don't know that **quelqu'un** means *someone*, you can't answer negatively or affirmatively! Table 8-1 reviews some of the words that come up in questions and the negative words that your answers have. (See Chapter 9 for more details about handling questions.)

Table 8-1	Responding Negatively to Questions
If the Question Has:	*Your Negative Answer Has:*
beaucoup (*a lot*)	**aucun** [+ noun] (*none*)
déjà (*already*)	**pas encore** (*not yet*)
déjà (*ever*)	**jamais** (*never*)
encore (*still*)	**plus** (*not any more/no longer*)
parfois (*sometimes*)	**jamais** (*never*)
quelque chose (*something*)	**rien** (*nothing*)
quelque part (*somewhere*)	**nulle part** (*nowhere*)
quelqu'un (*someone*)	**personne** (*no one*)
souvent (*often*)	**jamais** (*never*)

Here they are in action:

—**Il y a quelqu'un?** (*Is there someone?*)
—**Il n'y a personne.** (*There's no one.*)

—**Avez-vous beaucoup de chance?** (*Do you have a lot of luck?*)
—**Je n'ai aucune chance.** (*I have absolutely no luck.*)

—**Tu as déjà fini?** (*Have you already finished?*)
—**Je n'ai pas encore fini.** (*I haven't finished yet.*)

—**Vous êtes déjà allés en France?** (*Have you ever been to France?*)
—**Nous ne sommes jamais allés en France.** (*We've never been to France.*)

—**Elle joue encore à la poupée?** (*Does she still play with dolls?*)
—**Elle ne joue plus à la poupée.** (*She doesn't play with dolls any more.*)

Give a negative answer to these questions. Note that **du, de la, de l', un, une,** and **des** change to **de** in a negation, and be sure to check a French-English dictionary if you need help with the vocabulary. Here's an example:

Q. **Est-ce que vous sortez souvent?**

A. **Nous ne sortons jamais.**

21. **Est-ce que tu aimes quelqu'un?**

22. Allez-vous quelque part pour les vacances?

_____

23. Est-ce qu'ils veulent quelque chose?

_____

24. Est-ce qu'il y a quelque chose dans ce sac?

_____

25. Est-ce qu'elle danse parfois?

_____

Answer Key

1. Il ne réfléchit jamais.

2. Tu n'as plus besoin de ta voiture.

3. Ils n'aiment pas les animaux.

4. Vous ne sortez ni le samedi, ni le dimanche.

5. Je n'apprends pas encore la leçon.

6. Je n'ai pas de cigarettes.

7. Ils n'ont pas de voiture/Ils n'ont aucune voiture.

8. Je n'utilise pas de portable.

9. Je ne bois pas de café.

10. Il n'a pas de monnaie./Il n'a aucune monnaie.

11. Elle ne les écoute jamais.

12. Vous n'y allez pas.

13. Je n'en veux pas.

14. Tu ne la regardes pas.

15. Nous ne le finissons pas.

16. Je n'aime ni chanter ni danser.

17. Mes amis ne sont ni ennuyeux ni bêtes.

18. Nous n'avons ni oiseaux ni chiens à la maison.

19. Je ne mange ni au bureau ni à la maison le lundi.

20. Ce n'est ni moi, ni eux.

21. Je n'aime personne.

22. Nous n'allons nulle part.

23. Ils ne veulent rien.

24. Il n'y a rien dans ce sac.

25. Elle ne danse jamais.

Chapter 9

Handling Questions and Exclamations

Questions are a vital part of communicating. Being able to understand a question is important in order to answer it as well as possible, and it's equally important for you to be able to ask for what you need, especially if you travel. ("Can I keep my bag in the cabin?" "Where are the restrooms?" "Do you speak French?")

Questions come in two varieties: the yes/no questions and the information questions. This chapter helps you get a good grasp on how to build the question you need to ask as well as how to react enthusiastically with exclamations.

Composing and Answering Yes/No Questions

Yes/no questions don't give many options for the answer: *yes, no* . . . and of course the infamous *maybe* (which I think isn't a fair answer, because you either know or you don't, you either do or you don't, you either are or you aren't!).

In English, when you ask a yes/no question in present tense, you typically begin with *Do you,* and the verb follows. (For example, *Do you have a cat?*) French has two primary ways of asking the same question:

✔ Add **est-ce que** at the beginning of a sentence.

✔ Use inversion, but it's a bit more complex and usually reserved for written style/ expression.

In the following sections, I walk you through the mechanics of each option.

Using est-ce que

You can form a question by starting the sentence with the tag **est-ce que** and ending it with a question mark. **Est-ce que** doesn't translate in English, but it's the equivalent of *Do you* or *Are you*. Here are some examples:

Statement: **Mes amis vont au cinéma.** (*My friends go to the movies.*)

Question: **Est-ce que mes amis vont au cinéma?** (*Are my friends going to the movies?*)

Statement: **Je peux sortir.** (*I can go out.*)

Question: **Est-ce que je peux sortir?** (*Can I go out?*)

Statement: **C'est facile** (*It's easy.*)

Question: **Est-ce que c'est facile?** (*Is it easy?*)

If **est-ce que** precedes a subject that begins with a vowel, it changes to **est-ce qu'** as illustrated in the following example:

Est-ce qu'il pleut? (*Is it raining?*)

Put the following questions into French, using the **est-ce que** format. If you need help translating any words, check out a French-English dictionary. Here's an example:

0. *Do you speak French?*

A. **Est-ce que tu parles français?**

1. *Can I go out?* _____

2. *Do you* (singular informal) *like to dance?* _____

3. *Does he swim well?* _____

4. *Is it easy?* _____

5. *Are you* (plural) *tired?* _____

6. *Do they have a cat?* _____

7. *Do the children listen to their parents?* _____

8. *Is it cold today?* _____

9. *Does she have children?* _____

10. *Are we spending our vacation here?* _____

Using inversion

Using inversion to ask a question requires a litle tweaking in the order of the words of the statement. The subject pronoun and the verb get swapped around (inverted) and separated by a hyphen.

Here is a list of the subject pronouns you can use in inversion. Note how **je** (*I*) is not among them! You pretty much never invert **je** and the verb (unless you're a writer of melodramas in the 19th century).

- **tu** (*you* [singular informal])
- **il/elle/on** (*he/she/one*)
- **nous** (*we*)
- **vous** (*you* [singular formal or plural formal and informal])
- **ils/elles** (*they* [masculine or mixed/feminine])

And here are some of them in action:

> Statement: **Tu veux une glace.** (*You want an ice cream.*)
>
> Question with inversion: **Veux-tu une glace?** (*Do you want an ice cream?*)

> Statement: **Vous parlez italien.** (*You speak Italian.*)
>
> Question with inversion: **Parlez-vous italien?** (*Do you speak Italian?*)

Unfortunately, the rules for creating inversion don't stop there. But don't worry! In the following sections, I describe a few additional basics.

With verbs that end in a vowel in the third person

When you invert the subjects **il** (*he*), **elle** (*she*), or **on** (*one*) and a verb that ends in a vowel when conjugated in the present or future tense, pronunciation requires that you add **-t-** between the verb and subject inverted. This rule applies to the third person singular of **-er** verbs and the third person singular of **aller** (*to go*) in the present tense, and to the third person singular form in future tense. Here are a few examples of such forms:

> **Aime-t-elle la glace?** (*Does she like ice cream?*)
>
> **Parle-t-on anglais ici?** (*Does one speak English here?*)
>
> **Dinera-t-il avec nous?** (*Will he have dinner with us?*)

With a noun or a name as the subject

Inversion cannot be done when the subject is a noun (like **la fille**, which means *the girl*) or a name (like *Julie*). It can only be done between a subject pronoun and the verb. Here's how you get around that problem: You simply add the subject pronoun to the sentence while the noun or name sits at the beginning of the sentence. Here's how to proceed.

1. **Leave the original noun subject at the beginning.**

   For example, in **La petite fille veut un vélo** (*The little girl wants a bicycle*), leave **La petite fille** alone.

2. **Find the subject pronoun that matches the noun.**

   In this instance, you use **elle** (*she*) for **La petite fille**.

3. **Do inversion between the subject pronoun and the verb (be sure to add a hyphen) and add the question mark.**

   In this example, inversion produces **veut-elle.** And here's your question: **La petite fille veut-elle un vélo?**

Here are a few more examples, including some with the extra **-t-** that I talk about in the preceding section:

Statement: **Marie joue du violon.** (*Marie plays the violin.*)

Question with inversion: **Marie joue-t-elle du violon?** (*Does Marie play the violin?*)

Statement: **Ce fruit est bon.** (*This fruit is good.*)

Question with inversion: **Ce fruit est-il bon?** (*Is this fruit good?*)

Statement: **Le match finira tard** (*The match will end late.*)

Question with inversion: **Le match finira-t-il tard?** (*Will the match end late?*)

Apply inversion to the following sentences to form basic questions. Be sure to add a **-t-** when necessary and to add a subject pronoun if the question doesn't have one. Here's an example:

0. **Il dort.**

A. **Dort-il.**

11. **Tu as un chat.**

_____

12. **Vous parlez espagnol.**

_____

13. **Le petit garçon prend un bonbon.**

_____

14. **Paul sort ce soir.**

_____

15. **Vos amis dîneront avec vous.**

_____

16. Nous pouvons jouer ensemble.

_____

17. Ta soeur joue du piano.

_____

18. Elles invitent souvent leurs amies.

_____

19. Le témoin parle de l'accident.

_____

20. On déjeune ensemble aujourd'hui.

_____

In the compound past

A compound tense is formed by putting together a conjugated form of one of two helper verbs: **être** (*to be*) or **avoir** (*to have*) and the past participle of the verb. Here is an example of a compound tense made with **avoir** in the present perfect (**passé composé**):

Nous avons regardé la télé hier soir. (*We watched TV last night.*)

Here's an example that uses **être** to form the **passé composé**:

Tu es rentré très tard. (*You came home very late.*)

In the **passé composé** and all other compound tenses formed with an auxiliary verb + past participle, inversion works the same. You invert the conjugated verb and the subject. In this case, the conjugated verb is either **être** or **avoir**. Leave the past participle alone!

If you follow these easy guidelines, you will do just fine.

1. **Find the auxiliary verb (don't worry about the past participle).**

    The auxiliary verb is **être** (*to be*) or **avoir** (*to have*) in a conjugated form. For example, in the sentence **Ils ont bu du café** (*They drank coffee*), **ont** is the conjugated auxiliary verb.

2. **Switch around the conjugated auxiliary verb with the subject and put a hyphen between them, still leaving the past participle alone. Remember to add a -t- when the verb ends with a vowel and precedes il, elle, or on.**

    In the example, **ont** is the conjugated verb, and **ils** is the subject, so you invert them like this: **ont-ils**.

3. **Put the sentence back together with inversion instead of the original word order.**

    In the example, the question becomes **Ont-ils bu du café?** (*Did they drink coffee?*)

Here are a few more examples:

> **As-tu acheté un livre?** (*Did you buy a book?*)
>
> **A-t-elle parlé avec le prof?** (*Did she talk with the teacher?*)
>
> **Paul a-t-il dormi jusqu'à midi?** (*Did Paul sleep until noon?*)
>
> **Jules et Jim sont-ils arrivés en retard?** (*Did Jules and Jim arrive late?*)

Apply inversion to the following sentences to form questions in **passé composé**. Be sure to add a -**t**- when necessary and to add a subject pronoun if the question doesn't have one. Here's an example:

Q. **Tu as acheté le pain.**

A. **As-tu acheté le pain?**

21. **Jules et Jim ont dormi jusqu'à midi.**

_____

22. **Elle est arrivée en retard.**

_____

23. **Nous avons fini le travail.**

_____

24. **Vous avez parlé avec le prof.**

_____

25. **Tu as pris le bus.**

_____

In the near future

When you use the verb **aller** (*to go*) + infinitive in the near future (known as the **futur proche**; see Chapter 17), track down the conjugated form of **aller** to do inversion. Follow these steps:

1. **Find the conjugated form of aller, leaving the infinitive that follows it alone.**

   For example, in the sentence **Ils vont sortir ce soir** (*They are going to go out tonight*), the conjugated form of **aller** is **vont**.

2. **Switch around the conjugated form of aller with the subject and put a hyphen between them.**

   In the example, **vont** is the conjugated verb and **ils** is the subject, so you invert them like this: **vont-ils**.

3. **Now put the sentence back together with inversion instead of the original word order.**

   In the example, the finished question is **Vont-ils sortir ce soir?** (*Are they going to go out tonight?*)

Here are a few more examples.

> **Vas-tu acheter un livre?** (*Are you going to buy a book?*)
>
> **Julie va-t-elle parler avec le prof?** (*Is Julie going to talk with the teacher?*)
>
> **Allez-vous faire du vélo dimanche?** (*Are you going to ride your bike Sunday?*)

Apply inversion to the following sentences to form questions in **futur proche**. Be sure to add a -**t**- when necessary and to add a subject pronoun if the question doesn't have one. Here's an example:

Q. Tu vas acheter le pain.

A. Vas-tu acheter le pain?

26. Ils vont dormir jusqu'à midi.

_____

27. Elle va partir en vacances.

_____

28. Nous allons finir le travail.

_____

29. Vous allez parler avec le prof.

_____

30. Tu vas prendre le bus.

_____

Answering a yes/no question

Questions often start with *Do you . . .* in English, and short answers often use that very same helper verb: *I do* or *I don't.* French doesn't use an auxiliary to ask a question, so there's no such thing as *I do* either. For a short answer in French, your only options are **oui** (*yes*) and **non** (*no*). But you can add a few frills to that, like **bien sûr** (*of course*), or **pas du tout** (*not at all*). In the following list, I give you some good choices to use depending on how you want to color your answer. (For more negative expressions, see Chapter 8.)

- ✔ **avec plaisir** (*with pleasure*)
- ✔ **bien sûr** (*of course*)
- ✔ **certainement** (*certainly*)
- ✔ **jamais** (*never*)
- ✔ **pas du tout** (*not at all*)
- ✔ **pas encore** (*not yet*)

  ✔ **pas grand-chose** (*not much*)

  ✔ **pas question** (*no way*)

  ✔ **si** (*yes* [in response to a negative question])

Don't use **pas** alone as a response. It has to be with another word such as **pas encore** (*not yet*) or in combination with a stress pronoun as in **pas moi** (*not me*). Here's an example:

  —**Qui a fait ça?** (*Who did this?*) —**Pas moi.** (*Not me.*)

Asking for Specific Information with Question Words

Sometimes you need to know more than a simple yes or no; you may want to know when or where something happened and who came and what they did. In this case, you need to use an information question, and like in English, French information questions start with a question word (technically known as interrogative adverbs and adjectives). The following sections tell you what they are in French and how to use them.

Useful French question words

French has the same interrogative words and expressions as English. The following list introduces the most useful question words in French, with their English equivalents.

  ✔ **quand** (*when*)

  ✔ **à quelle heure** (*at what time*)

  ✔ **qui** (*who/whom*)

  ✔ **qui est-ce que** (*who*, object of the verb)

  ✔ **qui est-ce qui** (*who*, subject of the verb)

  ✔ **avec qui** (*with whom*)

  ✔ **pour qui** (*for whom*)

  ✔ **comment** (*how*)

  ✔ **combien (de)** (*how many/how much*)

  ✔ **où** (*where*)

  ✔ **d'où** (*from where*)

  ✔ **pourquoi** (*why*)

  ✔ **pour quelle raison** (*for what reason*)

  ✔ **quoi** (*what*)

  ✔ **qu'est-ce qui** (*what*, subject of the verb)

  ✔ **que/qu'est-ce que** (*what*, object of the verb)

  ✔ **quel** + noun (*what/which*)

The basics of using question words

The interrogative words are just an added block to the yes/no question block. In other words, you form a question like you would for a yes/no question and add the question word or expression at the beginning. The following sections show you how to proceed using the **est-ce que** and inversion formats (both of which I cover earlier in this chapter). I also provide some guidance on using a particularly tricky question word. (I provide details on using specific question words, such as *what* and *who*, later in this chapter.)

The est-ce que format

Follow these steps to include a question word in the **est-ce que** format:

1. **Start with a statement and add est-ce que to form a yes/no question.**

   For example, **Tu achètes un livre** (*You buy a book*) becomes **Est-ce que tu achètes un livre?** (*Do you buy a book?*)

2. **To ask a more specific question, just add the question word at the beginning of the yes/no question.**

   For example, if you want to know why someone buys a book, use the word **pourquoi** at the start of your question: **Pourquoi est-ce que tu achètes un livre?** (*Why do you buy a book?*)

Here are a few more examples of information questions using **est-ce que**:

Quand est-ce que tu vas en vacances? (*When do you go on vacation?*)

Combien d'enfants est-ce qu'ils ont? (*How many children do they have?*)

Qu'est-ce qu'on attend? (*What are we waiting for?*)

The question word **que** (*what*) turns into **qu'** before a vowel, as shown in the last example. However **qui** (*who/whom*) doesn't change.

Inversions

Follow these steps to include a question word in inversion format.

1. **Invert the verb and subject in the statement and put a hyphen between them.**

   For example, the statement **Tu achètes un livre** (*You buy a book*) becomes **Achètes-tu un livre?** (*Do you buy a book?*)

2. **Add the question word at the beginning, and don't forget the question mark at the end.**

   For example, if you want to know why someone buys a book, use the word **pourquoi** at the start of your question: **Pourquoi achètes-tu un livre?** (*Why do you buy a book?*)

   If the question includes a name or noun, it still has to go before the verb, at the beginning of the yes/no question. For example, **Pourquoi Pierre achète-t-il un livre?** (*Why does Pierre buy a book?*)

Here are additional examples of information questions using inversion:

Quand vas-tu en vacances? (*When do you go on vacation?*)

Combien d'enfants ont-ils? (*How many children do they have?*)

Qu'attend-on? (*What are we waiting for?*)

The rebel word où

The interrogative **où** (*where*) behaves differently from other question words. Actually, **où** is a complete rebel! The best way to ask a question that begins with **où** is to skip all the steps in the previous sections and build sentences this way: **où** + verb + any subject (pronoun or noun). If it is a subject pronoun, you still need to link it to the verb by a hyphen, as in the following examples:

Où as-tu trouvé ça? (*Where did you find that?*)

Où va Paul? (*Where is Paul going?*)

Où sont mes clés? (*Where are my keys?*)

Où allez-vous voyager? (*Where are you going to travel?*)

Ask the correct question based on the answer that is given to you. You can use the **est-ce que** or inversion form. Here's an example:

Q. Answer: **Elle est de Paris.**

A. Question: **D'où est-elle?**

31. Answer: **Vous devez partir maintenant.** (*You must leave now.*)

_____

32. Answer: **Nous allons au Mexique.** (*We're going to Mexico.*)

_____

33. Answer: **Tu conduis mal.** (*You drive poorly.*)

_____

34. Answer: **J'apprends le français parce que c'est une belle langue.** (*I'm learning French because it's a beautiful language.*)

_____

35. Answer: **Ils ont trois enfants.** (*They have three kids.*)

_____

36. Answer: **Je vais en vacances en été.** (*I go on vacation in the summer.*)

_____

37. Answer: **Il est né à Marseille.** (*He was born in Marseille.*)

_____

38. Answer: **Elle arrive ce soir.** (*She's arriving tonight.*)

_____

39. Answer: **On écrit mal sur un tableau.** (*One writes poorly on a blackboard.*)

40. Answer: **Elles partent à huit heures.** (*They leave at 8.*)

Discovering the Various Ways of Asking "What"

You can ask a question with *what* in several ways in French: **que**, **qu'est-ce que**, **qu'est-ce qui**, and **quel**. The following sections give you the scoop.

Untangling qu'est-ce que and qu'est-ce qui

The difference between **Qu'est-ce que tu veux?** (*What do you want?*) and **Qu'est-ce qui est arrivé?** (*What happened?*) is a matter of whether the interrogative *what* is the object of the verb or the subject of the verb.

Qu'est-ce que asks *what* when *what* is the object of the verb — that is, when it receives the action. In **Qu'est-ce que tu veux?**, **tu** (*you*) is the subject of the verb, so there can't be another subject. Because the interrogative **qu'est-ce que** can't be the subject, it must be the object. Here are a couple of other examples:

> **Qu'est-ce que vous voyez là-bas?** (*What do you see over there?*)
>
> **Qu'est-ce que c'est?** (*What is it?*)

Qu'est-ce que has a short version: **que**. However, if you want to use it, inversion must follow, which makes your sentence sound a bit pompous to French ears. Here are the two previous examples from before with the short version:

> **Que voyez-vous là-bas?** (*What do you see over there?*)
>
> **Qu'est-ce?** (*What is it?*)

With **qu'est-ce qui**, *what* is the subject of the verb. The sentence **Qu'est-ce qui est arrivé?** (*What happened?*) has no other subject. **Qu'est-ce qui** does not have a short version.

Follow these steps to choose between **qu'est-ce que** and **qu'est-ce qui**:

1. **Find the verb of the sentence and look for its subject.**

2. **If you can't find a noun or pronoun acting as the subject, the sentence probably doesn't have one, in which case *what* is the subject in your question.**

   In that instance, use **qu'est-ce qui**.

3. **If you do find a subject other than *what*, then *what* is the object of the verb in your question.**

   In that instance, use **qu'est-ce que**.

When a question begins with **que/qu'**, it's always asking about a thing.

As an example to illustrate the need for the subject *what*, start from a statement you may hear:

La pluie a causé la rupture du barrage. (*The rain caused the break of the dam.*)

Then imagine you didn't hear the first words. You'd be left with this incomplete sentence:

. . . **a causé la rupture du barrage.** (. . . *caused the break of the dam.*)

But you really want to know what caused the dam to break, so you ask just that, using **qu'est-ce qui** because the *what* is the subject of the sentence.

Qu'est-ce qui a causé la rupture du barrage? (*What caused the break of the dam?*)

Note how the first **qu-** in both **qu'est-ce que** and **qu'est-ce qui** never changes. The **qu-** word that alternates between **qui** and **que** is the second one.

Fill in the blank with either **qu'est-ce que** or **qu'est-ce qui**.

Q. _____ tu veux?

A. Qu'est-ce que

41. _____ tu as mangé? (*What did you eat?*)

42. _____ fait rire les enfants? (*What makes the kids laugh?*)

43. _____ est perdu? (*What is lost?*)

44. _____ elle a fait hier soir? (*What did she do last night?*)

45. _____ ils vont étudier? (*What are they going to study?*)

46. _____ je peux faire pour toi? (*What can I do for you?*)

47. _____ a causé l'accident? (*What caused the accident?*)

48. _____ va arriver maintenant? (*What is going to happen now?*)

49. _____ vous faites le dimanche? (*What do you do on Sundays?*)

50. _____ est sur la table? (*What is on the table?*)

Knowing when to use quel

Quel is an interrogative adjective that means *which* or *what*. Like most adjectives (see Chapter 4), it has four forms: masculine singular (**quel**) and plural (**quels**), and feminine singular (**quelle**) and plural (**quelles**). The following examples show all four forms in action:

Quel jour sommes-nous? (*What day is it?*)

Quelle heure est-il? (*What time is it?*)

Quels cours vas-tu prendre? (*Which classes will you take?*)

Quelles sont tes couleurs préférées? (*What are your favorite colors?*)

Both **quel** and **qu'est-ce que** (see the preceding section) are equivalent to *what*, so how do you choose? It isn't difficult when you know what to look for. **Quel** is an adjective, and an adjective describes a noun, so that's the big clue: Look for the noun that **quel** could accompany.

Here's an example in English: In the question *What dress will you wear tonight?*, the noun associated with *what* is *dress*. And in *What is the best restaurant around here?*, *what* is tied to the noun *restaurant*. So for those two questions, you use **quel** in French, like so:

Quelle robe vas-tu porter ce soir? (*What dress will you wear tonight?*)

Quel est le meilleur restaurant par ici? (*What is the best restaurant around here?*)

Now contrast those sentences with a question like *What did you do last night?* No noun is associated with *what* in this question, so you use **qu'est-ce que** in French.

Qu'est-ce que tu as fait hier soir? (*What did you do last night?*)

French uses **quel** in two specific ways, as you find out in the following sections.

Quel plus a noun

Quel can be directly in front of the noun, followed by a yes/no question formulated with **est-ce que** or inversion (as I explain earlier in this chapter). The following examples show you both versions:

Quelle robe est-ce que tu vas porter ce soir? (*What dress will you wear tonight?*)

Quelle robe vas-tu porter ce soir? (*What dress will you wear tonight?*)

In the format **quel** + noun + yes/no question, **quel** replaces the article that would normally precede the noun.

If the question includes a preposition like in *at what time*, use one of the following phrases:

preposition + **quel** + noun + yes/no question with **est-ce que**

preposition + **quel** + noun + yes/no question with inversion

For example, you can say **À quelle heure commencerons-nous?** (*At what time will we start?*)

Quel plus être plus a noun

The second way to use **quel** is by separating it from the noun. In this sentence construction, a conjugated form of the verb **être** (*to be*) always sits between **quel** and the noun like so:

Quels sont vos films préférés? (*What are your favorite films?*)

Quelle a été votre réaction? (*What was your reaction?*)

To get there, here's how you proceed:

1. **Find the noun the question is asking about and determine what its gender and number are in French.**

   For example, for *What was your reaction?*, **réaction** (*reaction*) is feminine singular.

2. **Match the proper version of quel to the noun.**

   The feminine singular version of **quel** is **quelle**. Now you have **quelle réaction**.

3. **Match the proper tense of être to the version of quel and the noun and insert it between the two words.**

   In this example, you need the past tense of **être** in the third person: **a été.** Insert it between **quelle** and **réaction.** Et voilà!

Fill the blanks with a form of **quel** or with **qu'est-ce que**, depending on what follows the blank.

Q. _____ tu as fait hier?

A. Qu'est-ce que

51. _____ tu préfères: le Coca ou le jus de fruit?

52. _____ boisson préfères-tu avec tes repas?

53. _____ tu bois le soir?

54. _____ sont vos films préférés?

55. _____ jour sommes-nous?

56. _____ vous faites le dimanche?

57. _____ nous devons faire après?

58. _____ est l'adresse correcte?

59. _____ ils prennent au petit-déjeuner?

60. _____ sports pratiquez-vous?

Asking "Who?"

The French equivalents of *who* are **qui**, **qui est-ce qui**, and **qui est-ce que**. The choice between the forms depends on whether **qui** is the subject or object of the verb.

"Who" as the subject

In **Qui est là?** (*Who's there?*), **qui** functions as the subject of the verb. Using **qui** this way is the most common and easiest way of asking *who*. To form this type of question, start with

qui, add the verb (always in third person singular) and the rest of the question, and complete the question with a question mark.

Here are a few examples of **qui** used as the subject.

> **Qui parle espagnol?** (*Who speaks Spanish?*)
>
> **Qui arrive toujours en retard?** (*Who is always late?*)
>
> **Qui veut un bonbon?** (*Who wants a candy?*)

"Who" as the object

Qui can also be the object of the verb in the question, and in proper English usage it's often a *whom*, as in *Whom do you prefer?* To form this question in French, start with **qui** and then use the **est-ce que** form or inversion of a yes/no question. Of course you finish with a question mark, like so:

> **Qui est-ce que tu préfères?** (*Whom do you prefer?*)
>
> **Qui préfères-tu?** (*Who do you prefer?*)

If the subject of the verb is a noun or a name, start with **qui** and then the noun or name, followed by inversion, as shown in the following examples:

> **Qui Paul préfère-t-il?** (*Whom does Paul prefer?*)
>
> **Qui les pompiers ont-ils aidé?** (*Whom did the firefighters help?*)

Like for **qui** subject, **qui** object has a long version: **qui est-ce que**. This time inversion can't be used, though, because you have **est-ce que** in the question. Use **qui est-ce que**, follow it with the subject (either a noun or a pronoun), and finish with the statement. Here are the previous examples in the long version so you can compare:

> **Qui est-ce que les pompiers ont aidé?** (*Whom did the firefighters help?*)
>
> **Qui est-ce que Paul préfère?** (*Whom does Paul prefer?*)

When a question begins with **qui**, it's always asking about a person.

Practice asking *who* by asking the questions that would get the following answers. Use the **qui/qui est-ce qui** or **qui/qui est-ce que** accordingly. The bolded word is who you're asking about. (Remember that when **qui** is subject of the verb, that verb has to be in third person singular.)

Q. <u>Anne</u> est arrivée.

A. Qui est arrivé?/Qui est-ce qui est arrivé?

61. Il a donné une bague <u>à sa fiancée</u>.

62. <u>Le président</u> a signé la lettre.

63. C'est <u>mon prof</u>.

64. <u>Tous les enfants</u> aiment le chocolat!

65. Il a vu <u>ses parents</u> récemment.

Including Prepositions in Questions

With questions such as *Who did you say that to?* and *What did you do it for?*, *to* and *for* are prepositions. In English, people understand your meaning if you put the preposition at the end (even though your English teacher may have taught you that it's improper). But in French, the preposition must come at the very beginning of the sentence, before **qui** if it's a *who* question and before **quoi** if it's a *what* question.

A preposition plus "who"

When you ask a question like *Who is it for?* or *Who did you play with?*, *who* is never the subject of the verb. So you need to use the kind of question with **qui** (*who*) as the object of the verb.

Here's a reminder of how easy it is to form this **qui** question (see the earlier section "'Who' as the object" for more info):

✔ For an **est-ce que** question, start with **qui**, add **est-ce que**, add the noun/pronoun subject, and then say the verb: **Qui est-ce que Paul aime?** (*Whom does Paul love?*)

✔ For a question in inversion format, start with **qui**, add the noun subject if the sentence has one, add the verb, and then add the pronoun subject (don't forget the hypen), like this: **Qui Paul aime-t-il?** (*Whom does Paul love?*)

To form a **qui** question with a preposition (like **de**, which means *of*) proceed like for a **qui** question, just adding the preposition in front of **qui** like this: **De qui est-ce que Paul est amoureux?** or **De qui Paul est-il amoureux?** (*Who is Paul in love with?*)

Here are a few more examples:

Avec qui travaillez-vous? or **Avec qui est-ce que vous travaillez?** (*With whom do you work?*)

De qui ont-ils hérité ce château? or **De qui est-ce qu'ils ont hérité ce château?** (*Whom did they inherit this castle from?*)

A preposition plus "what"

Say you want to ask your friend, *What do you do that with?* Your question is not just *what* but *with what*, using the preposition *with*. In this section I show you how to easily ask the same thing in French. The only tricky part is that **que** becomes **quoi** when it is used with a preposition.

1. **Start from a yes/no question with est-ce que, without any question word.**

   For example, you can say **Est-ce que tu fais ça?** (*Do you do that?*) (See the earlier section "Using **est-ce que**" for more info.)

2. **Choose the French preposition.**

   In this example, you need the equivalent of *with*: **avec.**

3. **Put your preposition at the beginning of the question, followed by quoi.**

   In this example, you use **avec quoi** (*with what*).

4. **Attach the yes/no est-ce que question you already have.**

   Here, you say **Avec quoi est-ce que tu fais ça?** (*What do you do that with?*)

Bravo, you're done!

You can ask the same type of question using inversion instead of the **est-ce que** format. Start with a yes/no question with inversion this time; for example, you can say **Fais-tu ça?** (*Do you do that?*) and attach **avec quoi** in front of it to get **Avec quoi fais-tu ça?** (*What do you do that with?*)

Here are more examples that use various prepositions, first in the **est-ce que** form and then in inversion form.

Dans quoi est-ce que tu mets ton portable? Dans quoi mets-tu ton portable? (*What do you put your cellphone in?*)

À quoi est-ce que tu veux jouer? À quoi veux-tu jouer? (*What do you want to play at?*)

Using either the **est-ce que** form or inversion, ask the following [*what* or *who* + preposition] questions in French. If you need help with any vocabulary, consult a French-English dictionary (I help you with a few words). Here's an example:

Q. *What is the cat sleeping under?*

A. **Sous quoi le chat dort-il?**

66. *What are they playing at?*

_____

67. *What do you* (informal) *put your glasses* (**tes lunettes**) *in?*

_____

68. *Who does he do that for?*

_____

69. *Who is she dancing with?*

_____

70. *Who are you* (formal) *talking to?*

_____

71. *What do you* (informal) *dream* (**rêver**) *of?*

_____

72. *What are we in need of?* (**avoir besoin de**)

_____

73. *What do they write with?*

_____

74. *Who is he in love with?*

_____

75. *Who are you* (informal) *talking about?*

_____

Expressing Surprise and Enthusiasm with Exclamations

Do you sometimes get excited to the point that you need to burst into an exclamation? You may exclaim with delight, as in *What a beautiful bird!*, or frustration, or even anger, as in *What a stupid thing to say!* The expressions you use are exclamatory, and French exclamatory expressions often use the same interrogative words that I list earlier in this chapter, like **quel** (*what* + noun), **que** (*how* + adjective), and **quoi** (*what*), as well as other expressions like **comme** (which literally means *as* but translates to *how* for exclamations).

Here are some exclamatory expressions that use them all:

> **Quel oiseau magnifique!** (*What a beautiful bird!*)
>
> **Que c'est laid!** (*How ugly it is!*)
>
> **Comme il est mignon!** (*How cute he is!*)
>
> **Quoi! Il a fait ça!** (*What! He did that!*)

In the following sections, I give you the scoop on exclamations that use a noun and exclamations that use only an adjective.

Including a noun

If you are marveling or griping about something in particular and you want to name that thing, use **quel** (*what*) + a noun without an article, followed by an exclamation mark, like in English.

> **Quel génie!** (*What a genious!*)
>
> **Quelle folie!** (*What a crazy thing to do!*)
>
> **Quels imbéciles!** (*What fools!*)
>
> **Quelles notes!** (*What grades!*)

Quel is an adjective and as such it must match the noun it describes in gender and number.

To make things even more specific, the noun can also be described by an adjective, as in **Quels grands arbres!** (*What tall trees!*). When you use an adjective, the rules of placement of adjectives apply (see Chapter 4 for details on placement of adjectives) and the BAGS adjectives come before the noun, whereas regular adjectives follow it. The following examples illustrate the difference between BAGS adjectives (which come before the noun) and regular adjectives (which come after the noun).

BAGS adjectives refer to beauty like **beau** (*beautiful/handsome*), age, like **jeune** (*young*), goodness, like **bon** (*good*) and size like **petit** (*small*), and they precede the noun they describe.

> **Quelle jolie fille!** (*What a pretty girl!*)
>
> **Quelle fille intelligente!** (*What a clever girl!*)

BAGS adjectives have an alternate masculine singular form when the noun they describe begins with a vowel, as in **bel oiseau** (*beautiful bird*).

Including just an adjective

When what you're exclaiming about is obvious enough, you don't need a noun in your exclamation and you can just say something like *How beautiful!*, skipping both a noun and the verb. To do the same thing in French, you can skip the noun, but you can't skip the verb. **C'est** (*it is*) must be included. But you have a choice for the exclamatory expression: You can use **que** or **comme**, which are totally interchangeable, or sometimes skip the exclamative word and make a very short sentence with just an exclamation mark. Check out these examples, which all convey the same message:

> **Que c'est beau!** (*How beautiful!*)
>
> **Comme c'est beau!** (*How beautiful!*)
>
> **C'est beau!** (*That's beautiful!*)

When you use just **c'est** + adjective, without an exclamatory word, sometimes **ça** (*that*) is added at the end for emphasis like this: **C'est fou, ça!** (Literally: *That's crazy, that!*)

After **c'est**, all adjectives are masculine when the noun is not expressed (included in the phrase), despite the gender of the noun. **C'est beau** can refer to either **la lune** (*the moon*) or **le soleil** (*the sun*).

Use the following list to find some very common exclamations that don't translate literally into English.

- **Quelle chance!/Quelle malchance!** (*How lucky/unlucky!*)

- **Quelle horreur!** (*How horrible!*)

- **Quel travail!** (*That's a lot of work!*)

- **Quel imbécile!** (*What an imbecile!*)

- **Quelle barbe!** (*What a bore!* [literally: *What a beard!*])

- **Comme c'est triste!** (*How sad!*)

- **C'est beaucoup!** (*That's a lot!*)

- **Quoi!** (*What!*)

- **Comme c'est gentil (à vous/toi)** (*How kind [of you]*)

- **Quel soulagement!** (*What a relief!*)

Translate the folowing exclamations. If you can say the same thing in two different ways, write both. Sentences marked with asterisks include idiomatic phrases that don't translate directly, so you can refer to the preceding list for help with those. Here's an example:

Q. *That's a lot!**

A. **C'est beaucoup!**

76. *What a bore!** _____

77. *How mean!* _____

78. *What intelligent students!* _____

79. *How unlucky!** _____

80. *How sad!** _____

81. *How interesting!* _____

82. *How kind!** _____

83. *How lucky!** _____

84. *What a good grade!* _____

85. *How tiny!* _____

Answer Key

1. Est-ce que je peux sortir?

2. Est-ce que tu aimes danser?

3. Est-ce qu'il nage bien?

4. Est-ce que c'est facile?

5. Est-ce que vous êtes fatigués?

6. Est-ce qu'ils ont un chat?

7. Est-ce que les enfants écoutent leurs parents?

8. Est-ce qu'il fait froid aujourd'hui?

9. Est-ce qu'elle a des enfants?

10. Est-ce que nous passons nos vacances ici?

11. As-tu un chat?

12. Parlez-vous espagnol?

13. Le petit garçon prend-il un bonbon?

14. Paul sort-il ce soir?

15. Vos amis dîneront-ils avec vous?

16. Pouvons-nous jouer ensemble?

17. Ta soeur joue-t-elle du piano?

18. Invitent-elles souvent leurs amies?

19. Le témoin parle-t-il de l'accident?

20. Déjeune-t-on ensemble aujourd'hui?

21. Jules et Jim ont-ils dormi jusqu'à midi?

22. Est-elle arrivée en retard?

23. Avons-nous fini le travail?

24. Avez-vous parlé avec le prof?

`25` **As-tu pris le bus?**

`26` **Vont-ils dormir jusqu'à midi?**

`27` **Va-t-elle partir en vacances?**

`28` **Allons-nous finir le travail?**

`29` **Allez-vous parler avec le prof?**

`30` **Vas-tu prendre le bus?**

`31` Question: **Quand est-ce que nous devons partir?/Quand devons-nous partir?**

`32` Question: **Où est-ce que vous allez?/Où allez-vous?**

`33` Question: **Comment est-ce que je conduis?**/(No inversion possible with **je**.)

`34` Question: **Pourquoi est-ce que tu apprends le français?/Pourquoi apprends-tu le français?**

`35` Question: **Combien d'enfants est-ce qu'ils ont?/Combien d'enfants ont-ils?**

`36` Question: **Quand est-ce que tu vas en vacances?/Quand vas-tu en vacances?**

`37` Question: **Où est-ce qu'il est né?/Où est-il né?**

`38` Question: **Quand arrive-t-elle?/Quand est-ce qu'elle arrive?**

`39` Question: **Comment est-ce qu'on écrit sur un tableau?/Comment écrit-on sur un tableau?**

`40` Question: **À quelle heure est-ce qu'elles partent?/À quelle heure partent-elles?**

`41` **Qu'est-ce que**

`42` **Qu'est-ce qui**

`43` **Qu'est-ce qui**

`44` **Qu'est-ce qu'**

`45` **Qu'est-ce qu'**

`46` **Qu'est-ce que**

`47` **Qu'est-ce qui**

`48` **Qu'est-ce qui**

`49` **Qu'est-ce que**

`50` **Qu'est-ce qui**

51 **Qu'est-ce que**

52 **Quelle**

53 **Qu'est-ce que**

54 **Quels**

55 **Quel**

56 **Qu'est-ce que**

57 **Qu'est-ce que**

58 **Quelle**

59 **Qu'est-ce qu'**

60 **Quels**

61 **À qui est-ce qu'il a donné une bague?/À qui a-t-il donné une bague?**

62 **Qui/qui est-ce qui a signé la lettre?**

63 **Qui est-ce?**

64 **Qui/qui est-ce qui aime le chocolat?**

65 **Qui a-t-il vu récemment?/Qui est-ce qu'il a vu récemment?**

66 **À quoi jouent-ils?/À quoi est-ce qu'ils jouent?**

67 **Dans quoi mets-tu tes lunettes?/Dans quoi est-ce que tu mets tes lunettes?**

68 **Pour qui fait-il ça?/Pour qui est-ce qu'il fait ça?**

69 **Avec qui danse-t-elle?/Avec qui est-ce qu'elle danse?**

70 **À qui parlez-vous?/À qui est-ce que vous parlez?**

71 **De quoi rêves-tu?/De quoi est-ce que tu rêves?**

72 **De quoi avons-nous besoin?/De quoi est-ce que nous avons besoin?**

73 **Avec quoi écrivent-ils?/Avec quoi est-ce qu'ils écrivent?**

74 **De qui est-il amoureux?/De qui est-ce qu'il est amoureux?**

75 **De qui parles-tu?/De qui est-ce que tu parles?**

76 **Quelle barbe!**

77 **Comme c'est méchant!**

78 **Quels étudiants intelligents!**

79 **Quelle malchance!**

80 **Comme c'est triste!**

81 **Comme c'est intéressant!**

82 **Comme c'est gentil (à vous)!**

83 **Quelle chance!**

84 **Quelle bonne note!**

85 **Comme c'est minuscule!**

Part III
Beefing Up Your Sentences

Common French Prepositions

French Preposition	English Translation
à	at, in, to
à cause de	because of
à côté de	next to
après	after
au lieu de	instead of
au milieu de	in the middle of
avant	before (temporal only)
avec	with
chez	at the place of someone
contre	against
dans	in
de	of/from
derrière	behind
devant	in front of
en	in
en face de	across from
entre	between
hors de	outside of
jusqu'à	until/as far as
loin de	far from
pendant	during/while
pour	for/in order to
sans	without
sauf	except
sous	under
sur	on
vers	toward

Find out how to use prepositions properly in French sentences in a free article at www.dummies.com/extras/frenchgrammar.

In this part . . .

- ✔ Use adverbs and prepositions to help you describe the when, where, and how of actions.

- ✔ Make comparisons with adjectives and adverbs, and use comparisons to discuss quantities.

- ✔ Figure out how to replace nouns with pronouns, and make your French communication more polished.

- ✔ Get the scoop on how to use gerunds to express simultaneous actions and to note when, why, and how something happened.

- ✔ Indicate that something has been done with the passive construction.

Chapter 10

Saying Where, When, and How with Adverbs

In This Chapter
▶ Discovering French adverbs dealing with time, place, and quantity
▶ Forming adverbs of manner from adjectives
▶ Placing adverbs in a sentence

Many words that give detail in French, like **maintenant** (*now*), **jamais** (*never*), and **peut-être** (*maybe*), are adverbs. **Les adverbes** (*adverbs*) modify verbs, adjectives, and sometimes even other adverbs; in French, they don't have to match any other word in a sentence in either gender or number. Adverbs can take different forms: They can be a single word or a whole expression (called an *adverbial expression*) like **tout de suite** (*right away*) or **avec joie** (*gladly*).

I split adverbs into two big categories in this chapter:

✔ Adverbs that answer the questions *when, where,* and *how much*
✔ Adverbs of manner that tell you how something is done

I also show you where to place adverbs in a sentence, depending on what they're modifying.

When, Where, and How Much: Getting to Know Adverbs of Time, Place, and Quantity

You've encountered these *very* common words *before*, and you will find more *here*! There, in just one sentence I used three adverbs! *Very* (**très**) is an adverb of quantity, *before* (**avant**) is an adverb of time, and *here* (**ici**) is an adverb of place. In the following sections, I sort adverbs into three categories, based on which question they answer: *when, where,* and *how much.*

Adverbs of time

Adverbs of time answer the question **quand** (*when*). Here are a few common adverbs of time.

- **actuellement** (*currently*)
- **après** (*after*)
- **aujourd'hui** (*today*)
- **avant** (*before*)
- **d'abord** (*first[ly]*)
- **déjà** (*already*)
- **demain** (*tomorrow*)
- **enfin** (*finally*)
- **ensuite** (*then, next*)
- **hier** (*yesterday*)
- **immédiatement** (*immediately*)
- **jamais** (*never*)
- **longtemps** (*a long time*)
- **maintenant** (*now*)
- **parfois** (*sometimes/occasionally*)
- **plus tard** (*later*)
- **rarement** (*rarely*)
- **souvent** (*often*)
- **tard** (*late*)
- **tôt** (*early*)
- **toujours** (*always*)
- **toujours** (*still*)
- **tout de suite** (*right away*)

Would you like to see a few of them in action?

> **Il fait toujours ses devoirs seul.** (*He always does his homework alone.*)

> **D'abord, elle se lève, puis elle prend son café.** (*First she gets up, then she has her coffee.*)

> **Ouvrez la porte tout de suite!** (*Open the door right away!*)

Adverbs of place

Adverbs of place answer the question **où** (*where*). Here are a few common adverbs of place:

- **où** (*where*)
- **ici** (*here*)
- **loin** (*far*)
- **partout** (*everywhere*)
- **quelque part** (*somewhere*)
- **nulle part** (*nowhere*)
- **devant** (*in front*)
- **derrière** (*behind*)
- **à l'interieur** (*inside*)
- **dehors** (*outside*)
- **sur** (*on*)
- **par-dessus/sur** (*over*)
- **sous** (*under*)
- **à droite** (*to the right*)
- **à gauche** (*to the left*)
- **en haut** (*up/upstairs*)
- **en bas** (*down/downstairs*)
- **en haut de** (*at the top*)
- **au fond** (*at the bottom*)
- **à côté** (*next door/next to*)
- **près (d'ici)** (*close/nearby*)

Check out some adverbs of place in the following sentences:

Le chat dort sous la table. (*The cat sleeps under the table.*)

Ils habitent loin. (*They live far away.*)

Tournez à droite. (*Turn right.*)

Adverbs of quantity

Adverbs of quantity answer the question **combien** (*how much/how many*). Here are some common adverbs of quantity:

- **assez** (*enough*)
- **autant** (*as much*)

- ✔ **beaucoup** (*a lot*)
- ✔ **combien** (*how much/how many*)
- ✔ **moins** (*less*)
- ✔ **peu** (*little*)
- ✔ **plus** (*more*)
- ✔ **presque** (*almost*)
- ✔ **tellement** (*so much*)
- ✔ **très** (*very*)
- ✔ **trop** (*too much*)

Here are a few of them in action:

> **Nous avons beaucoup mangé à Thanksgiving.** (*We ate a lot at Thanksgiving.*)
>
> **J'ai assez attendu!** (*I waited enough!*)
>
> **Tu es très gentil.** (*You are very kind.*)

Complete the following sentences with the correct adverb that's given in English. Here's an example.

0. Ils habitent _____. (*here*)

A. ici

1. Lave-toi les mains _____. (*right away*)

2. _____ il se lève, _____ il prend sa douche. (*first; then*)

3. J'ai cherché _____. (*everywhere*)

4. Ils sont _____ en vacances. (*currently*)

5. Il dîne _____ seul. (*always*)

6. Elle est partie _____. (*far*)

7. Tu vas tourner _____. (*to the right*)

8. J'ai _____ mangé! (*too much*)

9. Nous n'irons _____ pour les vacances. (*nowhere*)

10. Nous sommes _____ contents de vous rencontrer. (*very*)

That's the Way: Examining Adverbs of Manner

Adverbs that express *how* or *in what manner* something is done are recognizable by their *-ly* ending in English. The French equivalent is the **-ment** ending. *Unfortunately* (see what I did there?), the easy stuff stops there! Forming adverbs of manner in French has a few pitfalls but the following sections *quickly* show you how to avoid them *successfully*.

Forming regular adverbs of manner

Most adverbs of manner are derived from an adjective. For example, **lent** (*slow*) gives the adverb **lentement** (*slowly*). To form an adverb of manner, take the feminine singular form of the adjective (built from the masculine singular form) and add **-ment** to it. You follow this rule even for adjectives that have an irrregular feminine form, like **mou** (*limp*), **attentif** (*attentive*), **sot** (*silly*), and **doux** (*soft*). (For info on how to form the feminine of adjectives, see Chapter 4.) Table 10-1 gives some examples of this process, including irregular adjectives.

Table 10-1	From Adjective to Adverb		
Masculine Adjective	*Feminine Form*	*French Adverb*	*English Translation*
attentif	attentive	attentivement	*attentively*
discret	discrète	discrètement	*discreetly*
doux	douce	doucement	*softly*
fin	fine	finement	*finely*
franc	franche	franchement	*frankly/openly*
heureux	heureuse	heureusement	*fortunately*
lent	lente	lentement	*slowly*
long	longue	longuement	*at length/a long time*
mou	molle	mollement	*limply/half-heartedly*
naturel	naturelle	naturellement	*naturally*
nouveau	nouvelle	nouvellement	*newly*
parfait	parfaite	parfaitement	*perfectly*
sot	sotte	sottement	*in a silly way*
timide	timide	timidement	*timidly*

Check out a few adverbs of manner here:

Parle-moi franchement. (*Speak to me frankly.*)

Écoutons attentivement. (*Let's listen attentively.*)

Elle nous a serré la main mollement. (*She shook our hands limply.*)

C'est une épave nouvellement découverte. (*It's a newly discovered shipwreck.*)

Ils ont attendu longuement. (*They waited a long time.*)

A handful of adjectives are used as adverbs in specific expressions without adding **-ment.** The meaning of these adverbs is slightly different from the adjective itself, and they don't agree in gender or number with anything. The most common ones are

- **bas** (*low*), as in the expression **parler bas** (*to speak softly*)
- **bon** (*good*), as in **sentir bon** (*to smell good*)
- **cher** (*expensive*), as in **coûter cher** (*to cost a lot*)
- **clair** (*clear*), as in **voir clair** (*to see clearly*)
- **dur** (*hard*), as in **travailler dur** (*to work hard*)
- **faux** (*false*), as in **chanter faux** (*to sing out of pitch*)
- **fort** (*strong*), as in **parler fort** (*to speak loud*)
- **heureux** (*happy*), as in **ils vécurent heureux jusqu'à la fin** (*they lived happily ever after*)
- **juste** (*just*), as in **chanter juste** (*to sing in tune*)
- **mauvais** (*bad*), as in **sentir mauvais** (*to smell bad*)

Complete the sentences with an adverb from this list.

attentivement	finement	longuement
bas	franchement	parfaitement
cher	heureux	timidement
faux	lentement	

Q. **Il a parlé** _____. (*He spoke . . .*)

A. **longuement**

11. **À l'église, on parle** _____. (*In church, people speak . . .*)

12. **Dis la vérité! Parle** _____. (*Tell the truth! Speak . . .*)

13. **Tu as** _____ **compris.** (*You understood . . .*)

14. **Ces chaussures coûtent** _____. (*These shoes cost . . .*)

15. **Le vieil homme marchait** _____. (*The old man was walking . . .*)

16. Coupez les oignons _____. (*Cut the onions . . .*)

17. Les petits enfants parlent _____. (*Little kids speak . . .*)

18. Je chante _____. (*I sing . . .*)

19. Ecoutez _____! (*Listen . . .*)

20. Ils vécurent _____ jusqu'à la fin des temps. (*They lived . . . until the end of times.*)

Recognizing and forming irregular adverbs of manner

Some adverbs of manner take a route that's different from the one in the preceding section, and some adverbs of manner are completely irregular. The following sections show you the variations.

Straying slightly from the feminine adjective

Sometimes, an adverb of manner is not formed directly from the feminine of the adjective. Adjectives that end in **-e** in the feminine fall into this group. The **-e** changes to **-é** before adding the **-ment** ending of the adverb. Here are some examples:

- ✔ **précis/précise** form **précisément** (*precisely*)

- ✔ **énorme/énorme** form **énormément** (*enormously*)

- ✔ **profond/profonde** form **profondément** (*deeply*)

Avoiding the feminine adjective and going completely irregular

Some other adverbs don't go through the feminine form of the adjective at all. Here's their route:

- ✔ For adjectives ending in **-ant**, replace **-ant** with **-amment** to form the adverb, like this:

  courant → **couramment** (*fluently*); **bruyant** → **bruyamment** (*loudly*)

- ✔ For adjectives ending in **-ent**, replace **-ent** with **-emment** to form the adverb, like this:

  prudent → **prudemment** (*prudently*); **évident** → **évidemment** (*evidently*)

- ✔ For adjectives that end in **-i**, **-é**, or **-u**, add **-ment** directly, without the **-e** of the feminine. Such adjectives include:

  absolu → **absolument** (*absolutely*)

  passionné → **passionnément** (*passionately*)

  poli → **poliment** (*politely*)

  spontané → **spontanément** (*spontaneously*)

  vrai → **vraiment** (*really*)

And then come the completely irregular adverbs, those that don't follow any marked route! You have to memorize them. Table 10-2 gives you a sampling of the most common completely irregular adverbs of manner.

Table 10-2	Completely Irregular Adverbs		
Masculine Adjective	*Translation*	*Adverb*	*Translation*
bon	*good*	**bien**	*well*
bref	*brief*	**brièvement**	*briefly*
gentil	*kind*	**gentiment**	*kindly*
mauvais	*bad*	**mal**	*badly*
meilleur	*better*	**mieux**	*better*
rapide	*fast*	**vite** (although **rapidement** also exists)	*quickly*

Form the irregular adverbs for the following adjectives. Here's an example:

0. gentil

A. gentiment

21. énorme _____

22. courant _____

23. évident _____

24. vrai _____

25. meilleur _____

26. bref _____

27. mauvais _____

28. précis _____

29. bruyant _____

30. absolu _____

Knowing when no adverb of manner can work

Sometimes an adverb of manner just doesn't exist for what you want to say. For example, in English one such impossible adverbial situation is *He answered in a friendly way.* You can't say *He answered friendlyly!* French has similar work-arounds, which I list here.

✔ Use a verb + **d'une façon** (literally: *in a fashion*) + feminine singular adjective. For example:

Il a répondu d'une façon nonchalante. (*He answered in a nonchalant fashion.*)

✔ Use a verb + **d'une manière** (literally: *in a manner*) + feminine singular adjective. For example:

Elle parle d'une manière hautaine. (*She speaks in a haughty manner.*)

✔ Use a verb + **d'un air** (literally *with an air*) + masculine singular adjective. For example:

Ils écoutent d'un air distrait. (*They're listening with a distracted air.*)

✔ Use a verb + **avec** (*with*) + noun (without an article). For example:

Je le ferai avec plaisir. (*I will do it gladly.*)

Il fait son travail avec précision. (*He does his work with precision.*)

L'appartement est meublé avec goût. (*The apartment is furnished with taste.*)

Sometimes these expressions are used not for lack of an adverb but for stylistic reasons. My advice is to check a French-English dictionary to make sure the adverb you want to use exists.

Putting Adverbs in Their Place

Depending on whether they modify a verb, an adverb, or an adjective, adverbs move around quite a bit in the sentence. The following sections track them down for you.

In English, adverbs are sometimes placed right after the subject of the verb, like *she often sings.* In French, you can never place the adverb after the subject.

With verbs in a simple tense

When an adverb modifies a verb conjugated in a simple tense (a one-part verb form like the present tense in Chapter 6, the imperfect tense in Chapter 16, and the future tense in Chapter 17), the adverb follows the verb. Here are examples of the adverb placed after the verb:

Je mange rarement au restaurant. (*I rarely eat in a restaurant.*)

Il conduit vite. (*He drives fast.*)

Vous travaillez dur. (*You work hard.*)

Ils aiment beaucoup aller au cinéma. (*They really like to go to the movies.*)

You often find long adverbs at the end of a sentence, even if it means separating it from the conjugated verb. For example: **Vous écoutez le professeur attentivement.** (*You are listening to the professor attentively.*)

With verbs in the near future tense

When an adverb modifies a verb conjugated in the **futur proche** (*near future*; see Chapter 17), which consists of the verb **aller** (*to go*) + infinitive, the adverb follows **aller**, which is the conjugated verb. For example:

> **Tu vas probablement t'ennuyer.** (*You are probably going to be bored.*)
>
> **Il va sûrement gagner la course.** (*He is surely going to win the race.*)

With verbs in a compound tense

When an adverb modifies a verb conjugated in a compound tense like the **passé composé** (*present perfect*; see Chapter 15), the adverb usually follows the past participle of the verb. (The **passé composé** is made up of a conjugated form of the auxiliary **être** [*to be*] or **avoir** [*to have*] + the past participle of the verb.) For example:

> **Il s'est rasé rapidement.** (*He shaved quickly.*)
>
> **Elle s'est habillée élégamment.** (*She dressed elegantly.*)

However, some very common adverbs (especially short ones) must go between the auxiliary and the past participle, like this:

> **Tu as bien travaillé.** (*You worked well.*)
>
> **Elle est vite partie.** (*She left quickly.*)
>
> **Ils ont beaucoup aimé le film.** (*They liked the movie a lot.*)
>
> **Quelqu'un a mal fermé la porte.** (*Someone closed the door badly.*)

The adverbs that follow this pattern include: **vite** (*quickly*), **bien** (*well*), **mal** (*badly*), **déjà** (*already*), for the short ones, and **beaucoup** (*much*), **probablement** (*probably*), **tellement** (*so much*), **vraiment** (*really*), and **toujours** (*always*) for the long ones.

With adjectives and other adverbs

Adverbs that modify an adjective or another adverb come before those. Easy, right? Here are some examples:

> **Tu es mal coiffé.** (*Your hair looks terrible.*)
>
> **Il est vraiment petit.** (*He is really short.*)
>
> **Elle chante très bien.** (*She sings very well.*)

In the end: Certain adverbs of time

Adverbs of time that express specific days and times like **aujourd'hui** (*today*), **demain** (*tomorrow*), **hier** (*yesterday*), **tôt** (*early*), and **tard** (*late*) usually sit at the end of a sentence. Here are some examples:

> **Nous nous sommes levés tard.** (*We got up late.*)

> **Je ferai du sport demain.** (*I will play sports tomorrow.*)

Correctly place the adverbs in parentheses into the sentence, depending on the word that the adverb is modifying. Consult a French-English dictionary if you need help with any vocabulary. Here's an example.

Q. **Tu vas gagner! (sûrement)**

A. **Tu vas sûrement gagner.**

31. **Nous faisons nos devoirs. (sérieusement)**

32. **Ils ont perdu le match. (malheureusement)**

33. **Je t'aiderais si je pouvais. (avec plaisir)**

34. **Elle fera le ménage. (demain)**

35. **Il s'est levé. (tard)**

36. **Nous avons compris. (bien)**

37. **Ils font du yoga. (souvent)**

38. **Elle s'est trompée. (vraiment)**

39. **Vous allez réussir. (peut-être)**

40. **Tu as travaillé. (bien)**

Answer Key

1 tout de suite

2 D'abord; ensuite

3 partout

4 actuellement

5 toujours

6 loin

7 à droite

8 trop

9 nulle part

10 très

11 bas

12 franchement

13 parfaitement

14 cher

15 lentement

16 finement

17 timidement

18 faux

19 attentivement

20 heureux

21 énormément

22 couramment

23 évidemment

24 vraiment

25 mieux

26 brièvement

27 mal

28 précisément

29 bruyamment

30 absolument

31 Nous faisons nos devoirs sérieusement.

32 Malheureusement, ils ont perdu le match.

33 Je t'aiderais avec plaisir si je pouvais.

34 Elle fera le ménage demain.

35 Il s'est levé tard.

36 Nous avons bien compris.

37 Ils font souvent du yoga.

38 Elle s'est vraiment trompée.

39 Vous allez peut-être réussir.

40 Tu as bien travaillé.

Chapter 11

Picking Up Prepositions

. . . .

In This Chapter

▶ Focusing on the fundamentals of prepositions

▶ Deciphering tricky prepositions

▶ Knowing whether to say **à Paris** or **en Paris**

. . . .

Prepositions (**les prépositions**) are words that can answer questions like *where, when, with whom,* and so on. They are used in combination with other words in a sentence to form a prepositional phrase. You add more detail to a sentence with prepositional phrases, such as *in the kitchen* (**dans la cuisine**) or *with my friends* (**avec mes amis**).

French uses lots of prepositions. Some have an obvious English equivalent, like **avec** (*with*), **sur** (*on*), **contre** (*against*), and **devant** (*in front of*). Others are more mysterious, like **à** and **de**, which have several meanings. This chapter helps you sort out French prepositions.

Introducing the Basics of Prepositions

Prepositions can help you change the meaning of a sentence easily. They are *invariable words,* which means that you don't have to worry about making them agree with a noun, and their position in the sentence is not particularly crucial, unlike pronouns. So really, there's nothing not to like about them! This section shows you how easy using them is.

Presenting common prepositions

Like in English, there are different types of prepositions in French. Some are simple in their form, using a single word like **pour** (*for*) and **avec** (*with*). Others are compound, such as **à coté de** (*next to*), because they are made of two or more words. The following list provides a good sampling of French prepositions, both simple and compound.

- ✔ **à** (*at, in, to*)
- ✔ **à cause de** (*because of*)
- ✔ **à côté de** (*next to*)
- ✔ **après** (*after*)
- ✔ **au lieu de** (*instead of*)
- ✔ **au milieu de** (*in the middle of*)
- ✔ **avant** (*before*) (temporal only)

- ✔ **avec** (*with*)
- ✔ **chez** (*at the place of [someone]*)
- ✔ **contre** (*against*)
- ✔ **dans** (*in*)
- ✔ **de** (*of/from*)
- ✔ **derrière** (*behind*)
- ✔ **devant** (*in front of*)
- ✔ **en** (*in*)
- ✔ **en face de** (*across from*)
- ✔ **entre** (*between*)
- ✔ **hors de** (*outside of*)
- ✔ **jusqu'à** (*until/as far as*)
- ✔ **loin de** (*far from*)
- ✔ **malgré** (*in spite of*)
- ✔ **parmi** (*among*)
- ✔ **pendant** (*during/while*)
- ✔ **pour** (*for/in order to*)
- ✔ **sans** (*without*)
- ✔ **sauf** (*except*)
- ✔ **sous** (*under*)
- ✔ **sur** (*on*)
- ✔ **vers** (*toward*)

Here are some of these prepositions in action:

> **La voiture est devant le garage.** (*The car is in front of the garage.*)

> **Le chat dort sur le lit, avec sa balle.** (*The cat is sleeping on the bed with his ball.*)

> **Nous déjeunons à midi, avec nos amis, dans un bon restaurant.** (*We have lunch at noon with our friends, in a good restaurant.*)

Both **dans** and **en** mean *in*. Here are some pointers on how to sort them out.

- ✔ When both **dans** and **en** express a spatial *in*, think of **dans** as *inside something specific*, like **dans une boîte** (*in a box*) and **dans la maison** (*in the house*). **En**, on the other hand, tends to be less specific, as in **en Afrique** (*in Africa*) and **en banlieue** (*in the suburbs*).

- ✔ **Dans** and **en** can also express a temporal *in*, and here things get a little clearer! If *in* is a projection, like *in ten years*, use **dans**: **dans 10 ans**. If *in* means within a certain amount of time, choose **en**, as in **j'ai fini mon travail en une heure seulement** (*I finished my work in only one hour*). Also use **en** to express dates like **en 2012** (*in 2012*), **en hiver** (*in winter*), and **en juillet** (*in July*).

Another way to distinguish **en** from **dans** is that no article follows **en**. An article always follows **dans**.

Not all English prepositions have obvious French equivalents. For instance, in English you drink *out of a glass,* but in French you drink *in a glass* (**dans un verre**). So to play it safe, I recommend double-checking a French-English dictionary when you need to use a preposition you're not familiar with.

Choose a preposition from the following list to complete the sentences as shown in the example. (If you don't know some of the vocabulary, consult a French-English dictionary.)

à	dans	pour
au milieu de	jusqu'à	sans
avec	malgré	sur
chez		

0. Nous allons _____ la maison.

A. à

1. _____ leur fatigue, les athlètes sont contents.

2. La voiture est _____ le garage.

3. Je passe _____ mes amis.

4. Les livres sont _____ la table.

5. Ce cadeau est _____ toi!

6. Le chat joue _____ sa balle.

7. Tu as déjeuné _____ midi.

8. Le dimanche il dort _____ 11 heures.

9. Ne sors pas _____ ton manteau: il fait froid!

10. C'est une île _____ l'océan.

Using common prepositions properly

As you find out in the following sections, prepositions can be used in combination with lots of different words:

- With stress pronouns, like **avec moi** (*with me*)

- With nouns, like **avec sa balle** (*with his ball*)

- With interrogative words, like **à quelle heure?** (*at what time?*) and **dans quelle boîte?** (*in which box?*)

- With verbs, as in **pour dormir** (*in order to sleep*)

With stress pronouns and nouns

A *stress pronoun* is the pronoun you need after a preposition. It can only refer to people, not to things. (See Chapter 13 for more.) Here are the French stress pronouns:

- **moi** (*me*)
- **toi** (*you*) (singular informal)
- **lui** (*him*)
- **elle** (*her*)
- **nous** (*us*)
- **vous** (*you*) (singular formal and plural formal or informal)
- **eux** (*them*) (masculine)
- **elles** (*them*) (feminine)

To express phrases like *with me*, *for you*, and *on the table*, French proceeds like English, by simply using the preposition in front of the stress pronoun and the noun like this: **avec moi**, **pour toi**, **sur la table**.

Here are some prepositions in action with nouns:

> **Viens avec moi.** (*Come with me.*)
>
> **Il est chez lui.** (*He is at home.*)
>
> **Nous partirons sans eux.** (*We'll leave without them.*)

Here are some prepositions in action with nouns:

> **sans ton manteau** (*without your coat*)
>
> **au milieu de la nuit** (*in the middle of the night*)

With interrogative words

Sometimes when you want to ask a detailed question, you need more than a simple question word like *which* or *what*. You may need to ask something like *with which* or *at what*, using a preposition with the question word. It's very easy to do in French: Place the preposition before the interrogative and finish the question normally. (For details on how to ask a question, see Chapter 9.)

These examples show you prepositions combined with some question words.

> **Pour qui est ce cadeau?** (*For whom is this gift?*)
>
> **Dans quoi mets-tu les papiers?** (*What do you put the papers in?*) (Literally: *In what do you put the papers?*)

With verbs

When a French verb follows a preposition, it's usually in the infinitive form. Sometimes the verb is actually translated into English in the infinitive form; for example, **pour dormir** means *in order to sleep*. Often, though, the verb in a construction of preposition + verb is translated into a gerund instead of an infinitive: **sans parler** (*without talking*), **sans hésiter** (*without hesitating*).

However, constructions with the preposition **en** are an exception. After **en**, the French verb is in the gerund, and it expresses *while doing something* (see Chapter 14 for details on gerunds). For instance, **en regardant la télé** (*while watching TV*).

Here are some complete sentences that use prepositions with verbs:

> **Elle a besoin de trois oreillers pour dormir.** (*She needs three pillows to sleep.*)
>
> **Il est parti sans dire un mot.** (*He left without saying a word.*)
>
> **Nous dînons en regardant la télé.** (*We eat dinner while watching TV*)

Translate the following sentences using prepositions into French. Here's an example to get you started:

Q. *He eats while watching TV.*

A. **Il mange en regardant la télé.**

11. *This gift is for her.*

_____

12. *The car is next to the house.*

_____

13. *What is he thinking about?*

_____

14. *Under what chair is the ball?*

_____

15. *At what time do you leave?*

_____

16. *We live in a house.*

_____

17. *The book is on the table.*

_____

18. *He was born in 1999.*

_____

19. *Where will you be in one year?*

_____

20. *I'm going home.*

_____

Figuring Out Some Tricky Prepositions

A couple of French prepositions — **à** and **de** — are a little tricky. Why? They have multiple meanings in English, so you may not always know how and when to use them. In the following sections, I explain the various uses of these two prepositions.

Examining à

À is used most often to indicate travel to or location in a city. It is the equivalent of the English *to*, *in*, or *at*. Check out the following examples:

> **Il va à Paris.** (*He goes to Paris.*)

> **Il habite à Paris.** (*He lives in Paris.*)

When dealing with geography, **à** is not the only option in French. (Skip to the later section "A Geography Lesson: Using Prepositions with Destinations and Locations" for details.) But **à** has other uses, as you find out in the following sections.

À + noun

In French, most verbs that indicate communication have an indirect object introduced by **à**, as in **nous parlons à Julie** (*we talk to Julie*). A few other verbs have this particularity, too. The most common ones are detailed in the following list:

- **demander à quelqu'un** (*to ask someone*)

- **dire à quelqu'un** (*to tell someone*)

- **donner (quelque chose) à** (*to give [something] to*)

- **emprunter à quelqu'un** (*to borrow from someone*)

- **faire attention à quelqu'un/quelque chose** (*to pay attention to someone/something*)

- **parler à quelqu'un** (*to talk to someone*)

- **penser à quelqu'un/quelque chose** (*to think about someone/something*)

- **rendre visite à** (*to visit someone*)

> ✔ **répondre à quelqu'un/quelque chose** (*to answer someone*)
>
> ✔ **ressembler à quelqu'un/quelque chose** (*to look like someone*)
>
> ✔ **téléphoner à quelqu'un** (*to call someone*)

Here are a couple examples of how to use **à** with a noun:

> **Elle téléphone à ses grands-parents.** (*She phones her grandparents.*)
>
> **Ces enfants ressemblent à leur mère.** (*These kids look like their mother.*)

À + infinitive

Other French verbs must be followed by the preposition **à** if they introduce another verb (in the infinitive). The **à** doesn't change the meaning of the verb or its conjugation, and it isn't even translated in English, but it must be there. If no other verb follows, don't use the **à** after the verbs in the following list:

> ✔ **apprendre à** + infinitive (*to learn to do something*)
>
> ✔ **arriver à** + infinitive (*to manage to do something*)
>
> ✔ **commencer à** + infinitive (*to begin to [do something]*)
>
> ✔ **continuer à** + infinitive (*to continue to [do something]*)
>
> ✔ **hésiter à** + infinitive (*to hesitate to [do something]*)
>
> ✔ **obliger** (**quelqu'un**) **à** + infinitive (*to force [someone] to [do something]*)
>
> ✔ **réussir à** + infinitive (*to succeed in [doing something]*)
>
> ✔ **s'habituer à** + infinitive (*to get used to [doing something]*)
>
> ✔ **se préparer à** + infinitive (*to get ready to do*)

Here are some of them in action

> **On se prépare à partir.** (*We get ready to leave.*)
>
> **Est-ce que vous commencez à comprendre?** (*Are you beginning to understand?*)

Translate the following English sentences into French. Remember, when **à** precedes the definite articles **le** or **les**, it combines into **au** or **aux**.

Q. *I am beginning to understand.*

A. **Je commence à comprendre.**

21. *They're getting ready to go out.*

_____

22. *The little kids learn to write.*

_____

23. *She thinks about her husband.*

_____

24. *Answer the teacher!* (*you* plural)

_____

25. *I succeeded/managed to open the door.*

_____

Understanding de

The preposition **de** has a few clear translations in English. When it's used with a location, **de** means *from* (see the later section "A Geography Lesson: Using Prepositions with Destinations and Locations" for details). In front of most nouns that are not locations, it means *of*. However, when it introduces an infinitive, **de** loses a clear meaning, and most often it doesn't have an equivalent in English. The following sections give you the scoop.

Verb + de + noun

De can link a verb to a noun, as in the sentence **Il se moque de la sorcière** (*He makes fun of the witch*), but beware that the English equivalent of such verbs does not always include *of*. Here are many common verbs that require **de** before a noun, with their English equivalent, with or without *of*.

- **avoir besoin de** + noun (*to need*)
- **avoir envie de** + noun (*to want*)
- **avoir peur de** + noun (*to be afraid of*)
- **changer de** + noun (*to change*)
- **entendre parler de** + noun (*to hear of*)
- **être** + adjective + **de** + noun (*to be [adjective] of*)
- **faire la connaissance de** + noun (*to make the acquaintance of*)
- **jouer de** + noun (*to play an instrument*)
- **manquer de** + noun (*to not have enough of*)
- **parler de** + noun (*to talk about*)
- **profiter de** + noun (*to take advantage of/to enjoy*)
- **s'apercevoir de** + noun (*to realize*)
- **s'occuper de** + noun (*to take care of*)
- **se moquer de** + noun (*to make fun of*)
- **se servir de** + noun (*to use/utilize*)
- **se souvenir de** + noun (*to remember*)

Here are a couple of examples of how to use **de** to link a verb and a noun:

> **Occupe-toi de ta soeur s'il te plaît.** (*Take care of your sister, please.*)
>
> **Vous vous souvenez de vos vacances.** (*You remember your vacation.*)
>
> **Nous parlons de l'accident.** (*We're talking about the accident.*)

Translate the following sentences from English to French, incorporating the correct form of **de**.

_0._ *He plays guitar.*

_A._ **Il joue de la guitare.**

_26._ *She changed her name when she married.*

_____

_27._ *He uses a spoon to eat a pie.*

_____

_28._ *We're going to take advantage of the sales.*

_____

_29._ *I forgot to close the door!*

_____

_30._ *Did you hear about this actor?*

_____

Noun + de + noun

De can link two nouns, in expressing possession like English sometimes does. But how often do you say, *This is the car of my mother* (**La voiture de ma mère**)? You'd rather say, *It's my mother's car*, right? Well, in French you have only one option, and it's the **de** (*of*) way. Phrases like *John's dog* or *my mother's car* don't exist in literal French. But expressing those ideas is pretty easy to do when you use the following formula: object owned + **de** + owner. Here's the formula in action:

> **le chien** + **de** + **John** (*John's dog*)
>
> **la maison de mes parents** (*my parents' house*)
>
> **les livres des étudiants** (*the students' books*)

Think in terms of flipping things around. In the first example, **John** and **le chien** have opposite positions in the French sentence compared to the English sentence.

Note: When **de** is followed by the definite article **le**, it becomes **du**, and when followed by **les**, it becomes **des**, as in **les livres des étudiants** (literally: *the books of the students*).

Translate the following phrases that express possession into French.

0. *my parent's house* _____

A. **la maison de mes parents**

31. *my mother's car* _____

32. *Pierre's cat* _____

33. *the student' books* _____

34. *my friends' house* _____

35. *the teacher's bag* _____

De + infinitive

Just like quite a few French verbs must be followed by the preposition **à** if they introduce an infinitive, a number of French verbs must be followed by the preposition **de** when they introduce an infinitive. And like for **à**, **de** does not change the meaning of the verb and, in most cases it is not translated in English. In the following list, look at the English translation of a verb to see if it has *of* or not.

- ✔ **accepter de** + infinitive (*to accept to [do something]*)
- ✔ **arrêter de** + infinitive (*to stop/quit [doing something]*)
- ✔ **avoir peur/besoin/honte de** + infinitive (*to fear [doing something]/to need to [do something]/to be ashamed of [doing something]*)
- ✔ **choisir de** + infinitive (*to choose to [do something]*)
- ✔ **décider de** + infinitive (*to decide to [do something]*)
- ✔ **essayer de** + infinitive (*to try to [do something]*)
- ✔ **être** + adjective + **de** + infinitive (*to be [adjective] of [doing something]*)
- ✔ **être obligé de** + infinitive (*to have to [do something]*)
- ✔ **éviter de** + infinitive (*to avoid [doing something]*)
- ✔ **finir de** + infinitive (*to finish [doing something]*)
- ✔ **oublier de** + infinitive (*to forget to [do something]*)
- ✔ **refuser de** + infinitive (*to refuse to [do something]*)
- ✔ **se souvenir de** + infinitive (*to remember to [do something]*)

Here are a few of these verbs in action

Je veux arrêter de fumer. (*I want to stop smoking.*)

Elle a refusé de sortir. (*She refused to get out.*)

Vous essayez d'ouvrir la porte. (*You try to open the door.*)

Note: **De** turns to **d'** before a vowel or a mute **-h**.

Complete the following sentences with the verb + **de** indicated in parenthesis to be found in the preceding list.

Q. Tu _____ **manger.** (*finish*)

A. **finis de**

36. Tu _____ **fermer la porte à clé.** (*to forget to*)

37. Elle veut _____ **fumer.** (*quit*)

38. Il _____ **apprendre le français.** (*to decide to*)

39. Nous _____ **prendre des vacances.** (*need to*)

40. Elle _____ **sortir.** (*refuses to*)

A Geography Lesson: Using Prepositions with Destinations and Locations

Sometimes you don't know when to say **à Paris** or **en Paris** for instance. This section helps you conquer the tricky difference between different prepositions when dealing with geographical places, namely cities, states, countries, and regions.

Dealing with a preposition + a city

So you're planning to go *to* Paris? How long will you stay *in* Paris? The following sections reveal the French way to say those things.

Expressing a location or travel to a city

This is an easy one! To say that you're going *to* or staying *in* a particular city, use **à** followed by the name of that city. Don't forget that typically cities don't come with an article, except for some cities like **La Nouvelle Orléans** (*New Orleans*), **Le Caire** (*Cairo*), or **La Haye** (*the Hague*). Here are some examples using **à**:

Ils habitent à la Nouvelle Orléans. (*They live in New Orleans.*)

Nous allons à Madrid. (*We're going to Madrid.*)

Note: **à** + **le** contracts into **au**, and **à** + **les** contracts into **aux**.

After certain verbs + city, you just can't use the preposition **à**. These verbs require a direct object instead. They are **aimer** (*to like*) (and all verbs of preference; see Chapter 3), **visiter** (*to visit*), **quitter** (*to leave*), **connaître** (*to know*), and **voir** (*to see*). Here are a couple of examples:

Je voudrais visiter Rome. (*I'd like to visit Rome.*)

Est-ce que tu connais Vienne? (*Do you know Vienna?*)

Expressing travel from a city

Talking about traveling from a city is just as easy! To say that you're coming from a particular city, use **de** followed by the name of that city. Here are some examples:

Ils rentrent de Londres. (*They're returning from London.*)

Il vient de Paris. (*He comes from Paris.*)

Note: For cities that have a masculine singular article, like **Le Mans** or **Le Havre**, **de** + **le** contract into **du**. If the city has a plural article, like **Les Adrets**, contract **de** + **les** into **des**. Here are some examples:

Nous allons aux 24 heures du Mans cette année. (*We're going to the 24 hours of Le Mans this year.*)

Je rentre des Adrets. (*I am returning from Les Adrets.*)

Handling a preposition + a state or a country

To determine the right preposition to use before a state or a country, look at the gender of the state or country. Yes, states and countries have a gender in French! When you're talking about a state or a country, you have to use the proper article, like **la France** (*France*), **les États-Unis** (*The U.S.*), and **le Japon** (*Japan*). (Flip to Chapter 3 for details about nouns and gender.)

When saying you're going *to* that state or country, staying *in* it, or leaving *from* it, the choice of the preposition also depends on the gender. The following sections show you what you need to know.

Determining the gender of a state or a country

When the name of a country, region, or state ends with an **-e**, that country is feminine and uses the article **la**. However, a few exceptions end in **-e** but are masculine nonetheless. They are **le Mexique** (*Mexico*), **le Cambodge** (*Cambodia*), **le Mozambique** (*Mozambique*), and **le Zimbabwe** (*Zimbabwe*).

All other countries are masculine. For example: **le Canada** (*Canada*) and **le Danemark** (*Denmark*). All continents are feminine.

Expressing travel to and location in a state or a country

After you determine the gender of the place you're discussing, you can see how it affects the choice of words to express *in a country* or *to a country*.

To say you're *in* or going *to* a feminine state or country, use **en** followed directly by the name of the state or country, without its article. That's right, no article after **en**. Here are two examples:

Allons en Italie! (*Let's go to Italy!*)

Ils habitent en Turquie. (*They live in Turkey.*)

Any country, masculine or feminine, whose name starts with a vowel falls in this category also. So even though **Afghanistan**, **Ouganda**, and **Israël** are masculine countries because they don't end with an **-e**, they follow the preposition **en**, and you say **en Afghanistan**, **en Ouganda**, and **en Israël**.

To say you're *in* or going *to* a masculine country, use **à** + the article + the name of the country, like this: **à** + **le** + **Pérou: au Pérou**. Plural countries like **les États-Unis** (*the United States*) also fall into this category. (*Note:* When **à** is followed by the definite article **le**, it becomes **au**; when it's followed by **les**, it becomes **aux**.)

Expressing travel from a state or a country

To say you're traveling *from* a feminine country or a masculine country whose name starts with a vowel, use **de** followed directly by the name of the country without the article (note that when **de** precedes a noun that starts with a vowel or a mute **-h**, use **d'**). Here are two examples:

> **Il vient de France.** (*He comes from France.*)

> **Nous arrivons d'Irak.** (*We're arriving from Iraq.*)

To say you're traveling *from* a masculine or plural country, use **de** followed by the article **le** or **les**, which contract respectively into **du** and **des**, followed by the name of the country, like so:

> **Elle vient du Maroc.** (*She comes from Morocco.*)

> **Vous arrivez des Pays-Bas.** (*You're arriving from the Netherlands.*)

Complete each sentence with the correct geographical preposition or article. Remember that you can't use a preposition after some verbs, and cities don't have an article.

Q. J'irai _____ France cette année.

A. en

41. Ils partent _____ Italie pour les vacances.

42. Elle voudrait habiter _____ Paris.

43. Nous sommes allés _____ Europe récemment.

44. On parle un peu français _____ La Nouvelle Orléans.

45. Connaissez-vous _____ Texas?

46. Quand je serai _____ Egypte, je voyagerai _____ Caire.

47. Est-ce qu'il fait beau _____ États-Unis en été?

48. Lui, il veut visiter _____ Allemagne, mais elle voudrait aller _____ Vienne.

49. Tu reviens _____ Maroc.

50. Vous rentrez _____ Californie.

Answer Key

1 malgré

2 dans

3 chez

4 sur

5 pour

6 avec

7 à

8 jusqu'à

9 sans

10 au milieu de

11 Ce cadeau est pour elle.

12 La voiture est à coté de la maison.

13 À quoi est-ce qu'il pense?

14 Sous quelle chaise est la balle?

15 À quelle heure partez-vous?

16 Nous habitons dans une maison.

17 Le livre est sur la table.

18 Il est né en 1999.

19 Où seras-tu dans un an?

20 Je vais chez moi./Je rentre à la maison.

21 Ils se préparent à sortir.

22 Les petits enfants apprennent à écrire.

23 Elle pense à son mari.

24 Répondez au professeur!

25 J'ai réussi à ouvrir la porte.

26 Elle a changé de nom quand elle s'est mariée.

27 Il se sert d'une cuillère pour manger une tarte.

28 Nous allons profiter des soldes.

29 J'ai oublié de fermer la porte.

30 Est-ce que tu as entendu parler de cet acteur?

31 la voiture de ma mère

32 le chien de Pierre

33 les livres des étudiants

34 la maison de mes amis

35 le sac du professeur

36 oublies de

37 arrêter de

38 a décidé d'

39 avons besoin de

40 refuse de

41 en

42 à

43 en

44 à

45 le

46 en; au

47 aux

48 l'; à

49 du

50 de

Chapter 12

It's All Relative: Making Comparisons

In This Chapter

▶ Focusing on the basics of comparisons

▶ Including adjectives, adverbs, and quantities in comparisons

▶ Adding stress pronouns to comparisons

▶ Surveying superlatives

*W*hen describing things, people, and actions, you can use comparisons in order to give a more precise description. For example, you can say: **Julie est plus petite qu'Anne, mais elle court plus vite.** (*Julie is shorter than Anne, but she runs faster.*) In such a sentence, you compare the way two people are (using the comparative of an adjective, like *shorter*) and how they do something (using the comparative of an adverb, like *faster*). You can compare things and people several other ways, too, and this chapter reviews them all.

Comparing Two Elements: The Basics

A basic comparison contrasts two elements by putting them side by side. In English, you can say that one thing is more interesting than another thing, less interesting than another thing, or as interesting as another thing. The following sections give you an overview of how to make such comparisons in French.

Using three basic types of comparisons

A basic comparison starts with an element (either an adjective, a verb, or an adverb) and the type of comparison (*more, less,* or *as*):

▭ For *more/than*, French uses **plus/que**

▭ For *less/than*, French uses **moins/que**

▭ For *as/as*, French uses **aussi/que**

The first element is followed by **que** (*than, as*), which introduces the original element of a comparison (what you're comparing against). After **que**, the second part of the comparison can have any of the following words or phrases:

▭ A name: **que Julie** (*as Julie*)

▭ A noun: **que ma mère** (*than my mother*)

✔ A stress pronoun: **que toi** (*than you*) (I cover stress pronouns in more detail later in this chapter.)

✔ An indefinite pronoun: **que d'autres** (*than others*)

✔ A prepositional phrase: **qu'à Paris** (*than in Paris*)

✔ An expression of time: **que l'an dernier** (*than last year*)

Que becomes **qu'** before a vowel or a mute **-h**.

Here are some examples of basic comparisons:

> **Je suis plus petite que ma mère.** (*I'm shorter than my mother.*)
>
> **Ils sont aussi gentils que vous.** (*They are as kind as you.*)
>
> **Vous travaillez plus que d'autres.** (*You work more than others.*)
>
> **Cette année, ils ont moins de travail que l'an dernier.** (*This year they have less work than last year.*)

In English, a comparative is often marked by adding **-er** to the end of an adjective, like *smarter* and *taller*. This construction doesn't exist in French; you always have to use **plus** followed by the adjective, like this: **plus intelligent**.

Translate the following sentences into French. Don't forget that adjectives must agree in number and gender with the noun they describe (see Chapter 4).

0. *Our house is smaller than their house.*

A. **Notre maison est plus petite que leur maison.**

1. *They work more efficiently than me!*

_____

2. *I go to the grocery store less often than my mother.*

_____

3. *He runs less fast than the champion.*

_____

4. *This restaurant is more expensive than our favorite restaurant.*

_____

5. *Her room is as big as a palace.*

_____

Understanding unusual comparisons

Like their English counterparts, French comparatives have a few tricks in their bag. The following sections show you some handy tips to know.

Incomplete comparisons

In everyday talk, when describing something that's obvious to everyone because of the context, you can omit the second half of a two-item comparison — everything from **que** on. For example, you and a friend are eating two different pies; your friend tastes yours and declares: **Elle est moins bonne.** (*It's not as good.*) No need to say more — in other words, you don't need to say **Elle est moins bonne que ma tarte** (*It's not as good as my pie*). Or perhaps you're sitting outside and decide to take off your sweater because **il fait moins froid maintenant** (*it's less cold now*).

Increased comparisons

Did you know that you can increase a comparative? For example, at 6'5", a boy is not just *taller* but *much taller than* anyone else around him. To express that in French, use **beaucoup plus** (*much more*), like this: **Il est beaucoup plus grand que les autres.** (*He is much taller than the others.*) You can also use **beaucoup moins** (*much less*). Here are a couple more examples:

> **Ce chapitre est beaucoup plus intéressant que le précédent.** (*This chapter is much more interesting than the last one.*)

> **Nous sortons beaucoup moins cette année.** (*We go out a lot less this year.*)

More or Less: Using Adjectives and Adverbs in Comparisons

When you start a comparison, you can say that someone is *more* or *less* of a quality, using **être** (*to be*) and an adjective, or that he does things in more or less of a certain way, using a verb and an adverb. The following sections detail comparisons that use adjectives and adverbs.

Comparisons with adjectives

When you describe something as *more beautiful*, or *as big*, or *less expensive* than another thing, you're comparing qualities. The words *beautiful*, *big*, and *expensive* are adjectives that express the quality. In the following sections, I explain the basics of comparisons with adjectives, along with some unusual adjectives to know.

Focusing on fundamentals

In French, an adjective must agree in gender and number with the noun it describes (see Chapter 4 for details). That rule applies to adjectives in a comparison, as you probably assumed. But don't get carried away: Only the adjective varies, not the comparative words **plus**, **moins**, and **aussi** (which I introduce earlier in this chapter).

To make a comparison that includes an adjective, follow these easy steps:

1. **Start with subject + a conjugation of être (*to be*) + plus/moins/aussi + adjective that matches the subject.**

   For example: **il est plus grand** (*he is taller*). If you need help conjugating **être** in the present tense, see Chapter 6.

2. **Add que + the original noun that you're comparing against.**

   For example: **Il est plus grand que son frère.** (*He is taller than his brother.*)

Here are more examples that show the variations of the adjectives:

> **Ce sac est plus grand qu'une valise!** (*This bag is larger than a suitcase!*)
>
> **Cette maison est plus grande que notre maison.** (*This house is bigger than our house.*)
>
> **Ces sacs sont plus grands que des valises!** (*These bags are larger than suitcases!*)
>
> **Ces maisons sont plus grandes que les maisons du quartier.** (*These houses are bigger than the houses in the neighborhood.*)

When you want to use more than one adjective in the comparison, repeat the comparative word **plus**, **moins**, or **aussi** before each adjective, like this:

> **Pierre est aussi intelligent et aussi charmant que son frère.** (*Pierre is as intelligent and charming as his brother.*)
>
> **Mes nouvelles chaussures sont moins jolies et moins confortables que mes vieilles chaussures.** (*My new shoes are less pretty and less comfortable than my old ones.*)

Moving from good to better

Like its English equivalent *good*, the adjective **bon** has an irregular form in the comparative of superiority: **meilleur** (*better*). This word replaces the phrase **plus bon** (*more good*). Don't use **plus** and **meilleur** in the same sentence! Here are some examples:

> **Cette tarte est meilleure que l'autre.** (*This pie is better than that other one.*)
>
> **Les gâteaux sont meilleurs que le pain.** (*Cakes are better than bread.*)

Meilleur is still an adjective and, as such, it should match the noun it describes. Here are the four forms of **meilleur**:

- ✔ Masculine singular: **meilleur**
- ✔ Feminine singular: **meilleure**
- ✔ Masculine plural: **meilleurs**
- ✔ Feminine plural: **meilleures**

Compare the qualities of the following pairs using the adjectives in parentheses and a form of the verb **être** (*to be*). The sign before each adjective indicates which comparative to use: + indicates **plus**, – means **moins**, and = means **aussi**. Be sure to make each adjective agree with the noun it describes.

0. le vin californien, le vin chilien (= bon)

A. Le vin californien est aussi bon que le vin chilien.

6. la France, le Canada (– grand)

_____

7. Paris, Londres (= beau)

_____

8. les chats, les chiens (– bruyant)

_____

9. le chocolat, les gâteaux (+ bon)

_____

10. les matières grasses, les cigarettes (= mauvais pour la santé)

_____

11. le poisson, le boeuf (– bon)

_____

12. les étés, les hivers (+ chaud)

_____

13. ces bagues, ce bracelet (+ cher)

_____

14. ma mère, mon père (= âgé)

_____

15. Julie, Valérie (– sérieux)

_____

Talking about adjectives that don't need plus, moins, or aussi

Some adjectives, like *similar*, imply a comparison all to themselves; they don't need words like **plus**, **moins**, and **aussi**. You still start with a subject and a conjugated verb, followed by the adjective of your choice; after them, the second element of the comparison is introduced by **à** or **de** instead of **que**. Following is a list of some common adjectives of this type:

- ✔ **supérieur à** (*superior to*)
- ✔ **inférieur à** (*inferior to*)
- ✔ **identique à** (*identical to*)
- ✔ **semblable à** (*similar to*)
- ✔ **pareil à** (*same as*)
- ✔ **différent de** (*different from*)

Don't forget to make these adjectives agree in number and gender. For instance, **pareil** changes to **pareille** in the feminine singular, **supérieur** changes to **supérieure**, **inférieur** changes to **inférieure**, and **différent** switches to **différente**.

And here they are in some examples:

> **Ton résultat est différent de mon résultat.** (*Your result is different from my result.*)

> **Cette copie est identique à la photo originale.** (*This copy is identical to the original photo.*)

Comparisons with adverbs

How did you do your work? *Better than yesterday? More slowly? More gracefully?* These sentences compare how a person does a particular thing, and they use adverbs; that's what *better*, *slowly*, and *gracefully* are. French adverbs (see Chapter 10) fit into comparisons *as smoothly as* English adverbs do. (See what I did there? That's another adverb in a comparison!)

An adverb is a word that describes a verb, or how an action is done: *well, poorly, gracefully,* and so on. Adverbs are therefore invariable, so you don't have to worry about making them agree in gender and number with anything. I list some very common adverbs here.

- ✔ **bien** (*well*)
- ✔ **facilement** (*easily*)
- ✔ **gentiment** (*kindly*)
- ✔ **longtemps** (*a long time*)
- ✔ **mal** (*poorly/badly*)
- ✔ **précisément** (*precisely*)
- ✔ **prudemment** (*prudently/cautiously*)

✔ **rarement** (*rarely*)

✔ **souvent** (*often*)

✔ **tard** (*late*)

✔ **vite** (*quickly*)

To make a comparison using adverbs, follow these guidelines:

✔ **For a comparison of superiority, use this formula:**

> subject + verb + **plus** + adverb + **que** + second term of comparison

For example: **Il court plus vite que son adversaire.** (*He runs faster than his adversary.*)

The comparative of superiority of **bien** (*well*) is irregular. Say **mieux** instead of **plus bien**. For instance: **Elle parle italien mieux que moi.** (*She speaks Italian better than me.*) Also, English uses *worse* rather than *more badly*. French simply uses **plus mal**.

✔ **For a comparison of inferiority, use this formula:**

> subject + verb + **moins** + adverb + **que** + second term of comparison

For example: **Tu conduis moins prudemment que ta mère.** (*You drive less cautiously than your mother.*)

✔ **For a comparison of equality, use this formula:**

> subject + verb + **aussi** + adverb + **que** + second term of comparison

For example: **Vous travaillez aussi bien que les autres.** (*You work as well as the others.*)

Complete the following sentences with the correct comparative, using the adverbs indicated in English in the parentheses. Here's an example:

0. Leur équipe gagne _____ notre équipe. (*less often than*)

A. moins souvent que

16. Charlotte chante _____ toi! (*better than*)

17. Les docteurs écrivent _____ les secrétaires. (*worse than*)

18. J'ai fait cet exercice _____ la dernière fois. (*less easily than*)

19. Tu conduis _____ ton frère. (*more prudently than*)

20. Ils arrivent au bureau _____ moi. (*as late as*)

Good Stuff: Comparing Quantities

Quantities describe how much of a thing there is or how much a person does. In the following sections, I explain how to make comparisons of different quantities in French.

Quantities of an item

The comparative of a quantity looks a little different from its fellow comparatives in French — specifically, it uses **de** (*of*).

- For *more [of something]*, use this formula:

    plus de + noun + **que** + the original item of the comparison

    Example: **Il a plus de chance que son ami.** (*He has more luck than his friend.*)

- For *less [of something]*, use this formula:

    moins de + noun + **que** + the original item of the comparison

    Example: **On a moins de vacances que nos parents.** (*We have less vacation than our parents.*)

- For *as much/as many [of something]*, use this construction:

    autant de + noun + **que** + the original item of the comparison

    Example: **Il y a autant de soleil à Nice qu'à Cannes.** (*There's as much sun in Nice as in Cannes.*)

Note that before a vowel, **que** becomes **qu'** and **de** becomes **d'**.

Translate each phrase in parentheses to compare how much/how many of something the following pairs have; check out a French-English dictionary if you need help with vocabulary. Here's an example:

Q. La France a _____ l'Amérique. (*more bakeries than*)

A. **plus de pâtisseries que**

21. Louis a _____ mon école. (*more computers than*)

22. Les parents ont _____ les enfants. (*more money than*)

23. Chez moi, il y a _____ dans un café. (*less coffee than*)

24. Un prof a _____ un docteur. (*as much patience as*)

25. L'état d'Oregon a _____ le Texas. (*less sunshine than*)

Quantities of an action

You can also compare how much something is done, which is how you express things like *your little brother eats as much as an ogre* (**il mange autant qu'un ogre**). Because in this construction you don't express a quantity of something, the comparisons don't use **de**.

- To say someone does something *more than someone else*:

    verb + **plus que** + the second item of the comparison

    For example: **Il lit plus que sa femme.** (*He reads more than his wife.*)

✔ **To say that someone does something *less than someone else*:**

> verb + **moins que** + the second item of the comparison

For example: **Vous sortez moins que nous.** (*You go out less than us.*)

✔ **To say that someone does something *as much as someone else*:**

> verb + **autant que** + the second item of the comparison

For example: **Cet employé travaille autant que son patron.** (*This employee works as much as his boss.*)

Stressed Out: Using Stress Pronouns in a Comparison

A stress pronoun expresses *me* (**moi**), *you* (**toi**), *him* (**lui**), and so on, to refer to people. It can't be the subject of a verb, but it comes after a preposition like **pour** (*for*) or **avec** (*with*), after **c'est** (*it is/this is*), after **que** (*than, as*) in a comparison, or alone. Table 12-1 lists the stress pronouns with the equivalent subject pronouns, followed by the English translation.

Table 12-1	French Stress Pronouns	
Subject Pronoun	*Corresponding Stress Pronoun*	*Translation*
je	moi	*me*
tu	toi	*you* (singular informal)
il	lui	*him*
elle	elle	*her*
nous	nous	*us*
vous	vous	*you* (singular formal, and plural informal or formal)
ils	eux	*them* (masculine or a mixed group)
elles	elles	*them* (feminine)

Here are some examples with a stress pronoun in the second half of a comparison:

> **Tu chantes mieux que moi.** (*You sing better than me.*)

> **Jules est plus petit que toi.** (*Jules is shorter than you.*)

> **Nous avons plus de patience qu'eux.** (*We have more patience than them.*)

In front of **eux**, **elles**, and **elle**, **que** becomes **qu'**.

Translate the phrase in parentheses to complete each of the following comparative sentences. Use a stress pronoun. Here's an example.

Q. **Nous sommes plus sportifs** _____. (*than them*, masculine)

A. **qu'eux**

26. **Il est aussi riche** _____. (*than you*, singular informal)

27. **Julie est plus tolérante** _____. (*than me*)

28. **Les tortues sont moins rapides** _____. (*than us*)

29. **Les Françaises sont plus élégantes** _____. (*than them*, feminine)

30. **Je chante mieux** _____. (*than him*)

The Best of All: Superlatives

Someone has be the winner, and something is always the best of all those things we've been comparing. Who's *the most intelligent*? Who dances *best of all*? What's *the best restaurant*? What's *the cheapest*? The winner of each category is one of a kind, and you name it using a superlative that includes a definite article (*the*). The following sections discuss superlatives with adjectives, adverbs, and quantities.

Superlatives with adjectives

Pierre is not simply *more intelligent than the other kids in his class*, he is *the most intelligent in the school* (**le plus intelligent de l'école**). To express that someone (or thing) is *the* one out of so many, the superlative always includes the definite article *the*. In French you have to choose between **le**, **la**, or **les**, depending on the gender and number of the noun described. The superlative of superiority uses **le/la/les plus** (*the most*), and the superlative of inferiority uses **le/la/les moins** (*the least*). The following sections provide the basics of forming superlatives with adjectives and give pointers on some special circumstances.

Saying superlatives in two ways

Because French articles and adjectives show the gender and number of the noun they accompany (see Chapters 3 and 4 for details), for each superlative in English like *the most intelligent*, French has four: one for masculine singular (MS) and one for plural (MP), and one for feminine singular (FS) and one for the plural (FP). Be sure to match the definite article and the adjective to the subject you're describing.

For example, here are the four posssible forms of the superlative adjective **intelligent** in French:

- ✔ MS: **le plus intelligent**
- ✔ FS: **la plus intelligente**
- ✔ MP: **les plus intelligents**
- ✔ FP: **les plus intelligentes**

You can express the superlative in two ways:

- Use **le/la plus** or **le/la moins** + singular adjective in matching gender. For example: **la plus gentille** (*the kindest*).

  In plural, use **les plus/les moins** + plural adjective in matching gender. For example: **les moins grands** (*the least tall*).

  Use this formula after **c'est** (*he is/she is/it is/this is*), as in **C'est la plus gentille** (*She's the kindest*).

- Add a noun with a matching definite article in front of the superlative, like this: **le/la/les** + noun + **le/la/les plus** or **le/la/les moins** + adjective in matching gender and number.

  For example: **le garçon le moins intelligent** (*the least intelligent boy*), **la fille la plus intelligente** (*the most intelligent girl*), **les chiens les plus fidèles** (*the most faithful dogs*).

  Use this formula in the same context as the shorter version, or at the beginning or end of a complete sentence.

  - At the beginning: **La femme la plus bavarde est assise derrière moi.** (*The most chatty woman is sitting behind me.*)

  - At the end: **Ils ont adopté les chiens les plus fidèles.** (*They adopted the most faithful dogs.*)

Putting some special adjectives in their place

In French, most adjectives go after the noun they describe. For example: **une voiture rouge** (*a red car*). It's the opposite in English! However, some adjectives don't like to follow. For instance **beau** (*beautiful*), **jeune** (*young*), **grand** (*tall*), **petit** (*short*), **bon** (*good*), and a few more precede the noun they describe, like this: **une belle rose** (*a beautiful rose*). (See Chapter 4 for the rules of placement of adjectives).

To make a superlative with such adjectives, French has two options:

- Place the preceding adjective before the noun, following the rule of placement of such adjectives. (This option is the shortest.)
- Place the preceding adjective after the noun, like a regular adjective. (This option is longer.)

To form the shorter (and more common) superlative, follow these steps:

1. **Change the article to a definite one (if it isn't already), but leave the adjective before the noun.**

   For example, **une jolie fille** (*a pretty girl*) becomes **la jolie fille**.

2. **Add plus before the adjective.**

   Like this: **la plus jolie fille**. Easy, right?

To form the longer superlative, follow these steps:

1. **Change the article to a definite one (if it isn't already) and change the word order so that the adjective follows the noun.**

   For example, **une jolie fille** (*a pretty girl*) changes to **la fille jolie**.

2. **Insert le plus, la plus, or les plus before the adjective, making sure to match the number and the gender of the noun.**

   For example, you have **la plus jolie**, make sure both definite articles are the same, like this: **la fille la plus jolie** (*the prettiest girl*). Both articles must match the noun in gender and number.

Here are some more examples of the two versions of preceding adjectives in a superlative. Note how English has only one way of expressing the same thing:

la plus petite souris/la souris la plus petite (*the smallest mouse*)

les meilleures tartes/les tartes les meilleures (*the best pies*)

You have two placement options only with adjectives that typically come before the nouns they describe. For adjectives that normally follow nouns, there's only one place for the adjective in a superlative.

Make the superlative of superiority (*the most*) or inferiority (*the least*) of these adjectives, as indicated by the (+) or (–). If two options for adjective placement are possible, give both. Don't forget that you can only use definite articles in a superlative. Here's an example:

0. **un garçon intelligent** (+)

A. **le garçon le plus intelligent**

31. **des livres intéressants** (–) _____

32. **une route difficile** (+) _____

33. **une belle plante** (+) _____

34. **des résultats satisfaisants** (–) _____

35. **une bonne boisson** (+) _____

36. **des produits utiles** (–) _____

37. **une femme jalouse** (+) _____

38. **un travail lucratif** (+) _____

39. **une rue bruyante** (–) _____

40. **un grand secret** (+) _____

Adding a category

A superlative featuring an adjective can also express the category where that one perfect pearl comes from. In English, you can say *the smartest in the class*; or *the prettiest in the world*. To add categories in French, the superlative is followed by **de** (*of*) and the name of the category with the definite article like **de la classe** (*in the class*).

When **de** is followed by the definite article **le**, it changes to **du**. When it is followed by **les**, it changes to **des**. (See Chapter 3 for more details on these articles.)

Here are examples of the superlative with its origin expressed:

> **le plus intelligent de la classe** (*the smartest in the class*)
>
> **la plus belle fille du monde** (*the most beautiful girl in the world*)
>
> **le plus mignon des animaux** (*the cutest of animals*)
>
> **les meilleurs jours de l'année** (*the best days of the year*)

Superlatives with adverbs and quantities

To describe an action in superlative terms, French uses **le plus** or **le moins** followed by an adverb. (In superlatives with adverbs, the article is always **le**.) Easy enough right? Here's how to make the superlative using an adverb:

✔ For a superlative of superiority: subject + verb + **le plus** + adverb

✔ For *the best* (*the most well*): subject + verb + **le mieux**

> *The best* in French has an irregular form, like English. But the superlative of inferiority *the worst* has a regular French equivalent: just say **le moins bien**.

✔ For a superlative of inferiority: subject + verb + **le moins** + adverb

Here are some superlatives with adverbs in action:

> **Ma voiture va le plus vite.** (*My car goes the fastest.*)
>
> **Les chanteurs d'opéra chantent le mieux.** (*Opera singers sing the best.*)
>
> **Elle nage le moins bien.** (*She swims the worst.*)

For the most of a quantity, simply use the comparative **le plus de** or **le moins de** followed by the noun. Another easy one!

✔ For *the most of something*, use **le plus de** + noun.

Example: **Tu as le plus de chance.** (*You have the most luck.*)

✔ For *the least*, use **le moins de** + noun.

Example: **Cette région a le moins de soleil.** (*This region has the least sun.*)

Now you're ready to practice the superlative of adverbs and quantities. Answer the following questions using a superlative of superiority when you see (+), or a superlative of inferiority when you see (−). Here's an example:

Q. Est-ce qu'il conduit vite? (+)

A. Il conduit le plus vite!

41. Est-ce qu'elle chante bien? (+)

_____

42. Est-ce que ce stylo écrit bien? (−)

_____

43. Est-ce qu'ils ont beaucoup de chance? (−)

_____

44. Est-ce que la tortue marche vite? (−)

_____

45. Est-ce que tu joues bien au tennis? (+)

_____

46. Est-ce qu'il y a beaucoup de neige dans les Alpes? (+)

_____

47. Est-ce que vous travaillez sérieusement? (−)

_____

48. Est-ce que le prof a beaucoup de gadgets électroniques? (−)

_____

49. Est-ce que les frites ont beaucoup de matières grasses? (+)

_____

50. Est-ce que tu écris souvent des e-mails? (+)

_____

Answer Key

1 Ils travaillent plus efficacement que moi.

2 Je vais au supermarché moins souvent que ma mère.

3 Il court moins vite que le champion.

4 Ce restaurant est plus cher que notre restaurant préféré.

5 Sa chambre est aussi grande qu'un palace.

6 La France est moins grande que le Canada.

7 Paris est aussi beau que Londres.

8 Les chats sont moins bruyants que les chiens.

9 Le chocolat est meilleur que les gâteaux.

10 Les matières grasses sont aussi mauvaises pour la santé que les cigarettes.

11 Le poisson est moins bon que le boeuf.

12 Les étés sont plus chauds que les hivers.

13 Ces bagues sont plus chères que ce bracelet.

14 Ma mère est aussi âgée que mon père.

15 Julie est moins sérieuse que Valérie.

16 mieux que

17 plus mal que

18 moins facilement que

19 plus prudemment que

20 aussi tard que

21 plus d'ordinateurs que

22 plus d'argent que

23 moins de café qu'

24 autant de patience qu'

25 moins de soleil que

26 que toi

27 que moi

28 que nous

29 qu'elles

30 que lui

31 les livres les moins intéressants

32 la route la plus difficile

33 la plus belle plante (or la plante la plus belle)

34 les résultats les moins satisfaisants

35 la meilleure boisson (or la boisson la meilleure)

36 les produits les moins utiles

37 la femme la plus jalouse

38 le travail le plus lucratif

39 la rue la moins bruyante

40 le plus grand secret (Or le secret le plus grand)

41 Elle chante le mieux.

42 Ce stylo écrit le moins bien.

43 Ils ont le moins de chance.

44 La tortue marche le moins vite.

45 Je joue le mieux au tennis.

46 Il y a le plus de neige dans les Alpes.

47 Nous travaillons le moins sérieusement.

48 Le prof a le moins de gadgets électroniques.

49 Les frites ont le plus de matières grasses.

50 J'écris le plus souvent des e-mails.

Chapter 13

Using Pronouns

A pronoun is a very handy little word that replaces a bigger word or a phrase and allows you to talk without being redundant. For instance, you wouldn't want to have to say, "Mike came over, and I talked to Mike about my vacation and I showed Mike my photos." To give your sentences a more natural construction, you use subject pronouns like **il** (*he*) or **je** (*I*), indirect object pronouns like **lui** (*to him/to her*), and direct object pronouns like **le** (*him/it*), **la** (*her/it*), and so on. I introduce subject pronouns in Chapter 6; this chapter is all about object and stress pronouns.

I show you all the rules (and tricks) to use these pronouns like a native French speaker.

Digging into Direct Object Pronouns

In English, when someone asks you, "Do you like chocolate?" and you answer, "I like it," you're using a direct object pronoun. *It* is a pronoun because it replaces the noun *chocolate*, and it's direct because the verb *like* acts directly on it: You like what? You like *chocolate*.

French uses direct object pronouns, too. In the following sections, I list all the French direct object pronouns, I explain when to use them, and I show you how to construct sentences with them.

Meeting the direct object pronouns

French has seven direct object pronouns (DOPs) — and three more when you count the forms with an apostrophe. Here are the direct object pronouns and their English equivalents.

▶ **me** (**m'** in front of a vowel or mute **-h**) (*me*)

▶ **te** (**t'** in front of a vowel or mute **-h**) (*you* [singular informal])

✔ **le** (**l'** in front of a vowel or mute **-h**) (*him/it* [masculine])

✔ **la** (**l'** in front of a vowel or mute **-h**) (*her/it* [feminine])

✔ **nous** (*us*)

✔ **vous** (*you* [singular formal or plural informal and formal])

✔ **les** (*them*)

Because it replaces a noun, a pronoun takes the appearance of the noun as much as possible, kind of like a chameleon! The pronoun must match the noun in gender and number (see Chapter 3 for details). For example, when talking in the third person:

✔ If the noun to be replaced is masculine (such as **le père**, which means *the father*), the pronoun must be masculine (**le**).

✔ If the noun to be replaced is feminine (such as **la voiture**, which means *the car*), the pronoun must be feminine (**la**).

✔ If the noun to be replaced is plural masculine or feminine (such as **ses enfants**, which means *his/her children*), the pronoun must be plural (**les**).

In the following sentences, underline the direct object. Then write which DOP you would use in French, in parentheses. If you need help with the vocabulary, check out a French-English dictionary. Keep in mind that the direct objects are all preceeded by a specific determiner, such as a definite article, a possessive, or a demonstrative (see Chapter 3). Here's an example:

0. J'aime le chocolat.

A. J'aime <u>le chocolat</u>. (le)

1. **Nous respectons nos parents.** _____

2. **Est-ce que tu aimes la musique classique?** _____

3. **Le prof écoute moi et les autres étudiants.** _____

4. **Les étudiants font leurs devoirs.** _____

5. **Est-ce que vous voyez moi?** _____

6. **Il regarde toi.** _____

7. **Est-ce que vous connaissez le président?** _____

8. **Ils ont trouvé la solution.** _____

9. **Elle influence Pierre et toi.** _____

10. **Nous cédons notre place dans le bus.** _____

Knowing when to use direct object pronouns

When you can go directly from a verb to its object (what the verb acts upon), you are dealing with a direct object (*I give money*). If there is a preposition (*I give **to** charity*) between the verb and an object, then you have an indirect object. (I talk about indirect object pronouns later in this chapter.)

You can use a direct object pronoun to replace any noun, as long as the following two conditions are met:

✔ The noun to be replaced refers to a person or a thing. For example:

Elle aime ses enfants. (*She likes her kids.*) → **Elle les aime.** (*She likes them.*)

Il aime le fromage. (*He likes cheese.*) → **Il l'aime.** (*He likes it.*)

✔ The noun you want to replace is specific — that is, it's preceded by a specific determiner such as a definite article (**le**, **la**, or **les** [*the*]), a possessive (**mon** [*my*], **ton** [*your*], and so on), or a demonstrative (**ce** [*this*]). (Flip to Chapter 3 for more about articles, possessives, and demonstratives.) If the noun you want to replace is preceded by an indefinite determiner such as **un**, **une**, or **des** (*a, an, some*), don't use the DOP.

Here's a little trick that will really make the process of deciding if the object is specific easier for you. Proceed like this:

Question: Is the object I'm considering an "it/them" or a "some"?

Answer: It's an "it/them" → Use the DOP.

Answer: It's a "some" → Don't use the DOP, and read the later section about the pronouns **en** and **y**.

For example, in *I like my comfort* (**J'aime mon confort**), "my comfort" is definitely an "it," but in *I want some comfort* (**Je veux du confort**), you would not be able to use the direct object pronoun to replace it because of the word *some* (**du**).

Writing a sentence with a direct object pronoun

Now you're ready to start building sentences that include a DOP. Here's how to proceed:

1. **Find the noun or phrase that is the direct object of the verb.**

   For example, **Paul aime les pommes.** (*Paul likes apples.*)

2. **Choose the DOP that matches the direct object in number (singular or plural) and gender (feminine or masculine).**

   Les pommes is feminine plural, so the corresponding DOP is **les**.

3. **Remove the entire direct object from your sentence.**

   In this example, you're left with **Paul aime.**

4. **Replace the direct object with the pronoun and place the pronoun properly in the sentence.**

   In most sentences, you place the pronoun before the verb, but exceptions exist. See the later section "Positioning Pronouns Properly" for more information. In this example, you wind up with **Paul les aime.**

Replace the underlined part of each sentence with the correct direct object pronoun. Be sure to spot the determiner so you know the gender of the noun.

0. Bébé mange <u>sa soupe</u>.

A. Bébé la mange.

11. Nous aimons <u>les pommes</u>. _____

12. Elle apprend <u>ses leçons</u>. _____

13. Vous achetez <u>le journal</u>. _____

14. Ils visitent <u>l'Italie</u>. _____

15. Je retrouve <u>mes amis</u> au café. _____

Investigating Indirect Object Pronouns

In the sentence **Nous parlons <u>à</u> nos parents** (*We talk <u>to</u> our parents*), the preposition **à** (*to*) stands in the path of the verb object. Meet an indirect object! To replace those types of objects, you now need the indirect object pronoun, or IOP. In the following sections, I list all the French indirect object pronouns, note some verbs that always use them, and show you how to construct sentences with them.

Introducing the indirect object pronouns

French has six indirect object pronouns, plus two more when you count the forms with an apostrophe. Here are the indirect object pronouns and their English equivalents.

- ✔ **me** (**m'** in front of a vowel or mute **-h**) (*me/to me*)
- ✔ **te** (**t'** in front of a vowel or mute **-h**) (*you/to you* [singular informal])
- ✔ **lui** (*him/her, to him/her*)
- ✔ **nous** (*us/to us*)
- ✔ **vous** (*you/to you* [singular formal or plural formal and informal])
- ✔ **leur** (*them/to them*)

Note that the IOPs are the same as the DOPs that I listed earlier in this chapter, except for the third person singular (**lui**) and plural (**leur**). Also notice that the singular form has no gender distinction: both *him* and *her* are **lui** in French.

Knowing the verbs that require an indirect object

You use an indirect object pronoun only to replace a noun that refers to a person, as in **Paul parle à Marie** (*Paul talks to Marie*). Certain verbs are always followed by the preposition **à** when they have a human object, so you have to use indirect objects (and IOPs) with them. Here are some common ones with their English equivalents.

- ✔ **annoncer à quelqu'un** (*to announce to someone*)
- ✔ **donner à quelqu'un** (*to give to someone*)
- ✔ **dire à quelqu'un** (*to tell to someone*)
- ✔ **faire la bise à quelqu'un** (*to kiss someone [on the cheek]*)
- ✔ **obéir à quelqu'un** (*to obey someone*)
- ✔ **parler à quelqu'un** (*to talk to someone*)
- ✔ **poser des questions à quelqu'un** (*to ask someone questions*)
- ✔ **prêter à quelqu'un** (*to lend to someone*)
- ✔ **rendre visite à quelqu'un** (*to pay a visit to someone*)
- ✔ **ressembler à quelqu'un** (*to look like someone*)
- ✔ **téléphoner à quelqu'un** (*to call someone*)

Some common French verbs, like **regarder** (*to look at*), **écouter** (*to listen to*), **chercher** (*to look for*), and **attendre** (*to wait for*), use direct objects when their English counterparts use indirect objects. It goes the other way, too: Some English verbs use direct objects, like **téléphoner à** (*to call*), **dire à** (*to tell*), and **rendre visite à** (*to visit*) when their French equivalents take indirect objects. You can see the differences in the following examples where I underline the preposition that makes the object indirect, whether in French or in English:

> **Nous attendons nos amis.** (*We are waiting <u>for</u> our friends.*)

> **Je rends visite <u>à</u> Julie.** (*I visit Julie.*)

When dealing with pronouns, a verb + **à** + a human object generally triggers the use of an IOP. But as always, you can count on a few verbs to resist the common rule, and sometimes, even if you have a verb + **à** + a human object, you can't use the IOP. Zut alors! What are you to do? Well, another pronoun called the *stress pronoun* can save the day; I discuss stress pronouns in detail later in this chapter.

Determine if the following objects (underlined) are to be replaced by a DOP or an IOP. Write "DOP" or "IOP"and the correct IOP or DOP after the sentence. Be aware that **à** is not underlined; it is up to you to spot it.

Don't forget that **le** and **la** become **l'** before a vowel. Here's an example:

Q. **Il aime le chocolat.**

A. DOP. **le**

16. **Vous rendez visite à <u>vos amis</u>.** _____

17. **Vous aimez <u>votre vieille voiture</u>.** _____

18. **Ils écoutent <u>le professeur</u>.** _____

19. **Nous donnons des fleurs à <u>Maman</u>.** _____

20. Est-ce que vous comprenez <u>mes questions</u>? _____

21. Il parle à <u>son prof</u>. _____

22. Paul aime <u>Jeanne</u>. _____

22. Elle regarde <u>les enfants</u>. _____

24. Tu présentes ton ami à <u>tes parents</u>._____

25. Je réponds à <u>Charlotte</u>. _____

Putting together a sentence with an indirect object pronoun

Use an indirect object pronoun when you have a verb + **à** + human object (that is, a person or group of people) in a sentence. Proceed like this to replace the indirect object by the IOP:

1. **Spot the à + object right after the verb.**

   For example: **Paul parle <u>à sa mère</u>.** (*Paul talks to his mother.*)

2. **Choose the IOP that matches the indirect object in number only (no gender distinction with the IOP).**

   The IO, **à sa mère**, is third person singular, so you choose **lui**.

3. **Remove the entire indirect object group that you have underlined, including the à.**

   In this example, you wind up with **Paul parle**.

4. **Replace the indirect object group with the pronoun you chose and place the pronoun properly in the sentence.**

   In most sentences, you place the pronoun before the conjugated verb, but exceptions exist. Check out the later section "Positioning Pronouns Properly" for the scoop. In this example, you finish with **Paul lui parle.**

The best way to identify an indirect object is by spotting the **à** that follows the verb. However our little **à** likes to play tricks and wear a mask sometimes. It will appear as **au** (contracted form of **à** + **le**) or as **aux** (contracted form of **à** + **les**). Don't be fooled! The following examples illustrate the contracted forms of **à**.

> **Nous posons des questions <u>au</u> (à + le) professeur.** (*We ask the professor questions.*)
>
> **Le prof parle <u>aux</u> (à + les) étudiants.** (*The professor talks to the students.*)

In the following sentences, replace the indirect objects with an indirect object pronoun. Be sure to distinguish the indirect object from other elements in the sentence. Rewrite the entire sentence. Here's an example:

Q. Tu écris souvent à tes amis.

A. Tu leur écris souvent.

26. Je parle aux voisins.

_____

27. Elle pose des questions au docteur.

_____

28. Pierre et Marine ressemblent à leur mère.

_____

29. Vous offrez des fleurs à votre fiancée.

_____

30. Nous faisons la bise à nos amies.

_____

Working with Pronouns that Replace Phrases

Replacing nouns of things and people with direct and indirect object pronouns is simple, but sometimes you also need to replace whole phrases. If someone asks you whether the car is in the garage, which part of the question are you likely to not repeat in the response?

Chances are you'll say something like "Yes, it's there." The word *there* is a special pronoun in French — the letter **y** — to replace the phrase *in the garage* so you don't have to repeat it.

If that same person asks if lots of grocery bags are in the car, you would probably say something like, "Yes, there are lots (of them)." To say the same thing in French, this time you use the pronoun **en** (*of it/of them*). In the following sections I explain how to use pronouns to express phrases like these and more.

Using y to replace a variety of prepositional phrases

The pronoun **y** replaces a prepositional phrase that indicates location, like **dans le garage** (*in the garage*). Such phrases begin with a preposition, like *at*, *under*, *in*, and so on. Here's how to proceed to replace this type of prepositional phrase with **y**:

1. **Find the phrase that's introduced by the preposition.**

   For example: **Jeanne va <u>à la plage</u>.** (*Jeanne goes to the beach.*)

2. **Remove the entire prepositional phrase, including the preposition itself.**

   In this case, you're left with **Jeanne va**.

3. **Add the pronoun y to the sentence.**

In most sentences, you place the pronoun before the conjugated verb, but exceptions exist. Flip to the later section "Positioning Pronouns Properly" for details. In this example, you wind up with **Jeanne y va.**

Note: When the pronoun **y** is preceded by **je**, **je** changes to **j'.**

See **y** in action in the following examples:

Tu dormiras <u>dans une tente</u>. (*You will sleep in a tent.*) → **Tu y dormiras.**

Le chat est <u>sous la table</u>. (*The cat is under the table.*) → **Le chat y est.**

Nous allons <u>au Québec</u>. (*We're going to Quebec.*) → **Nous y allons.**

A phrase beginning with the preposition **de** (*from*) can't be replaced by the pronoun **y**, even if the phrase indicates place. (Instead, you use the pronoun **en**, which I discuss in the next section.) See this distinction in action in the following two examples:

Tu vas <u>à</u> la pharmacie. (*You go to the pharmacy.*) → **Tu y vas.**

Tu reviens <u>de</u> la pharmacie. (*You're coming back from the pharmacy.*) → **Tu en reviens.**

The pronoun **y** is not used just to indicate location. Use it when you want to replace a phrase with the pattern [**à** + thing], as in: **Je pense à mes vacances** (*I think about my vacation*) → **J'y pense.**

Okay, at this point you're confused because I say earlier in this chapter that the preposition **à** is the hint to use the IOP. Here's the help you needed: The IOP is only used in the case of [**à** + person]! Here are some examples that show the difference between **à** + a person and **à** + a thing:

Je parle à mes amis. (*I talk to my friends.*) → **Je leur parle.** (*I talk to them.*)

Il obéit à son père. (*He obeys his father.*) → **Il lui obéit.** (*He obeys him.*)

Elle pense à ses vacances. (*She thinks about her vacation*) → **Elle y pense.** (*She thinks about it.*)

Nous réfléchissons au problème. (*We ponder/reflect on the problem.*) → **Nous y réfléchissons.** (*We ponder/reflect on it.*)

When **penser à** is followed by a thing, use **y**, but when **penser à** is followed by a person, use the stress pronoun (see the later section "Staying Strong with Stress Pronouns").

Decide whether the objects underlined should be replaced by the indirect object pronoun (**à** + person) or by **y** (**à** + thing). Write IOP or **y**. Here's an example:

0. **Ils obéissent <u>au règlement</u>.** (*They obey the rule.*)

A. **y**

31. **Je téléphone rarement <u>à mon père</u>.** _____

32. **Allons <u>au cinéma</u> ce soir.** _____

33. Cet enfant ne parle pas <u>aux adultes</u>. _____

34. Je vais rester <u>à la maison</u>. _____

35. Répondez <u>à ma question</u> s'il vous plait. _____

Using en to replace expressions of quantities and certain prepositional phrases

The pronoun **en** replaces phrases that indicate quantities (of things or people). These quantities can be expressed with

> ✔ A number: **J'ai trois chats.** (*I have three cats.*)
>
> ✔ An expression + **de**: **Il a beaucoup de CDs.** (*He has a lot of CDs.*)
>
> ✔ An indefinite article: **Nous avons une voiture bleue.** (*We have a blue car.*)
>
> ✔ A partitive article: **Ils ont de la chance.** (*They have some luck.*)

En also replaces many prepositional phrases that begin with **de** (which means *of, from,* and more depending on the prepositional phrase). The following sections detail the phrases that can be replaced by **en**.

When **en** is preceded by **je**, **je** changes to **j'**.

Expressions of quantity with numbers or de

The word **de** in an expression of quantity like **un peu de** (*a little bit of*) or just a number + noun is replaced by the pronoun **en**. But don't lose track of that specific quantity when you are using the pronoun: Eating "a lot of chocolate" is not the same as eating "a little bit of chocolate"! How do you keep track of the quantity? That's super easy: Just put the quantity you're talking about at the end of the sentence, no matter where **en** is in the sentence.

Here's how to proceed:

1. **Find the quantity phrase.**

   For example, in **Les athlètes ont beaucoup de médailles** (*The athletes have a lot of medals*), the expression of quantity is **beaucoup de médailles**.

2. **Remove the entire phrase: the expression of quantity (+ de) + noun.**

   In this example, you're left with **Les athlètes ont**.

3. **Replace the phrase with the pronoun en and place the pronoun properly in the sentence — in this sentence, before the conjugated verb.** For more details on placement of the pronouns, see the next section.

   In this case, you have **Les athlètes en ont**.

4. **Add the expression of quantity (same one or a new one), without de, at the very end of the sentence.**

   Here, you wind up with **Les athlètes <u>en</u> ont <u>beaucoup</u>.** (*The athletes have a lot of them.*)

Here are a few examples using different expressions of quantity of this type.

Je bois <u>un verre de lait</u>. (*I drink a glass of milk.*) → **J'<u>en</u> bois <u>un verre</u>.** (*I drink a glass of it.*)

Elle a <u>un portable</u>. (*She has a cellphone.*) → **Elle <u>en</u> a <u>un</u>.** (*She has one [of them].*)

Le champion a gagné <u>neuf médailles</u>. (*The champion won nine medals.*) → **Le champion <u>en</u> a gagné <u>neuf</u>.** (*The champion won nine [of them].*)

Note: The indefinite article **un** (*a, an*) counts as a specific quantity and has to be taken up as such in the new sentence with **en**. This fact also applies to the indefinite article **une** (*a*) but not to the indefinite article **des** (*some*).

This construction is particularly useful when you are asked how many of something you have or want.

—**Combien d'animaux est-ce que tu as chez toi?** (*How many pets do you have?*)
—**J'<u>en</u> ai <u>trois</u>: un chien, un chat et un poisson rouge.** (*I have three: a dog, a cat, and a goldfish.*)

—**Tu bois du lait le matin?** (*Do you drink any milk in the morning?*)
—**Oui, j'en bois un verre.** (*Yes, I drink a glass of it.*)

Indefinite determiners

Indefinite determiners include the plural indefinite article **des** (*some*); the partitives **du, de la, de l'** (*some/any*); and **de** (which takes the place of those articles after a negative verb). (See Chapter 3 for details on articles.) The following examples show you different types of articles being replaced by **en**.

Nous mangeons <u>du fromage</u>. (*We eat [some] cheese.*) → **Nous <u>en</u> mangeons.** (*We eat some.*)

Tu as <u>de la chance</u>. (*You have luck.*) → **Tu <u>en</u> as.** (*You have some.*)

Elle ne veut pas <u>de chien</u>. (*She doesn't want a dog.*) → **Elle n'<u>en</u> veut pas.** (*She doesn't want one.*)

To replace this type of phrase, proceed like this:

1. **Find the phrase that is introduced by the indefinite determiner:**

   For example, **Paul a <u>des enfants</u>.** (*Paul has some kids.*)

2. **Remove the entire quantity phrase:**

   In this case, you're left with **Paul a**.

3. **Place the pronoun en properly in the sentence.**

   In most sentences, you place the pronoun before the conjugated verb, but exceptions exist. Check out the later section "Positioning Pronouns Properly" for the scoop. In this example, you wind up with **Paul <u>en</u> a**.

De + a thing with certain verbs

When certain verbs are followed by a non-human object, you use the pronoun **en** to replace the whole phrase. For example, when using the verb **avoir peur de** (*to be afraid of*), **j'ai peur**

de l'orage (_I am afraid of the storm_) becomes **j'en ai peur** (_I am afraid of it_). Following are some common verbs of this type and their English equivalents. The noun you're referring to (or simply **quelque chose** [_something_]) comes after each phrase:

- ✔ **avoir besoin de** (_to need_)
- ✔ **avoir envie de** (_to want_)
- ✔ **avoir peur de** (_to be afraid of_)
- ✔ **entendre parler de** (_to hear of_)
- ✔ **[être** + adjective] **de** ([_to be_ + adjective] _of_)
- ✔ **jouer de** (_to play_ [an instrument])
- ✔ **parler de** (_to talk about_)
- ✔ **profiter de** (_to take advantage of/to enjoy_)
- ✔ **s'occuper** (_to take care of_)
- ✔ **se servir de** (_to utilize_)
- ✔ **se souvenir de** (_to remember_)

To replace this type of **de** phrase, proceed like for the object pronoun **y** when it replaces **à** + non-human object: Remove the whole prepositional phrase including **de** and replace it with **en**, and then place it into the sentence. (See the earlier section "Using **y** to replace a variety of prepositional phrases" for details.) Here are a few examples.

> **Bébé a peur de la nuit.** (_Baby is afraid of the night._) → **Bébé en a peur.** (_Baby is afraid of it._)

> **Il profite de ses vacances pour se reposer.** (_He takes advantage of his vacation to rest up._) → **Il en profite pour se reposer.** (_He takes advantage of it to rest up._)

If the verb is pronominal, such as **se souvenir de** (to _remember_), then **en** must follow the reflexive pronoun and **me, te,** and **se** (only those three) change to **m', t',** and **s'**. For example: **Il s'en souvient.** (_He remembers it._)

The **de** phrase must refer to a thing, not a person. If it is **de** + person, you can't replace it with **en**, and you have to resort to a stress pronoun, as illustrated here (I talk about stress pronouns later in this chapter):

> **Bébé a besoin de sa mère.** (_Baby needs his mother._) → **Bébé a besoin d'elle.** (_Baby needs her._)

A prepositional phrase that starts with de

When **de** expresses _from_, as in **Les athlètes rentrent de Londres** (_The athletes return home from London_), use the pronoun **en** to replace that whole phrase: **Les athlètes en rentrent.**

To replace this type of **de** prepositional phrase, proceed like this:

1. **Find the phrase that is introduced by de.**

   For example, **Nous faisons partie de cette équipe.** (_We are part of this team._)

2. **Remove the entire prepositional phrase, including de itself.**

   In this case, you wind up with **Nous faisons partie.**

3. **Replace the prepositional phrase with the pronoun en and place it properly in the sentence.**

   In most sentences, you place the pronoun before the conjugated verb, but exceptions exist. (See the later section "Positioning Pronouns Properly" for more info.) In this example, your sentence is **Nous en faisons partie.** (*We are part of it.*)

Rewrite the sentences, replacing the prepositional phrases with **de** with the pronoun **en**. Remember that **de** may appear as **du**, **de l'**, **de la**, or **des**.

Q. **Il joue de l'harmonica**

A. **Il en joue.**

36. **Elle se sert de son ordinateur.**

_____

37. **Vous êtes déçus du résultat.**

_____

38. **Je me souviens de cette date.**

_____

39. **Il est satisfait de sa médaille.**

_____

40. **Nous sommes contents de notre travail.**

_____

Positioning Pronouns Properly

In this section, I tell you how to place any pronoun in a sentence. I begin with just one pronoun per sentence (or command), and then I show you how to juggle two, but you should not try to put more than two in the same sentence. (Even though it is technically possible, it would sound weird and contrived to native speakers.)

In affirmative and negative sentences

As you may have noticed so far through the examples I've been giving you in this chapter, in French the pronoun precedes the verb most of the time.

Il mange du chocolat. (*He eats some chocolate.*) → **Il en mange.** (*He eats some.*)

Nous préférons la glace. (*We prefer ice cream.*) → **Nous la préférons.** (*We prefer it.*)

How did I get there? That's easy if you follow these steps. Consider them a shortcut for the steps I provide earlier in this chapter:

1. **First find the object of the verb, and decide what kind of pronoun you should use.**

   For example, in **Nous préférons <u>la glace</u>** (*We prefer ice cream*), **la glace** (*ice cream*) is the direct object of the verb **préférons** (*prefer*). You need the direct object pronoun **la**. (See previous sections on how to choose the pronoun.)

2. **Switch the order of the object and the verb.**

   You now have **Nous <u>la glace</u> préférons.**

3. **Replace the object with the specific pronoun you need.**

   There you are: **Nous la préférons.**

If the sentence is negative, it works the same way. The pronoun and the verb are still switched around, and you need to make sure you're using the right type of pronoun. For **Il n'aime pas le chocolat** (*He doesn't like chocolate*), the verb is **aime**, so switch it with **le chocolat** (**Il ne le chocolat aime pas**) and then replace **le chocolat** with the direct object pronoun **l'**: **Il ne l'aime pas.**

Keep in mind that the word **ne** (*not*) is not tied to the verb and can be pushed back some. On the other hand, the pronoun always stays right by the verb. Flip to Chapter 8 for full details on negative words and expressions.

In the following affirmative and negative sentences, the object of the verb is underlined. Replace it with the pronoun in parentheses and rewrite the whole sentence. Remember that **ne** changes to **n'** before **y** and **en**.

0. Vous allez <u>au restaurant</u>. **(y)**

A. **Vous y allez.**

41. Vous ne faites jamais <u>la cuisine</u>. **(la)**

_____

42. Tu ne seras pas <u>chez toi</u> ce soir. **(y)**

_____

43. Ils aiment <u>ce film</u>. **(le)**

_____

44. Il ne met jamais <u>de lait</u> dans son café. **(en)**

_____

45. Je parle souvent <u>à mes voisins</u>. **(leur)**

_____

In a sentence that has more than one verb

What should you do if a sentence has several verbs, as in **Il aime regarder la télé** (*He likes to watch TV*), and how can you be sure to place the pronoun in front of the right verb of the two? The answer is in a question actually: "Who do you go with?"

What you need to do is find the noun or phrase you want to replace and then find the verb it goes with (usually the verb is right before its object). In our example, he may *like* TV, but what you're saying is that he likes to *watch* TV, so *watch* is the verb that matters. Now you can proceed with the steps in the preceding section as if there was only one verb: **Il aime la regarder.** (*He likes to watch it.*)

In a sentence in the passé composé

In the **passé composé** (*present perfect*), which I cover in Chapter 15, what is considered the verb is the whole verb unit: auxiliary verb + past participle. For instance, in **je suis allé** (*I went*), the verb unit is **suis allé**, and so the pronoun goes in front of **suis**, like this: **j'y suis allé** (*I went there*).

Don't confuse the **passé composé** conjugated with **être** or **avoir** (**je suis allé**) and the **futur proche** (*near future;* see Chapter 17) conjugated with **aller**, as in **je vais aller** (*I am going to go*). Both are two-word verb forms, but the rule for placement is different for each.

✔ In the following sentence, in **futur proche**, the verb that has an object is **partir**, not **vais**; therefore the pronoun goes before **partir**.

> **Je vais partir au Brésil.** (*I am going to leave for Brasil.*) → **Je vais y partir.** (*I am going to leave for there.*)

✔ But in the following sentence, in **passé composé**, what constitutes the verb is **suis parti**, so the pronoun goes in front of it.

> **Je suis parti au Brésil.** (*I left for Brasil.*) → **J'y suis parti.** (*I left for there.*)

In the following sentences in **passé composé** or **futur proche**, the object of the verb is underlined. Replace it with the pronoun in parentheses and rewrite the whole sentence.

Q. **Vous allez diner <u>au restaurant</u>.** (y)

A. **Vous allez y diner.**

46. Il a acheté <u>des CDs</u>. (en)

_____

47. Tu vas rester <u>chez toi</u> ce soir? (y)

_____

48. Je vais attendre <u>le bus</u>. (le)

_____

49. Elle a parlé <u>à son professeur</u>. (lui)

_____

50. Nous allons vendre <u>notre voiture</u>. (la)

_____

In affirmative and negative commands

Commands are unusual verbal forms, because you don't use the subject of the verbs in a command. The grammatical name for this conjugation is **l'impératif** (*imperative*), and it is detailed in Chapter 20. For now, you just need to know that this conjugation has three forms only: **tu** (*you* [singular informal]), **nous** (*we*), and **vous** (*you* [singular formal or plural formal and informal]), which are borrowed from the present tense conjugation for most verbs. For **parler**, the three forms of the imperative are **parle** (*speak* [singular informal]), **parlons** (*let's speak*), and **parlez** (*speak* [singular formal or plural formal and informal]).

To place the pronoun in an affirmative imperative, you don't switch anything around as you do in regular sentences. In fact, the position of the pronoun is the same as in English, after the verb, and this is how it's done:

1. **Find the object of the verb and determine which pronoun should replace it.**

    For example, **Regarde <u>le chat</u>** (*Look at the cat*), **le chat** is the direct object of the verb, so use the DOP **le.**

2. **Replace the object with the correct pronoun and attach it after the verb with a hyphen.**

    You wind up with **Regarde-le.** (*Look at it.*)

When the pronouns **me** (*me/to me*) and **te** (*you/to you*) are after the verb, they are replaced by the equivalent stress pronouns **moi** and **toi.** (I talk about stress pronouns later in this chapter.) For example:

Parle-moi! *Talk to me.*

Achète-toi une nouvelle voiture. *Buy yourself a new car.*

In the imperative, the **-er** verbs (including **aller**) lose the **-s** of the **tu** form of the present tense conjugation. However, when the pronoun following the verb is **y** or **en**, you put the **-s** back on, mainly for pronunciation's sake. Table 13-1 shows you what can happen when **y** or **en** follow the **tu** form of those verbs.

Table 13-1	Tu Imperative + En or Y	
Present Tense	*Imperative*	*Imperative with Y or En*
tu parles	**parle** (*talk*)	**parles-en** (*talk about it*)
tu manges	**mange** (*eat*)	**manges-en** (*eat some*)
tu vas	**va** (*go*)	**vas-y** (*go there*)

To form negative commands, you still omit the subject pronoun and use only the three relevant forms of the present tense (**tu**, **nous**, **vous**). You use the negatives **ne** and **pas** to surround the verb, like in a regular negative sentence: **Ne regarde pas le chat!** (*Don't look at the cat!*) For the pronoun placement, you switch around the object pronoun and the verb like for a regular sentence. Here are the three forms of the negative imperative in examples (note that **ne** becomes **n'** before a vowel):

> **Ne le regarde pas.** (*Don't look at him/it.*)
>
> **N'y allons pas.** (*Let's not go there.*)
>
> **N'en mangez pas.** (*Don't* [you, plural] *eat any.*)

In the following affirmative and negative commands, replace the underlined expression with the corresponding object pronoun and rewrite the sentence. Here's an example:

0. Mange <u>la pomme</u>.

A. Mange-la.

51. Ne mangez pas <u>de bonbons</u>.

_____

52. Offre quelque chose <u>à ton ami</u>.

_____

53. Raconte <u>des histoires</u>.

_____

54. N'écoutez pas <u>cet homme</u>.

_____

55. Allons <u>au cinéma</u>.

_____

In a sentence or command that needs two pronouns

Sometimes you need to use two pronouns in the same sentence, like to answer **As-tu mis les livres sur le bureau?** (*Did you put the books on the desk?*): **Oui, je les y ai mis** (*Yes, I put them there*).

With two pronouns, you have several possible combinations that can include (two at a time) the IOPs, DOPs, **y**, **en**, and the reflexive pronouns (**me**, **te**, **se**, **nous**, **vous**, **se**). (For information on those pronouns, see Chapter 7.) As a general rule, the pronouns that are common to all lists (**me**, **te**, **nous**, **vous**) and **se** always come first of the pair. Also, **en** always comes last when combined with another pronoun. The table summarizes the possible combinations. Read it from left to right. For example, if you need to use the pronouns **te** and **y** in your sentence, **te** will be first and **y** will follow. Or if you need to use **lui** and **en**, then **lui** comes first and **en** follows.You can pick any two as long as you go from left to right.

me	le	lui	y	en
te	la	leur		
se	les			
nous				
vous				

Here are a few examples that show the double pronouns in action.

>**Je te le dis.** (*I am telling it to you.*)

>**Il s'y promène.** (*He walks there.*)

When you combine **me**, **te**, **le**, **la**, or **se** with **y** or **en**, you use an apostrophe before **y** or **en** whether or not the verb is a command.

Other pronoun combinations don't require anything except for the hyphen in commands when the pronouns are after the verb.

>**Parle-lui-en.** (*Talk to him/her about it.*)

>**Donne-m'en.** (*Give me some.*)

Replace the underlined expression(s) with the pronoun(s) given in parentheses and rewrite the sentence with two pronouns. Sometimes the second pronoun is already in the sentence. Here's an example:

Q. **Je nous prépare <u>le diner</u>.** (le)

A. **Je nous le prépare.**

56. **Nous mettons <u>le livre</u> <u>sur la table</u>.** (le, y)

_____

57. **Elle me dira <u>la vérité</u>.** (la)

_____

58. **Je vais donner <u>mon numéro de téléphone</u> <u>à Louis</u>.** (le, lui)

_____

59. Nous donnons <u>du chocolat</u> <u>aux enfants</u> pour Pâques. **(en, leur)**

_____

60. Ne fais pas <u>tes devoirs</u> <u>dans ton lit</u>. **(les, y)**

_____

Staying Strong with Stress Pronouns

As you find out in the following sections, a stress pronoun replaces or emphasizes a human object. You can find it alone, after **c'est** (*it is*; see Chapter 3), or after a preposition. The beauty of this pronoun is that it's *nonintegrated,* which means you don't need to worry about where to put it in the sentence: It goes right after the preposition or **c'est**! There are eight stress pronouns.

- **moi** (*me*)
- **toi** (*you* [singular informal])
- **lui** (*him*)
- **elle** (*her*)
- **nous** (*us*)
- **vous** (*you* [singular formal or plural formal and informal])
- **eux** (*them* [masculine])
- **elles** (*them* [feminine])

Replacing a noun

After the expression **c'est** (*this is*), or also used alone, the stress pronoun emphasizes or points out someone, like in these examples:

—**Est-ce que c'est Paul, là-bas?** (*Is that Paul over there?*) —**Oui c'est lui.** (*Yes, that's him.*)

—**C'est toi qui as fait ça?** (*Did you do this?*) —**Oui, c'est moi.** (*Yes, it's me./Yes, I did.*)

—**Qui veut du chocolat?** (*Who wants some chocolate?*) —**Nous.** (*Us./We do.*)

Using **c'est** + the stress pronoun is a good equivalent to using the English *I did* or *we do,* which don't really translate into French otherwise.

After prepositions like **avec** (*with*), **pour** (*for*), and **chez** (*at the house of*), the stress pronoun replaces a noun to avoid a repetition. Here's an example:

—**Tu viens avec nous, ou tu pars <u>avec Pierre et Julie</u>?** (*Are you coming with us, or are you leaving with Pierre and Julie?*) —**Je pars avec eux.** (*I am leaving with them.*)

You also use a stress pronoun after certain verbs + **de**, like **avoir besoin de** (*to need*) and **être amoureux de** (*to be in love with*), when the object of these verbs is a person, not a thing. (For other such verbs, see the list in the earlier section "**De** + a thing with certain verbs.") Check out these examples:

> **Il a peur de son prof de math.** (*He is afraid of his math teacher.*) → **Il a peur de lui.** (*He is afraid of him.*)

> **L'enfant a besoin de ses parents.** (*The child needs his parents*) → **L'enfant a besoin d'eux.** (*The child needs them.*)

When verbs like **penser à** (*to think about*) and **s'intéresser à** (*to be interested in*) are followed by a human object, you have to use a stress pronoun in place of an indirect object pronoun. Here are some common verbs of this kind.

- ✔ **penser à** (*to think about someone*)
- ✔ **tenir à** (*to hold someone dear*)
- ✔ **faire attention à** (*to pay attention to someone*)
- ✔ **être à** (*to belong to someone*)
- ✔ **s'intéresser à** (*to be interested in someone*)

Here they are in action:

> **Il pense <u>à ses amis</u>.** (*He thinks about his friends*) → **Il pense à <u>eux</u>.** (*He thinks about them.*)

> **Ce livre est <u>à Anne</u>.** (*This book belongs to Anne*) → **Ce livre est à <u>elle</u>.** (*This book belongs to her.*)

Reinforcing a noun

The stress pronoun can also reinforce the subject of a verb, for effect. As long as it refers to a person, that subject can be a noun, like **son mari** (*her husband*), or the subject pronoun (**je, tu,** and so on). In both cases, the stress pronoun is placed right after the subject, often separated by a comma.

> **Jeanne part en vacances; son mari, lui, travaille.** (*Jane is going on vacation; but her husband, he's working.*)

> **Moi, je me suis bien amusé samedi. Et vous?** (*Personally, I had a lot of fun Saturday. And you?*)

The stress pronoun can reinforce a subject pronoun, but it can never replace it. In other words, the stress pronoun can never be the subject of the verb. Don't say **Moi mange beaucoup de chocolat.** (*Me, I eat a lot of chocolate.*) You still have to use the subject pronoun (underlined in the example): **Moi, <u>je</u> mange beaucoup de chocolat.** (*Me, I eat a lot of chocolate.*)

Answer the questions using a stress pronoun. If the question has **tu**, answer with **je**, and if there's **vous**, answer with **nous**.

Q. Est-ce que ces gants sont à toi?

A. Oui, ces gants sont à moi.

61. Est-ce qu'il pense souvent à sa fiancée?

_____

62. Est-ce que tu te souviens de ton premier prof de français?

_____

63. Est-ce que vous êtes fiers de vos enfants?

_____

64. Est-ce que tu as acheté ce cadeau pour moi?

_____

65. Est-ce que nous irons chez Isabelle et Anne?

_____

Answer Key

1 Nous respectons <u>nos parents</u>. (les)

2 Est-ce que tu aimes <u>la musique classique</u>? (la)

3 Le prof écoute <u>moi et les autres étudiants</u>. (nous)

4 Les étudiants font <u>leurs devoirs</u>. (les)

5 Est-ce que vous voyez <u>moi</u>? (me)

6 Il regarde <u>toi</u>. (te)

7 Est-ce que vous connaissez <u>le président</u>? (le)

8 Ils ont trouvé <u>la solution</u>. (la)

9 Elle influence <u>Pierre et toi</u>. (vous)

10 Nous cédons <u>notre place</u> dans le bus. (la)

11 Nous les aimons.

12 Elle les apprend.

13 Vous l'achetez.

14 Ils la visitent.

15 Je les retrouve au café.

16 IOP. **leur**

17 DOP. **l'**

18 DOP. **l'**

19 IOP. **lui**

20 DOP. **les**

21 IOP. **lui**

22 DOP. **l'**

23 DOP. **les**

24 IOP. **leur**

25 IOP. **lui**

26 Je leur parle.

27 Elle lui pose des questions.

28 Pierre et Marine lui ressemblent.

29 Vous lui offrez des fleurs.

30 Nous leur faisons la bise.

31 IOP

32 y

33 IOP

34 y

35 y

36 Elle s'en sert.

37 Vous en êtes déçus.

38 Je m'en souviens.

39 Il en est satisfait.

40 Nous en sommes contents.

41 Vous ne la faites jamais.

42 Tu n'y seras pas ce soir.

43 Ils l'aiment.

44 Il n'en met jamais dans son café.

45 Je leur parle souvent.

46 Il en a acheté.

47 Tu vas y rester ce soir?

48 Je vais l'attendre.

49 Elle lui a parlé.

50 Nous allons la vendre.

51 N'en mangez pas.

52 Offre-lui quelque chose.

53 Racontes-en.

54 Ne l'écoutez pas.

55 Allons-y.

56 Nous l'y mettons.

57 Elle me la dira.

58 Je vais le lui donner.

59 Nous leur en donnons pour Pâques.

60 Ne les y fais pas.

61 Oui, il pense à elle.

62 Oui, je me souviens de lui/d'elle.

63 Oui, nous sommes fiers d'eux.

64 Oui, je l'ai acheté pour toi.

65 Oui, nous irons chez elles.

Chapter 14

Adding the Gerund and the Passive to Your Repertoire

In This Chapter

▶ Getting the scoop on gerunds

▶ Expressing the passive

Gerunds and passive voice are two ways to describe how things happen. Writing sentences with gerunds is a way of describing actions that occurred simultaneously (such as when *you enjoyed yourself while reading this book*). The passive construction lets you talk in a sort of distant, impersonal way about something being done by someone else (whether or not that person is named). In this chapter I get you up to speed on sentences that use gerunds or the passive so that you have two more options for speaking and writing French in a natural way.

While Doing Something: The Gerund

If you read your mail while *eating* dinner, *watching* the news and *talking* to your cat, you're using **le gérondif** (*the gerund*). The gerund is also useful to explain how you do something. How do you stay in shape? By *exercising*. How are you going to learn French grammar? By *reading* this book, right? So the gerund is a very handy little verb form. And what's even better news is that it has only one form in French!

In the following sections, I explain how gerunds differ in English and French, tell you how to build them from present participles, and describe when to use them.

Comparing gerunds in English and French

A gerund in English is easily recognizable by its *-ing* form. A French gerund is also easily recognizable: it's an **-ant** verb form. This form by itself is called the *present participle;* adding the preposition **en** (which translates as *by*, *in*, or *while*) in front of it forms **le gérondif**.

The -*ing* form is very common in English, but often it doesn't have a direct translation in French. Therefore, you can't automatically use a French gerund as the translation for an English gerund. For instance:

- ✔ Most English verb tenses have an -*ing* form. The present tense can be expressed by either *I do* or *I am doing*. In French, however, the present can only be expressed in one form: **je fais** (see Chapter 6 for more about the present tense).

- ✔ English also uses the -*ing* form to express the past: *I was doing*. The French equivalent here is the **imparfait** (*imperfect*; see Chapter 16), absolutely not the gerund: **je faisais**.

- ✔ You can say *I will be doing something* in English, but in French you'd have to use regular future tense (see Chapter 17): **je ferai**.

Forming present participles

To create a French gerund, you need the present participle. Forming the present participle is easy for most verbs, regular and irregular. Take the **nous** form of the present tense, drop the **-ons** ending, and replace it with **-ant**. Do not keep the subject pronoun **nous**. You're done! Table 14-1 shows how some common verbs form their present participle.

Table 14-1	Forming the Gerund of Some Common Verbs	
Infinitive	*Nous Form of Present*	*Present Participle*
aller (*to go*)	**nous allons** (*we go*)	**allant** (*going*)
arriver (*to arrive*)	**nous arrivons** (*we arrive*)	**arrivant** (*arriving*)
commencer (*to begin*)	**nous commençons** (*we begin*)	**commençant** (*beginning*)
dire (*to say*)	**nous disons** (*we say*)	**disant** (*saying*)
dormir (*to sleep*)	**nous dormons** (*we sleep*)	**dormant** (*sleeping*)
faire (*to do*)	**nous faisons** (*we do*)	**faisant** (*doing*)
finir (*to finish*)	**nous finissons** (*we finish*)	**finissant** (*finishing*)
manger (*to eat*)	**nous mangeons** (*we eat*)	**mangeant** (*eating*)
ouvrir (*to open*)	**nous ouvrons** (*we open*)	**ouvrant** (*opening*)
parler (*to talk*)	**nous parlons** (*we talk*)	**parlant** (*talking*)
répéter (*to repeat*)	**nous répétons** (*we repeat*)	**répétant** (*repeating*)
tenir (*to hold*)	**nous tenons** (*we hold*)	**tenant** (*holding*)
travailler (*to work*)	**nous travaillons** (*we work*)	**travaillant** (*working*)
vendre (*to sell*)	**nous vendons** (*we sell*)	**vendant** (*selling*)
voir (*to see*)	**nous voyons** (*we see*)	**voyant** (*seeing*)

You only have to worry about three irregular gerunds in French. They are:

- ✔ **avoir** (*to have*), which becomes **ayant** (*having*)

- ✔ **être** (*to be*), which becomes **étant** (*being*)

- ✔ **savoir** (*to know*), which becomes **sachant** (*knowing*)

Give the gerund of the following regular and irregular verbs. See Chapter 6 to find the present tense of the verbs you don't know. Here's an example.

Q. partir

A. partant

1. voir _____

2. tenir _____

3. faire _____

4. ouvrir _____

5. commencer _____

6. manger _____

7. lire _____

8. parler _____

9. réussir _____

10. jouer _____

Creating and knowing when to use gerunds

The French gerund is used with the preposition **en**. It is equivalent to the English *while* + *-ing*, as in *while eating* (**en mangeant**); *upon* + *-ing*, as in *upon arriving* (**en arrivant**); and *by* + *-ing*, as in *by exercising* (**en faisant de la gym**). But you have to keep one important thing in mind: The action expressed by the gerund is performed by the *same subject* as the conjugated verb. For example, to say that *Upon arriving, Papa kissed the kids*, say: **En arrivant Papa a embrassé les enfants.** But if you say: **En arrivant les enfants ont embrassé Papa** (*Upon arriving, the kids kissed Papa*), the **en arrivant** refers to **les enfants**, not Papa, because the verb **embrassé** (*kissed*) is the kids' action, not Papa's.

The placement of a gerund in a sentence doesn't really matter. It can be at the beginning or at the end, and people tend to put it at the end.

> **En mangeant une pomme j'ai mordu ma lèvre.** (*While eating an apple, I bit my lip.*)

> **J'ai mordu ma lèvre en mangeant une pomme.** (*I bit my lip while eating an apple.*)

Pronominal verbs (which I discuss in Chapter 7) have to keep their reflexive pronoun in the gerund, and the pronoun needs to match the subject of the main verb. You place the pronoun between **en** and the present participle. I use the verb **se promener** (*to take a walk*) as an example:

 ✔ If the subject of the main verb is **je**, the pronominal verb in the gerund is **en me promenant**.

 ✔ If the subject of the main verb is **tu**, the pronominal verb in the gerund is **en te promenant**.

✔ If the subject of the main verb is **il**, **elle**, **on**, **ils**, or **elles**, the pronominal verb in the gerund is **en se promenant**.

✔ If the subject of the main verb is **nous**, the pronominal verb in the gerund is **en nous promenant**.

✔ If the subject of the main verb is **vous**, the pronominal verb in the gerund is **en vous promenant**.

Use the gerund in the following instances:

✔ To express simultaneous actions. For example:

> **Elle conduit en écoutant la radio.** (*She drives while listening to the radio.*)
>
> **Nous prenons une douche en chantant.** (*We take a shower while singing.*)

✔ To answer the question "how/why." For example:

> **Je suis tombé en courant.** (*I fell because I was running/while running.*)
>
> **Il gagne sa vie en vendant des hot-dogs.** (*He earns a living by selling hot dogs.*)

✔ To say when something happened. For example:

> **Elle a crié en voyant la souris.** (*She screamed upon seeing the mouse.*)
>
> **Ferme la porte en partant.** (*Close the door upon leaving.*)

Explain how the following people make a living using the verb in parentheses in the gerund form. Here's an example:

0. **Julie est professeur. (enseigner)**

A. **Elle gagne sa vie en enseignant.**

11. **Charles est chanteur. (chanter)**

_____

12. **Conrad est écrivain. (écrire)**

_____

13. **Paul est chauffeur de taxi. (conduire)**

_____

14. **Wolf est pianiste. (jouer du piano)**

_____

15. **Josie est vendeuse. (vendre)**

_____

Using the gerund of the verb in parentheses, say when or why the following things happened. Then translate each sentence; consult a French-English dictionary if you need help with the vocabulary. Here's an example:

0. **Elle a eu un accident de voiture. (parler sur son portable)**

A. **Elle a eu un accident de voiture en parlant sur son portable.** (*She had an accident by/while talking on her cell phone.*)

16. **Il s'est bléssé. (être imprudent en vélo)**

_____

_____

17. **Julie a fait des progrès. (s'entrainer beaucoup)**

_____

_____

18. **Je me suis cassé une dent. (manger des noix)**

_____

_____

19. **Tu as perdu tes clés. (se promener au parc)**

_____

_____

20. **Nous avons appris la nouvelle. (téléphoner à nos amis)**

_____

_____

Building Sentences in a Different Way: The Passive Construction

In a passive construction, the person doing the action (officially called the *agent*) is kind of absent, but the action gets done somehow. Here's an example: **Cette maison a été vendue.** (*This house has been sold.*) In this sentence, **cette maison** (*this house*) is the apparent subject because the verb is in the third person singular, but you don't know who actually sold it! In other words, the agent remains mysterious, as long as you're not told *by whom* (**par qui**) it was sold.

A fun way to decide if you're dealing with passive voice is to test whether you can add "by mutants" after the subject and verb. For instance, you can say *This house has been sold by mutants,* so you know that my previous example is legit. On the other hand, it doesn't really make sense to say *She sold the house by mutants,* so that sentence isn't passive.

The following sections show you how to form the passive, with or without revealing the agent.

Note: The passive is often called *passive voice,* and most grammar books use that term. I prefer the term *construction* to *voice* because it better highlights that the passive involves a different way of building sentences. *Voice* doesn't tell you much of anything!

Pairing être with a past participle in a passive construction

The passive construction involves a conjugated form of **être** (*to be*), in any tense, simple or compound, followed by the past participle of the verb. I break down both parts of the construction in the following sections.

Starting with the past participle

Here's how to form the past participle for regular verbs (see Chapter 15 for full details on forming past participles):

- For **-er** verbs, drop the **-er** of the infinitive and replace it with **-é**, like this: **parler** (*to talk*) → **parlé** (*talked*).

- For **-ir** verbs, drop the **-ir** of the infinitive and replace it with **-i**, like this: **finir** (*to finish*) → **fini** (*finished*).

- For **-re** verbs, drop the **-re** of the infinitive and replace it with **-u**, like this: **vendre** (*to sell*) → **vendu** (*sold*).

A past participle is basically a verb turned into an adjective. That means it has to agree in gender (masculine or feminine) and number (singular or plural) with the subject of the verb. In the example **les nouvelles seront annoncées** (*the news will be announced*), the past participle **annoncées** refers to **les nouvelles** (feminine plural) and therefore takes the mark of the feminine (**-e**) and the plural (**-s**). Here's how it works, using **fini** (*finished*) as an example of a past participle (but this works for any past participle):

- If **fini** refers to a masculine singular subject, it remains **fini**.

- If **fini** refers to a masculine plural subject, add an **-s**: **finis**.

- If **fini** refers to a feminine singular subject, add an **-e**: **finie**.

- If **fini** refers to a feminine plural subject, add **-es**: **finies**.

Adding être

Here are the formulas to form the passive in the main tenses:

- **For present tense** (see Chapter 6):

  Subject + form of **être** conjugated in present + past participle.

  Here's an example: **La maison est construite.** (*The house is being built.*)

✔ **For present perfect tense** (see Chapter 15):

Subject + form of **être** conjugated in **passé composé** + past participle.

Here's an example: **Nous avons été informés.** (*We were told.*)

✔ **For the imperfect tense** (see Chapter 16):

Subject + form of **être** conjugated in **imparfait** + past participle.

Here's an example: **Le courrier était distribué avant midi.** (*The mail used to be distributed by noon.*)

✔ **For the future tense** (see Chapter 17):

Subject + form of **être** conjugated in future + past participle.

Here's an example: **Les nouvelles seront annoncées.** (*The news will be announced.*)

✔ **For the conditional** (see Chapter 18):

Subject + form of **être** conjugated in conditional + past participle.

Here's an example: **Elle serait facilement trompée.** (*She would be easily duped.*)

✔ **For pluperfect tense** (see Chapter 21):

Subject + form of **être** conjugated in pluperfect + past participle.

Here's an example: **La porte avait été fermée.** (*The door had been closed.*)

✔ **For future perfect** (see Chapter 21):

Subject + form of **être** conjugated in future perfect + past participle.

Here's an example: **Les nouvelles auront été annoncées.** (*The news will have been announced.*)

✔ **For past conditional** (see Chapter 21):

Subject + form of **être** conjugated in past conditional + past participle.

Here's an example: **On aurait été punis.** (*We would have been punished.*)

Translate the following sentences into French, being very careful with the verb tense you choose for **être** and the agreement of the past participle with the subject. Consult a French-English dictionary if you need help with any vocabulary. Here's an example:

0. *The cat is scolded.*

A. **Le chat est grondé.**

21. *The mice have been eaten.*

_____

22. *The house will have been sold.*

_____

23. *Julie has been informed.*

_____

24. *They* (masculine) *would have been arrested.*

_____

25. *They* (feminine) *would be helped.*

_____

26. *The house will be built.*

_____

27. *The books are being read.*

_____

28. *The car has been repaired.*

_____

29. *Dinner was always served.*

_____

30. *The date had been chosen.*

_____

Uncovering the mysterious agent

If you choose to reveal the identity of the agent by saying who or what is really performing the action, then after the passive verb you need to use **par** (*by*) + agent. Here's how to construct a passive sentence with the agent expressed:

Subject + conjugated form of **être** + past participle + **par** + agent.

Here are a few examples from the preceding section with agents to illustrate.

La maison est construite par un architecte. (*The house is being built by an architect.*)

Nous avons été informés par nos voisins. (*We were told by our neighbors.*)

Le courrier était distribué par le facteur avant midi. (*The mail used to be distributed by the mailman before noon.*)

Les nouvelles seront annoncées par la presse. (*The news will be announced by the press.*)

Answer Key

1 voyant

2 tenant

3 faisant

4 ouvrant

5 commençant

6 mangeant

7 lisant

8 parlant

9 réussissant

10 jouant

11 Charles gagne sa vie en chantant.

12 Conrad gagne sa vie en écrivant.

13 Paul gagne sa vie en conduisant.

14 Wolf gagne sa vie en jouant du piano.

15 Josie gagne sa vie en vendant.

16 Il s'est bléssé en étant imprudent en vélo. (*He got hurt by not being prudent on his bike.*)

17 Julie a fait des progrès en s'entrainant beaucoup. (*Julie improved by practicing a lot.*)

18 Je me suis cassé une dent en mangeant des noix. (*I broke a tooth while eating nuts.*)

19 Tu as perdu tes clés en te promenant au parc. (*You lost your keys while taking a walk in the park.*)

20 Nous avons appris la nouvelle en téléphonant à nos amis. (*We learned the news by calling our friends.*)

21 Les souris ont été mangées.

22 La maison aura été vendue.

23 Julie a été informée.

24 Ils auraient été arrêtés.

25 Elles seraient aidées.

26 La maison sera construite.

27 Les livres sont lus.

28 La voiture a été réparée.

29 Le dîner était toujours servi.

30 La date avait été choisie.

Part IV
Talking about the Past or Future

Some Common Irregular Past Participles

Infinitive	Past Participle
avoir (*to have*)	**eu** (*had*)
boire (*to drink*)	**bu** (*drunk*)
connaître (*to know*)	**connu** (*known*)
devoir (*to have to*)	**dû** (*had to*)
dire (*to tell*)	**dit** (*told*)
écrire (*to write*)	**écrit** (*written*)
être (*to be*)	**été** (*been*)
faire (*to do/make*)	**fait** (*done/made*)
lire (*to read*)	**lu** (*read*)
mettre (*to put*)	**mis** (*put*)
mourir (*to die*)	**mort** (*died*)
naître (*to be born*)	**né** (*been born*)
plaire (*to please*)	**plu** (*pleased*)
pleuvoir (*to rain*)	**plu** (*rained*)
pouvoir (*to be able to*)	**pu** (*been able to*)
prendre (*to take*)	**pris** (*taken*)
savoir (*to know*)	**su** (*known*)
tenir (*to hold*)	**tenu** (*held*)
venir (*to come*)	**venu** (*come*)
voir (*to see*)	**vu** (*seen*)
vouloir (*to want*)	**voulu** (*wanted*)

web extras

Enjoy additional French grammar basics on nouns, adjectives, and pronominal verbs on the Cheat Sheet at www.dummies.com/extras/frenchgrammar.

In this part . . .

✔ Discover how to properly use the **passé composé** (*present perfect*) tense, which names past actions.

✔ Understand the **imparfait** (*imperfect*) tense, which expresses ongoing or habitual past actions.

✔ Look forward with future tense verb conjugations, and recognize when to use the future tense instead of the near future tense.

Chapter 15

Noting Past Actions with the Present Perfect

*W*hat did you do Saturday night? Did you go out, or did you stay home and watch a movie? In French, asking such questions requires the **passé composé**, the tense that's called *present perfect* in English. The **passé composé** is the most widely used of all French past tenses. It's a compound tense, which means it's made up of two components instead of just one. The two components are

✔ A conjugated auxiliary verb (sometimes called a *helping verb*) — either **être** (*to be*) or **avoir** (*to have*) — in the present tense

✔ A past participle, which is a set form of the verb you're using

For example, to say *we danced* or *we have danced* in French, use the **nous** form of **avoir** (the auxiliary verb) in the present tense and the past participle of the verb **danser** (*to dance*), to make the **passé composé**: **nous avons dansé**.

And now, let's make those components dance! In this chapter, I show you how to build the **passé composé** from past participles and auxiliary verbs, and I explain how to use the **passé composé** properly.

Forming the Past Participle

The *past participle* is a set form of a verb used in a compound tense (such as the **passé composé**) in combination with the auxiliary verb. (I discuss auxiliary verbs later in this chapter.) The past participle doesn't get conjugated. In English, most past participles end in **-ed**, like *danced*, *walked*, and *rested*. In French, regular past participles end in **-é**, **-i**, or **-u**, depending on whether the verb ends in **-er**, **-ir**, or **-re**. And then, as always with verb forms, you have irregular past participles that follow different rules. The following sections show you how to form both regular and irregular past participles.

Regular past participles

Forming the past participle of most verbs is easy, because each of the three conjugation types (-**er**, -**ir**, and -**re** verbs; see Chapter 6 for an introduction) has one single form of its own. Instead of trying to memorize an individual verb's past participle, just remember the pattern for each of the three types of verbs. Easy!

-er verbs

For regular -**er** verbs, remove the -**er** of the infinitive and replace it with -**é**. For instance, to form the past participle of **danser** (*to dance*), remove -**er** and add -**é** to **dans-** to form **dansé**. Here are a few examples of -**er** verbs in the infinitive, followed by their past participle and their English translation.

- ✔ **aller** → **allé** (*to go* → *gone*)
- ✔ **commencer** → **commencé** (*to begin* → *begun*)
- ✔ **montrer** → **montré** (*to show* → *shown*)
- ✔ **parler** → **parlé** (*to talk* → *talked*)

-ir verbs

For regular -**ir** verbs, remove the -**ir** of the infinitive and replace it with -**i**. For instance, to form the past participle of **finir** (*to finish*), remove -**ir** and add -**i** to **fin-** to form **fini**. Here are a few examples of -**ir** verbs in the infinitive, followed by their past participle and English translation.

- ✔ **dormir** → **dormi** (*to sleep* → *slept*)
- ✔ **grossir** → **grossi** (*to get big* → *gotten big*)
- ✔ **partir** → **parti** (*to leave* → *left*)
- ✔ **sortir** → **sorti** (*to go out* → *gone out*)

-re verbs

For regular -**re** verbs, remove the -**re** of the infinitive and replace it with -**u.** For instance, to form the past participle of **vendre** (*to sell*), remove -**re** and add -**u** to **vend-** to form **vendu**. Following are a few examples of -**re** verbs in infinitive form, followed by their past participle and English translation:

- ✔ **descendre** → **descendu** (*to go down* → *gone down*)
- ✔ **entendre** → **entendu** (*to hear* → *heard*)
- ✔ **mordre** → **mordu** (*to bite* → *bitten*)
- ✔ **répondre** → **répondu** (*to answer* → *answered*)

Give the past participle of these regular verbs. Here's an example:

Q. dormir

A. dormi

1. descendre _____

2. casser _____

3. parler _____

4. sortir _____

5. entendre _____

6. grossir _____

7. répondre _____

8. commencer _____

9. perdre _____

10. monter _____

Irregular past participles

As you probably expected, irregular past participles do exist. These participles don't follow any sort of pattern; you just have to memorize them. (Sorry!) In Table 15-1, I present common verbs with irregular past participles.

Table 15-1	Some Common Irregular Past Participles
Infinitive	*Past Participle*
apprendre (*to learn*)	**appris** (*learned*)
avoir (*to have*)	**eu** (*had*)
boire (*to drink*)	**bu** (*drunk*)
comprendre (*to understand*)	**compris** (*understood*)
connaître (*to know*)	**connu** (*known*)
devoir (*to have to*)	**dû** (*had to*)
dire (*to tell*)	**dit** (*told*)
écrire (*to write*)	**écrit** (*written*)
être (*to be*)	**été** (*been*)
faire (*to do/make*)	**fait** (*done/made*)
falloir (*to be necessary*)	**fallu** (*been necessary*)
lire (*to read*)	**lu** (*read*)
mettre (*to put*)	**mis** (*put*)
mourir (*to die*)	**mort** (*died*)
naître (*to be born*)	**né** (*been born*)

(continued)

Table 15-1 *(continued)*

Infinitive	Past Participle
plaire (*to please*)	**plu** (*pleased*)
pleuvoir (*to rain*)	**plu** (*rained*)
pouvoir (to be able to)	**pu** (*been able to*)
prendre (*to take*)	**pris** (*taken*)
savoir (*to know*)	**su** (*known*)
tenir (*to hold*)	**tenu** (*held*)
venir (*to come*)	**venu** (*come*)
voir (*to see*)	**vu** (*seen*)
vouloir (*to want*)	**voulu** (*wanted*)

Adding the Auxiliaries Être and Avoir

Although most French verbs use **avoir** (*to have*) to form the **passé composé**, a few take **être** (*to be*) as the auxiliary. Because fewer verbs use **être**, I start with those, and then you can assume that all other verbs take **avoir** to form their **passé composé**. (Watch out, though; a few verbs can use either one!)

Entering the house of être

I call these verbs the *house of **être*** verbs, and here's why: These verbs more or less describe everything that can happen around a house. To visualize the house of **être**, (and make it useful for you), think of verbs of motion, such as **entrer/sortir** (*to enter/exit*), and **monter/descendre** (*to go up/down*). To those, you can add personal care actions described by reflexive verbs (that typically take place at home, too) like **se réveiller** (*to wake up*), **se coucher** (*to go to bed*), **se laver** (*to wash up*), and **se brosser les dents** (*to brush one's teeth*), and by extension all other pronominal verbs, like **s'amuser** (*to have fun*), **s'ennuyer** (*to be bored*), and so on (see Chapter 7 for details on pronominal verbs).

Using verbs of motion

Following is a list of verbs of motion that belong in the house of **être**. Some are regular, and some are irregular.

- ✔ **aller** (*to go*)
- ✔ **arriver** (*to arrive*)
- ✔ **descendre** (*to go down*); **redescendre** (*to come back down*)
- ✔ **devenir** (*to become*)

- **entrer** (*to go in*)
- **monter** (*to go up*); **remonter** (*to go back up*)
- **mourir** (*to die*)
- **naître** (*to be born*); **renaître** (*to be reborn*)
- **partir** (*to leave*); **repartir** (*to leave again*)
- **passer** (*to pass/stop by*); **repasser** (*to pass by again*)
- **rentrer** (*to come home*)
- **rester** (*to stay*)
- **retourner** (*to return*)
- **sortir** (*to go out*); **ressortir** (*to go out again*)
- **tomber** (*to fall*); **retomber** (*to fall again*)
- **venir** (*to come*); **revenir** (*to come again/to return home*)

To form the **passé composé** of these verbs of motion, conjugate **être** in the present tense and add the past participle. To start you off, here's the present tense conjugation of **être** for your reference (see Chapter 6 for more info).

être (*to be*)	
je **suis**	nous **sommes**
tu **es**	vous **êtes**
Il/elle/on **est**	ils/elles **sont**

Easy enough? Well, that's not all — now comes the agreement of the past participle! Whenever a verb is conjugated with **être** to form a compound tense like the **passé composé**, its past participle must agree in number and gender with the subject of **être**. Here's how the agreement of the past participle works:

- If the subject of **être** is masculine singular, leave the basic past participle alone, like this: **Il est arrivé** (*He arrived*).
- If the subject of **être** is feminine singular, the past participle must agree in gender with that subject by taking an **-e** for feminine: **Elle est arrivée** (*She arrived*).
- If the subject of **être** is masculine plural, or a mixed group of feminine and masculine, the past participle must agree in number with that subject and take an **-s** for plural: **Ils sont arrivés** (*They arrived*); **nous sommes arrivés** (*we arrived*); **vous êtes arrivés** (*you all arrived*).
- If the subject of **être** is feminine and plural, the past participle must agree in gender and number with that subject and take an **-es** for feminine plural: **Elles sont arrivées** (*They* [females] *arrived*); **nous sommes arrivées** (*we* [females] *arrived*); **vous êtes arrivées** (*you* [females] *arrived*).

Form the **passé composé** with **être** of the following verbs of motion using the subject indicated in the parentheses. Don't forget to make the past participles agree with the subjects. Here's an example:

0. arriver (**je** [feminine]) _____

A. **je suis arrivée**

11. mourir (**il**) _____

12. monter (**tu** [masculine]) _____

13. partir (**elles**) _____

14. venir (**elle**) _____

15. aller (**nous** [feminine]) _____

16. naître (**vous** [plural masculine]) _____

17. entrer (**je** [masculine]) _____

18. rester (**on**) _____

19. descendre (**ils**) _____

20. tomber (**tu** [feminine]) _____

Putting pronominal verbs in the passé composé

A pronominal verb is conjugated with an extra pronoun, hence its name (see Chapter 7 for details). For instance, **se préparer** (*to get oneself ready*) is a pronominal verb. Here's a reminder of the present tense form of such a verb so you can see what happens with the placement of the added pronoun (for more detail, flip to Chapter 7):

se préparer (to get oneself ready)	
je **me prépare**	nous **nous préparons**
tu **te prépares**	vous **vous préparez**
il/elle/on **se prépare**	ils/elles **se préparent**

In the **passé composé,** you keep the combination **je me**; **tu te**; **il se**; and so on and drop the verb form per se. You replace it by the matching form of **être** in the present tense, and then you add the past participle of the verb. For example: To say *I got ready* (assuming the subject refers to a man), use **je me**, add the **je** form of **être** (**suis**), and then add the past participle (**préparé**). In **elle s'est préparée** (*she got ready*), the past participle **préparée** agrees with the feminine singular subject **elle**.

Note: Te becomes **t'** before the second person singular of **être** (**es**); and **se** becomes **s'** before the third person singular of **être** (**est**).

Here is the complete conjugation for **se préparer** in **passé composé**, with all the possible agreements of the past participles in parentheses.

se préparer (*to get oneself ready*)	
je **me suis préparé(e)**	nous **nous sommes préparé(e)s**
tu **t'es préparé(e)**	vous **vous êtes préparé(e)s**
il/on **s'est préparé**	ils **se sont préparés**
elle **s'est préparée**	elles **se sont préparées**

Form the **passé composé** with **être** for the following pronominal verbs, using the subject indicated in the parentheses. The past participle can be regular or irregular. Don't forget to make the past participles agree with the subjects.

0. **se préparer (je** [masculine]) _____

A. **je me suis préparé**

21. **se laver (je** [feminine]) _____

22. **s'ennuyer (tu** [feminine]) _____

23. **s'amuser (ils)** _____

24. **s'excuser (vous** [plural masculine]) _____

25. **se lever (nous** [feminine]) _____

26. **se dépêcher (elles)** _____

27. **se trouver (on)** _____

28. **se marier (ils)** _____

29. **se laver (elle)** _____

30. **s'habiller (il)** _____

Conjugating everything else with avoir

Most French verbs take **avoir** (*to have*) to form a compound tense like the **passé composé**. You simply use the present tense of **avoir** along with the past participle. This conjugation doesn't need agreement between the past participle and the subject, unlike with **être** (whew!).

To start you off, here's the present tense conjugation of **avoir** (see Chapter 6 for more details).

avoir (*to have*)	
j'**ai**	nous **avons**
tu **as**	vous **avez**
il/elle/on **a**	ils/elles **ont**

You can break verbs that use **avoir** into several groups. First, **être** and **avoir** take **avoir** to form the **passé composé** (you can see their irregular past participles earlier in this chapter). Here's the conjugation of **être** in the **passé composé**.

être (*to be*)	
j'**ai été**	nous **avons été**
tu **as été**	vous **avez été**
il/elle/on **a été**	ils/elles **ont été**

Here's the conjugation of **avoir** in the **passé composé**:

avoir (*to have*)	
j'**ai eu**	nous **avons eu**
tu **as eu**	vous **avez eu**
il/elle/on **a eu**	ils/elles **ont eu**

And here they are in action:

> **Nous avons été en classe.** (*We were in class.*)
>
> **Qu'est-ce que tu as eu dans ton sac?** (*What did you have in your bag?*)

Next, impersonal verbs such as **pleuvoir** (*to rain*) and **falloir** (*to be necessary*) take **avoir** to form their **passé composé** (both of these verbs are conjugated only in the **il** form). Here are a couple of examples:

> **Il a plu toute la semaine.** (*It rained all week.*)
>
> **Il a fallu quitter la maison.** (*It became necessary to leave the house.*)

All other verbs that are not in the "house of **être**" (see the preceding section) form their **passé composé** with **avoir**. Here are a few examples:

> **Elle a mangé une pomme.** (*She ate an apple.*)
>
> **Nous avons beaucoup voyagé.** (*We traveled a lot.*)

Ils ont visité la Grèce l'été dernier. (*They visited Greece last summer.*)

Les enfants ont joué au jardin. (*The children played in the backyard.*)

Put the following verbs in **passé composé** using the subject indicated in parentheses. All the verbs have a regular past participle.

0. manger (il) _____

A. **il a mangé**

31. rendre (il) _____

32. répéter (tu) _____

33. choisir (elle) _____

34. préparer (je) _____

35. vendre (nous) _____

36. entendre (ils) _____

37. finir (vous) _____

38. écouter (elles) _____

39. payer (nous) _____

40. obéir (je) _____

Considering verbs that can take either être or avoir

All the "house of **être**" verbs of motion (which I list earlier in this chapter) are *intransitive verbs,* which means that they can't take an object. For example, in English, *to arrive* is intransitive because you can't *arrive something* (*something* would be the direct object of *arrive*). It works the same way in French: **arriver**, like its English equivalent, cannot take an object: It is also an intransitive verb. However, five of the house of **être** verbs can actually have a direct object. When that happens, you need to be aware of two consequences: The meanings of the verbs change slightly, and they form the **passé composé** with **avoir** instead of **être**. These five verbs are **passer** (*to pass/stop by*), **sortir** (*to go out*), **rentrer** (*to come home*), **monter** (*to go up*), and **descendre** (*to go down*). The following sections explore each of these verbs in more detail.

Monter and descendre

When it denotes motion, **monter** is intransitive, and it means *to go up.* You use **être** to form its **passé composé**, as shown, and make the past participle agree with the subject.

Ils sont montés au sommet de la Tour Eiffel. (*They climbed to the top of the Eiffel Tower.*)

But **monter** can also mean *to take something up*. In this sense, it's transitive (*something* is the direct object) and is conjugated with **avoir** in **passé composé** as shown below.

Il a monté un plateau de petit-déjeuner à sa femme. (*He took a breakfast tray up[stairs] to his wife.*)

When it denotes motion, **descendre** is intransitive, and it means *to go down*. You use **être** to form its **passé composé**, as shown, and make the past participle agree with the subject.

Elle est descendue à la cave. (*She went down to the cellar.*)

But **descendre** can also mean *to take something down*. In this sense, it's transitive (*something* is the direct object) and is conjugated with **avoir** in **passé composé** as shown below.

Tu as decendu la valise sur le quai. (*You took the suitcase down onto the [train] platform.*)

Passer

When it denotes motion, **passer** is intransitive, and it means *to pass by/to pass/to stop by*. You form its **passé composé** with **être**, as shown, and make the past participle agree with the subject.

Hier nous sommes passés chez nos amis. (*Yesterday we stopped by our friends' house.*)

But **passer** can also mean *to spend time*. In this sense, it is transitive (*time* is the direct object) and is conjugated with **avoir** in **passé composé** as shown:

Dimanche elle a passé la soirée avec sa famille. (*Sunday she spent the evening with her family.*)

Rentrer

When it denotes motion, **rentrer** is intransitive, and it means *to come home*. You use **être** to form its **passé composé**, as shown, and make the past participle agree with the subject.

Tu es rentré très tard hier soir. (*You came home very late last night.*)

But **rentrer** can also mean *to bring something in*. In this sense, it's transitive (*something* is the direct object) and is conjugated with **avoir** in **passé composé** as shown below.

Papa a rentré la voiture au garage. (*Dad drove the car into the garage.*)

Sortir

When it denotes motion, **sortir** is intransitive, and it means *to go out*. Form its **passé composé** with **être** as shown and make the past participle agree with the subject.

Samedi soir, vous êtes sortis. (*Saturday night you went out.*)

But **sortir** can also mean *to take something out*. In this sense, it is transitive (*something* is the direct object) and is conjugated with **avoir** in **passé composé** as shown.

Le magicien a sorti un lapin du chapeau. (*The magician pulled a rabbit out of the hat.*)

Using the Passé Composé Correctly

After you know how to form the **passé compose** with auxiliary verbs and past participles, you have all you need to function in the past! In the following sections, I explain the purposes of the present perfect tense, note some expressions of time to help you know when to use it, and show you how to create negative statements with it.

Knowing the basic uses

The **passé composé** tells about things that happened at one time or several times in the recent or remote past. Here are the uses of the **passé composé**:

✔ To relate an occurence in the past, an event that is completely finished:

- **Elle est allée en Italie il y a cinq ans.** (*She went to Italy five years ago.*)
- **Hier nous avons mangé du poisson.** (*Yesterday we ate fish.*)

✔ To list actions that ocurred one after the other

- **D'abord je suis rentré, puis j'ai pris une douche, et je me suis couché.** (*First I went home, then I showered, and I went to bed.*)
- **Nous avons déjeuné, puis nous sommes sortis.** (*We had lunch; then we went out.*)

✔ To interrupt an ongoing action (which is expressed in the **imparfait**; flip to Chapter 16 for details):

- **J'étudiais quand le téléphone a sonné.** (*I was studying when the phone rang.*)
- **Quand il est rentré, les enfants dormaient.** (*When he came home, the kids were sleeping.*)

Saying no

A French negative always has two parts that surround the conjugated verb: **ne** and **pas**, as in **il ne parle pas** (*he does not talk*). **Pas** can be replaced by a negative word such as **personne** (*no one*), **rien** (*nothing*), or **jamais** (*never*). When you negate the **passé composé**, you put **ne** before the auxiliary verb and put the second negative word right after the auxiliary verb — with two exceptions. (See Chapter 8 for more on negatives.)

Here are some regular negative statements in the **passé composé**:

Je n'ai pas compris la question. (*I did not understand/have not understood the question.*)

Vous n'avez jamais vu Notre-Dame. (*You never saw/you've never seen Notre Dame.*)

Two second negative words don't follow the same format. They are **personne** (*no one*) and **nulle part** (*nowhere*). Instead of placing them after the auxiliary verb, you place them after the past participle. The position of **ne** doesn't change. Here are two examples:

Elle n'a reconnu personne. (*She did not recognized anyone.*)

Ils ne sont allés nulle part hier. (*They didn't go anywhere yesterday.*)

To form the negative **passé composé** of a pronominal verb, put **ne** before the reflexive pronoun and put **pas** after the auxiliary verb (which is always **être**). Here are some pronominal verbs in negative **passé composé**:

> **Elle ne s'est pas maquillée.** (*She did not put makeup on.*)
>
> **Ils ne se sont pas vus.** (*They did not see to each other.*)

Negate the following sentences. (If you need more info on negative words, you can refer to Chapter 8.)

O. **Il est parti.** (*He left.*)

A. **Il n'est pas parti.**

41. **J'ai mangé quelque chose.** (*I ate something.*)

_____

42. **Nous avons chanté.** (*We sang.*)

_____

43. **Il y a eu un accident.** (*There was an accident.*)

_____

44. **Ils sont rentrés.** (*They came home.*)

_____

45. **Tu t'es amusé.** (*You had fun.*)

_____

46. **Elle a rencontré quelqu'un.** (*She met someone.*)

_____

47. **Vous avez fait quelque chose.** (*You did something.*)

_____

48. **Elles se sont excusées.** (*They apologized.*)

_____

49. **J'ai toujours aimé les fraises.** (*I've always liked strawberries.*)

_____

50. **Tu as déjà fini.** (*You've already finished.*)

_____

Answer Key

1. descendu

2. cassé

3. parlé

4. sorti

5. entendu

6. grossi

7. répondu

8. commencé

9. perdu

10. monté

11. il est mort

12. tu es monté

13. elles sont parties

14. elle est venue

15. nous sommes allées

16. vous êtes nés

17. je suis entré

18. on est resté

19. ils sont descendus

20. tu es tombée

21. je me suis lavée

22. tu t'es ennuyée

23. ils se sont amusés

24. vous vous êtes excusés

25. nous nous sommes levées

26. elles se sont dépêchées

27. on s'est trouvé

28. ils se sont mariés

29. elle s'est lavée

30. il s'est habillé

31. il a rendu

32. tu as répété

33. elle a choisi

34. j'ai préparé

35. nous avons vendu

36. ils ont entendu

37. vous avez fini

38. elles ont écouté

39. nous avons payé

40. j'ai obéi

41. Je n'ai rien mangé.

42. Nous n'avons pas chanté.

43. Il n'y a pas eu d'accident.

44. Ils ne sont pas rentrés.

45. Tu ne t'es pas amusé.

46. Elle n'a rencontré personne.

47. Vous n'avez rien fait.

48. Elles ne se sont pas excusées.

49. Je n'ai jamais aimé les fraises.

50. Tu n'as pas encore fini.

Chapter 16

Reminiscing and Describing Ongoing Past Actions with the Imperfect

▶ Saying what you used to do with the imperfect tense

▶ Knowing when and how to use the imperfect

The **imparfait** (*imperfect*) is used to describe an action that was taking place in the past, with no precise indication of time, or to talk about what you used to do. It is the second most common past tense in French, after the **passé composé** (*present perfect*; see Chapter 15). A major difference between these two past tenses is the form: The **imparfait** is a single word verb form, as in **je parlais** (*I was talking/I used to talk*), whereas the **passé composé** is a compound form (conjugated auxiliary + past participle) as in **j'ai parlé** (*I spoke/I have spoken*). In this chapter, I start by explaining how to form the **imparfait**; I then explain when and how to use it properly.

Forming the Imperfect Properly

I have good news for you: Only one verb has an irregular **imparfait** conjugation: **être** (*to be*). All other verbs follow the same pattern to form the **imparfait**, and it all begins with the **nous** (*we*) form of their present tense conjugation. There's a caveat: You need to know the present tense conjugations before starting on the **imparfait**. So using the imperfect isn't quite as easy as it first seems, especially if I tell you that verbs that are irregular in the present tense maintain their irregularity in the **imparfait**. But no worries — in the following sections, I help you through various present tense forms so you can smoothly move on to the **imparfait**.

Getting acquainted with imperfect endings

To form the **imparfait** of all verbs except **être** (*to be*), take the **nous** (*we*) form of the present tense, drop the **-ons** ending to get the stem you need, and add one of the following endings to the stem, depending on the subject you're using: **-ais**, **-ais**, **-ait**, **-ions**, **-iez**, or **-aient**. Easy enough? I have even better news: The **imparfait** has only one set of endings, and they fit all verbs — **-er**, **-ir**, **-re**, and irregular alike!

Here's an example of an **-er** verb for you: the **imparfait** conjugation of **parler** (*to talk*). It starts with the **nous** form of the present tense (**parlons**); you then remove **-ons** and add endings to the stem:

parler (*to talk*)	
je **parlais**	nous **parlions**
tu **parlais**	vous **parliez**
il/elle/on **parlait**	ils/elles **parlaient**

The following table shows the imperfect for a regular **-ir** verb, **finir** (*to finish*). It starts with the **nous** form of the present tense (**finissons**); you then remove **-ons** and add endings to the stem.

finir (*to finish*)	
je **finissais**	nous **finissions**
tu **finissais**	vous **finissiez**
il/elle/on **finissait**	ils/elles **finissaient**

The following table shows the imperfect for a regular **-re** verb, **vendre** (*to sell*). It starts with the **nous** form of the present tense (**vendons**); you then remove **-ons** and add endings to the stem.

vendre (*to sell*)	
je **vendais**	nous **vendions**
tu **vendais**	vous **vendiez**
il/elle/on **vendait**	ils/elles **vendaient**

Be ready to apply the formula to any verb (except **être**), even if you end up with double **i**'s! Verbs that end in **-ier**, like **étudier** (*to study*), **se marier** (*to get married*), and **crier** (*to shout*), for instance, end up with a **-iions** and **-iiez** ending in the **nous** and **vous** forms of their **imparfait**. Here are some examples:

Nous étudiions ensemble au lycée. (*We used to study together in high school.*)

Vous criiez beaucoup au match de foot. (*You used to shout a lot at the soccer game.*)

And verbs ending in **-yer** like **payer** (*to pay*) or **s'ennuyer** (*to be bored*) end up with **-yions** and **-yiez** endings in the **imparfait**, like this:

> **Nous payions.** (*We used to pay.*)

> **Vous payiez.** (*You used to pay.*)

Form the **imparfait** of the following verbs using the subject in parentheses. (If you need help with the **nous** form in the present tense before you form the **imparfait,** check out Chapter 6.)

0. déjeuner (je)

A. je déjeunais

1. regarder (tu) _____

2. grandir (il) _____

3. s'amuser (elle) _____

4. attendre (nous) _____

5. réfléchir (ils) _____

6. étudier (nous) _____

7. agir (vous) _____

8. aimer (elles) _____

9. entendre (on) _____

10. réussir (je) _____

Working with verbs ending in -cer and -ger

In the present tense, verbs ending in **-cer** and **-ger** have a spelling change in the **nous** form (see Chapter 6 for more details). This change is carried over into the conjugation of the **imparfait**, but in different ways; I give you the scoop in the following sections.

Verbs that end in -cer

When conjugated, French verbs typically keep the pronunciation of the stem consistent with the infinitive. Most of the forms in the present tense of **-cer** verbs, like **placer** (*to place*), have a soft *c* sound, but the **nous** form doesn't. To maintain the soft *c* sound throughout the entire present tense conjugation, a **ç** replaces the regular **c** before the **-ons** ending like this: **nous plaçons** (*we place*). Without the **ç**, **c** + **o** would have a hard *c* sound. (See Chapter 2 for more about pronunciation.)

In the **imparfait**, a hard *c* sound would come from **c + a** of the **-ais**, **-ais**, **-ait**, and **-aient** endings, so those forms keep the **ç** from the present tense's **nous** form to maintain a soft *c* sound. The **nous** and **vous** forms of the **imparfait** (ending in **-ions** and **-iez**) don't need the **ç** because **c + i** is already a soft sound. The following table shows the conjugation of **placer** in the imperfect so you can see the differences:

placer (*to place*)	
je **plaçais**	nous **placions**
tu **plaçais**	vous **placiez**
il/elle/on **plaçait**	ils/elles **plaçaient**

Other verbs in this case are **agacer** (*to annoy*), **commencer** (*to begin*), and **effacer** (*to erase*).

Verbs that end in -ger

In the present tense, verbs that end in **-ger** add an **e** before the **-ons** of the **nous** form for pronunciation's sake. For instance, the infinitive of **ranger** (*to put away*) has a soft *g* sound that transfers to the stem **rang-**, as long as the endings you add to it begin with **e**. Because **g + e** is a soft sound, the **je**, **tu**, **il/elle/on**, **vous**, and **ils/elles** forms have no problem. The **-ons** ending of the **nous** form breaks the pattern, though, because **g + o** make a hard sound. To fix it, add **e** between the **-ons** ending and the stem like this: **rangeons** (*we put away*). (Chapter 2 has more info on pronunciation.)

In the **imparfait,** you still want to maintain the soft sound throughout, but most of the endings begin with **a** (**-ais**, **-ais**, **-ait**, and **-aient**). And **g + a** makes a hard sound. What to do? Simply keep the **e** of the **nous** present tense ending for those forms. The **nous** and **vous** endings of the **imparfait** are **-ions** and **-iez**, and so they don't need the extra **-e** because **g + i** is already soft. The following table shows the conjugation of **ranger** in the imperfect so you can see the differences.

ranger (*to put away*)	
je **rangeais**	nous **rangions**
tu **rangeais**	vous **rangiez**
il/elle/on **rangeait**	ils/elles **rangeaient**

Other verbs in this case are **plonger** (*to dive*), **manger** (*to eat*), **nager** (*to swim*), and **voyager** (*to travel*).

Form the **imparfait** of the follow **-cer** and **-ger** verbs, using the subjects in parentheses.

0. **plonger (vous)**

A. **vous plongiez**

11. **manger (tu)** _____

12. **voyager (je)** _____

13. annoncer (vous) _____

14. avancer (elle) _____

15. obliger (vous) _____

16. placer (je) _____

17. commencer (ils) _____

18. nager (on) _____

19. mélanger (il) _____

20. menacer (nous) _____

Tackling verbs with irregular stems in the present tense

All irregular verbs behave regularly in the **imparfait** because they follow the same formula that I provide in the earlier section "Getting acquainted with imperfect endings": Take the **nous** form of the present tense, however irregular it may be, drop the **-ons** ending, and replace it with one of the following endings, depending on your subject: **-ais**, **-ait**, **-ions**, **-iez**, or **-aient**. Because the present tense is where the irregularity occurs, in Table 16-1 I give you the **nous** forms of the present tense of some very common irregular verbs.

Table 16-1	Irregular Verbs in the Present Tense and Their Stems in the Imperfect		
Infinitive	*English*	*Present Tense of Nous Form*	*Stem for Imperfect*
aller	*to go*	nous allons	all-
avoir	*to have*	nous avons	av-
devoir	*to have to*	nous devons	dev-
dire	*to tell*	nous disons	dis-
dormir	*to sleep*	nous dormons	dorm-
faire	*to do*	nous faisons	fais-
lire	*to read*	nous lisons	lis-
mettre	*to put*	nous mettons	mett-
pouvoir	*to be able to*	nous pouvons	pouv-
prendre	*to take*	nous prenons	pren-
venir	*to come*	nous venons	ven-
vouloir	*to want*	nous voulons	voul-

And now, here are a few irregular verbs in action in the imperfect:

Elle devait aider sa mère. (*She had to help her mother.*)

Nous prenions le bus pour aller à l'école. (*We used to take the bus to go to school.*)

Ils faisaient toujours leurs devoirs ensemble. (*They always used to do their homework together.*)

Forming the imperfect of être

Être (*to be*) is the only verb that's formed irregularly in the **imparfait**. It is irregular because it doesn't follow the pattern you apply to all other verbs, as I describe in the preceding sections. Its endings are the same (**-ais, -ait, -ions, -iez,** and **-aient**), but its stem is off the wall. Here's what I mean: Do you know the **nous** form of **être** in the present tense? (I'll wait while you check Chapter 6.) Yes, **nous sommes** (*we are*). Now glance at the following table, which gives you the **imparfait** of **être**! Very far from **nous sommes**, isn't it?

être (*to be*)	
j'**étais**	nous **étions**
tu **étais**	vous **étiez**
il/elle/on **était**	ils/elles **étaient**

Putting the Imperfect to Work in Everyday Situations

In English, the **imparfait** can be translated as several past forms. For instance, **je dansais** can be translated as *I danced, I used to dance,* or *I was dancing.* What will give you a clue is the context, and some expressions of time that I detail in the following sections.

Talking about past habits

You use the imperfect to discuss something *habitual,* meaning something you used to do on a regular basis in the past. If you *used to visit your grandma on Sundays when you were little,* in French you say, **Je rendais visite à ma grand-mère le dimanche, quand j'étais petit.**

You see how the expressions of time *on Sundays* (**le dimanche**) and *when I was little* (**quand j'étais petit**) helped you spot the habitual aspect? Many such expressions are used in French; here are some common ones:

- ✔ **tous les jours/les ans/les mois** (*every day/year/month*)
- ✔ **chaque jour/mois/année** (*each day/month/year*)
- ✔ **le lundi/mardi/. . .** (*on Mondays/Tuesdays/. . .*)
- ✔ **tout le temps** (*all the time*)
- ✔ **jamais** (*never*)
- ✔ **d'habitude** (*usually*)
- ✔ **rarement** (*rarely*)
- ✔ **comme** (at the beginning of a sentence) (*as*)
- ✔ **pendant que** (*while*)
- ✔ **autrefois** (*formerly*)
- ✔ **quand + [the imparfait]** (*when*)

Here are some of these habit expressions in action:

Chaque année, elle allait en vacances à la mer. (*Each year, she used to go on vacation at the beach.*)

Quand nous étions petits, nous jouions souvent au foot. (*When we were little, we used to play soccer often.*)

Form the imparfait of the following verbs.

Q. Il _____ toujours tard. (**partir**)

A. **partait**

21. Tu _____ leurs parents. (**connaître**)

22. Elle _____ un beau jardin. (**avoir**)

23. Vous _____ dans notre quartier. (**habiter**)

24. J' _____ beaucoup. (**étudier**)

25. Ils _____ tout. (**partager**)

Telling a story

When you're reminiscing or telling a story, you need to set the scene before you tell what happened. That explanation may include descriptions of

- ✔ Weather
- ✔ Time and day
- ✔ Scenery
- ✔ Feelings and mental states
- ✔ Appearance of people and things
- ✔ What actions were ongoing

To set a scene this way, French uses the **imparfait**. Here's one example:

> **Le jour de leur mariage, il faisait beau, les invités étaient contents, et la mariée était très belle.** (*On their wedding day, the weather was nice, all the guests were happy, and the bride was very beautiful.*)

In this example, you have several descriptions:

- ✔ **il faisait beau** (*the weather was nice*)
- ✔ **étaient contents** (*were happy*)
- ✔ **était très belle** (*was very beautiful*)

Here's another example:

> **Samedi dernier, il pleuvait. Il y avait beaucoup de circulation et il était 8h 30 quand je suis enfin arrivé à la maison. J'étais très fatigué!** (*Last Saturday, it was raining. There was a lot of traffic, and it was 8:30 when I finally got home. I was very tired!*)

In this example, you have several descriptions:

- ✔ **il pleuvait** (*it was raining*)
- ✔ **il y avait beaucoup de circulation** (*there was a lot of traffic*)
- ✔ **il était 8h 30** (*it was 8:30*)
- ✔ **j'étais très fatigué** (*I was very tired*)

Decide whether the underlined verbs of these sentences would be in **imparfait** if the text was in French. Write yes if so or no.

0. *This morning I <u>got</u> up early.*

A. no

26. *It <u>was</u> cold when he left last night.* _____

27. *<u>Did you take</u> the bus to school when you were little?* _____

28. *What <u>did you do</u> last night?* _____

29. *What <u>was she doing</u> when you arrived?* _____

30. *They all cried when the bride <u>said</u> "I do."* _____

Noting continuous past actions

Sometimes you need to talk about several ongoing actions that were happening at the same time. In this case, French uses the **imparfait** for all the verbs. When two actions are happening at the same time, they can be linked by **et** (*and*) or by **pendant que** (*while*). Here are a couple of examples:

> **Maman lisait pendant que papa regardait la télé.** (*Mom was reading while Dad was watching TV.*)

> **Il pleuvait et la rivière grossissait dangereusement.** (*It was raining, and the river was swelling dangerously.*)

In other situations, one ongoing action is suddenly interrupted. Imagine that you were sleeping when suddenly you heard a loud noise in the kitchen. In this situation, French uses the **imparfait** in combination with the **passé composé** (*present perfect*; see Chapter 15 for details). A verb in the **imparfait** indicates what was going on (the continuous action), and an action conjugated in **passé composé** interrupts it. Here's what the sentence looks like in French:

> **Je dormais quand j'ai entendu un grand bruit à la cuisine.** (*I was sleeping when I heard a loud noise in the kitchen.*)

> **Ils faisaient un pique-nique, quand la pluie a commencé.** (*They were having a picnic when the rain started.*)

As demonstrated in these two examples, the clause in the **passé composé** (that interrupts what was going on) usually occurs last, after the word **quand** (*when*).

For each underlined verb in the English sentence, indicate whether the tense should be **passé composé** or **imparfait**. Write **passé composé** or **imparfait** (separated by a slash if there's more than one verb) in the blanks provided.

0. *I <u>came</u> to your house, but you <u>were</u> not there.*

A. **passé composé/ imparfait**

31. *Last year I <u>read</u> the paper every morning.* _____

32. *Yesterday, we <u>went</u> out.* _____

33. *When he <u>was</u> 10, he <u>broke</u> his bike.* _____

34. *He <u>used to like</u> cherries, but one day he <u>got</u> very sick.* _____

35. *Last time you traveled, where <u>did you go</u>?* _____

Discussing hypothetical situations

Do you know the song "If I Were a Rich Man"? The fiddler on the roof is using very proper English (*if I were*) to express a daydream, a hypothetical situation. This hypothetical situation is part of a sentence that starts with the imperfect and continues with a verb in the conditional to express what he *would do*, indeed. For instance, he could sing:

> **Si j'étais riche, je construirais un château.** (*If I were rich, I would build a castle.*)

> **Si elle faisait du sport, elle serait plus en forme.** (*If she exercised, she would be in better shape.*)

> **S'ils habitaient en France, ils parleraient français tous les jours.** (*If they lived in France, they would speak French every day.*)

As you can see, French describes a hypothetical situation the same way English does, using **si** (*if*) + **imparfait** to express the dream and the conditional with **construirais** (*would build*), **serait** (*would be*), and **parleraient** (*would talk/speak*) to express its result. You can find out all about the conditional by turning to Chapter 18.

Offering suggestions

In an informal context, **si** (*if*) + **imparfait** can be used to extend an invitation or suggest an activity like this: **Si on allait au cinéma?** (*What about going to the movies?*) Here's are a couple of additional examples:

> **Si tu faisais tes devoirs au lieu de regarder la télé?** (*What about doing your homework instead of watching TV?*)

> **Si on sortait ce soir?** (*What about going out tonight?*)

Match each of the following sentences in **imparfait** with one of the categories that best (most precisely) describes it.

Continuous action   Suggestion   Past habit
Storytelling   Hypothesis

Q. La baby-sitter regardait la télé pendant que les enfants dormaient.

A. Continuous action

36. Quand nous étions petits, nous prenions le bus scolaire.

37. Autrefois, il faisait un voyage chaque année.

38. Elle travaillait quand le bébé a commencé à pleurer.

39. Il était minuit et il pleuvait.

40. Si tu achetais une moto, Maman serait inquiète.

41. Si on sortait ce soir?

42. Quand les enfants étaient au lycée, ils rentraient à la maison tous les soirs.

43. Je dînais quand le téléphone a sonné.

44. Avec le soleil, tout le monde était heureux.

45. Papa lisait pendant que nous faisions nos devoirs.

Answer Key

1	regardais	17	commençaient	33	imparfait/passé composé
2	grandissait	18	nageait	34	imparfait/passé composé
3	s'amusait	19	mélangeait	35	passé composé
4	attendions	20	menacions	36	Past habit
5	réfléchissaient	21	connaissais	37	Past habit
6	étudiions	22	avait	38	Continuous action
7	agissiez	23	habitiez	39	Storytelling
8	aimaient	24	étudiais	40	Hypothesis
9	entendait	25	partageaient	41	Suggestion
10	réussissais	26	yes	42	Past habit
11	mangeais	27	yes	43	Continuous action
12	voyageais	28	no	44	Storytelling
13	annonciez	29	yes	45	Continuous action
14	avançait	30	no		
15	obligiez	31	imparfait		
16	plaçais	32	passé composé		

Chapter 17

Projecting Forward with the Future

· ·

In This Chapter

▶ Using the simple future

▶ Handling irregular future verbs

▶ Discussing the future in other ways

▶ Finding out other uses of the future

· ·

*W*hen you're making plans, such as imagining what you'll do when your family comes for Thanksgiving or how your life will be different after you adopt that new pup, you need the future tense (**le futur**) in French. Forming the future tense is quite simple, so I'm confident that you can begin using it in no time. In this chapter, you discover how to form regular and irregular future conjugations, find out alternate ways to talk about the future, and identify other uses for the future tense.

Forming the Simple Future Tense of Regular Verbs

Unlike the English future tense, which uses two words (for example, *will go*), the future tense in French is simple. It's a one-word form of a verb, and the conjugation only affects the ending of the verb. You do have to know the conjugation, but it's super easy because the French simple future is formed from the complete infinitive (see Chapter 6 for more about infinitives). In the following sections, I walk you through forming the simple future tense of regular -**er**, -**ir**, and -**re** verbs.

The future tense of -er and -ir verbs

To form the future tense of all regular -**er** and -**ir** verbs, proceed like this:

1. **Start with the complete infinitive, without dropping any part of it.**

2. **Add one of the following endings, depending on the subject you're using: -ai, -as, -a, -ons, -ez, or -ont.**

   Be sure to choose the ending that matches the subject you need: For **je**, choose the -**ai** ending; for **tu**, choose -**as**; and so on. (See Chapter 6 for more about subjects and verb endings.)

As you can see, these endings look a lot like the present tense of the verb **avoir**! You can keep that in mind if it helps you remember the future tense endings. (See Chapter 6 for more about this verb.)

Would you like to see these steps in action? Here's the complete conjugation of **le futur** for **parler** (*to speak*), a regular -**er** verb.

parler (to speak)	
je **parlerai**	nous **parlerons**
tu **parleras**	vous **parlerez**
il/elle/on **parlera**	ils/elles **parleront**

Be aware that the **é** sound of the infinitive for an -**er** verb like **jouer** (*to play*) changes from **é** to a closed **e**, or even becomes silent, when you add the new ending to it. For **étudier** (*to study*), the -**er** ending has an **é** sound. But in **il étudiera** (*he will study*), it sounds like ey-tew-dee-rah — the **é** sound of the -**er** is gone! (See Chapter 2 for the basics of sounding out French words.)

Here's the complete conjugation for **finir** (*to finish*), a regular -**ir** verb.

finir (to finish)	
je **finirai**	nous **finirons**
tu **finiras**	vous **finirez**
il/elle/on **finira**	ils/elles **finiront**

The -**er** or -**ir** verb of each of the following sentences is given to you in the infinitive form, in parentheses. Put the verb in the future tense. Be sure to match the ending to the subject. Here's an example:

Q. Je _____ chez toi ce soir. (**passer**)

A. **passerai**

1. Ils _____ la porte à clé. (**fermer**)

2. Je _____ pour prendre des nouvelles. (**téléphoner**)

3. Vous _____ avant la fin du film. (**partir**)

4. Tu _____ en France un jour. (**habiter**)

5. Il _____ de voiture l'année prochaine. (**changer**)

6. Ils _____ en automne. (se marier)

7. On _____ pour l'examen. (étudier)

8. Elle _____ le chien. (nourrir)

9. Nous _____ vite. (réagir)

10. Elles _____ la bonne réponse. (choisir)

The future tense of -re verbs

To form the future of regular **-re** verbs, proceed like this:

1. **Starting with the infinitive, drop the final -e.**

2. **Add one of the following endings, depending on the subject you're using: -ai, -as, -a, -ons, -ez, or -ont.**

   Be sure to choose the ending that matches the subject you need: For **je**, choose **-ai**; for **tu**, choose **-as**, and so on.

Need an example? Here's the complete conjugation for **vendre** (*to sell*), a regular **-re** verb.

vendre (*to sell*)	
je **vendrai**	nous **vendrons**
tu **vendras**	vous **vendrez**
il/elle/on **vendra**	ils/elles **vendront**

The **-re** verb of each of the following sentences is given to you in the infinitive, in parentheses. Put it in the future. Be sure to match the ending to the subject. Here's an example:

Q. Je _____ dans un bon hôtel. (descendre)

A. descendrai

11. Nous _____ le train pour voyager. (prendre)

12. Tu _____ la vérité. (dire)

13. Je _____ un chapeau. (mettre)

14. Nous _____ le journal. (lire)

15. Ils _____ patiemment. (attendre)

Dealing with Irregular Forms of the Simple Future Tense

The simple future tense of regular verbs, which I discuss earlier in this chapter, is pretty easy to form. Unfortunately, some verbs refuse to fall in with the rest, and they behave differently. They are the dreaded irregular verbs. So what does "irregular" mean in the future? You still use **-ai**, **-as**, **-a**, **-ons**, **-ez**, and **-ont** as your endings (I talk about them earlier in this chapter), but you don't add them to just the complete infinitive. This easy stem of the future tense now has to be replaced by a set of irregular stems. The following sections guide you through the various irregular stem changes of verbs in the simple future tense.

Creating the future tense of -yer and -ayer verbs

Verbs that have an infinitive ending in **-yer**, such as **employer** (*to employ*), **nettoyer** (*to clean*), and **s'ennuyer** (*to get/be bored*), have a slight irregularity in the future tense. Follow these directions carefully to form their future:

1. **Start with the infinitive and change the y of the infinitive to an i.**

2. **Add the usual future endings to it, choosing the one that matches your subject: -ai, -as, -a, -ons, -ez, or -ont.**

Here's the complete conjugation for **employer** so you can see the change from **y** to **i**.

employer (*to employ*)	
j'**emploierai**	nous **emploierons**
tu **emploieras**	vous **emploierez**
il/elle/on **emploiera**	ils/elles **emploieront**

Now here's one irregularity that you're going to love: verbs that end in **-ayer**, such as **payer** (*to pay*) and **essayer** (*to try*), may or may not lose their **y** and exchange it for an **i**. In other words, you could see **payeras** *or* **paieras**, for example (for the singular informal *you* form). Both forms are correct and accepted. I suggest you pick one way (maybe the no-change form with the **y**) and stick to it. If you want to use the alternate form (with the **i**), just follow the preceding steps.

Here's the complete conjugation for **essayer**, with the two versions.

essayer (*to try*)	
j'**essaierai/essayerai**	nous **essaierons/essayerons**
tu **essaieras/essayeras**	vous **essaierez/essayerez**
il/elle/on **essaiera/essayera**	ils/elles **essaieront/essayeront**

The irregular verb of each of the following sentences is given to you in the infinitive, in parentheses. Put the verb in the correct form of the future tense, matching the ending to the subject. If the verb has an alternate form, write it also. Here's an example:

O. Il _____ plus tard. (essayer)

A. **essayera/essaiera**

16. La prochaine fois, il _____ une amende. (payer)

17. Tu ne _____ pas. (s'ennuyer)

18. Ils _____ des gens honnêtes. (employer)

19. Vous _____ votre chambre. (nettoyer)

20. Elle _____ une nouvelle robe. (essayer)

Handling appeler and jeter in the future

For **appeler** (*to call*) and **jeter** (*to throw*), all you need to do is double the consonant that precedes the infinitive ending and add the future endings. That's not too difficult. Here's how to form these irregular conjugations:

1. **Drop the -er ending from the infinitive.**

   Appeler turns into **appel-**, and **jeter** turns into **jet-**.

2. **Double the last consonant you see (l for appeler and t for jeter) and put the -er ending back on.**

   You now have **appel + l + er** and **jet + t + er**.

3. **Add the future ending that matches your subject: -ai, -as, -a, -ons, -ez, or -ont.**

Here's the complete conjugation of **appeler**:

appeler (*to call*)	
j'**appellerai**	nous **appellerons**
tu **appelleras**	vous **appellerez**
il/elle/on **appellera**	ils/elles **appelleront**

The following examples will help you see the future forms of **appeler** in action:

> **J'appellerai mes parents dimanche.** (*I will call my parents Sunday.*)

> **Ils appelleront leur chien Brutus.** (*They will call their dog Brutus.*)

Here's the complete future tense conjugation for **jeter**.

jeter *(to throw)*	
je **jetterai**	nous **jetterons**
tu **jetteras**	vous **jetterez**
il/elle/on **jettera**	ils/elles **jetteront**

Here are a couple of examples of using **jeter** in the future:

> **Vous ne jetterez pas vos papiers par terre.** (*You will not throw your papers on the floor.*)
>
> **Elle jettera ces vieux livres.** (*She will throw away these old books.*)

Knowing what to do with verbs ending in e/é + consonant + -er

Putting aside the irregular verbs I introduce in the previous two sections, all other irregular verbs that have **e/é** + consonant immediately before the **-er** of the infinitive ending follow their own rule in the simple future: They change that **e/é** to an **è** on all forms of the future. Some common verbs of this kind include: **acheter** (*to buy*), **amener** (*to bring*), **préférer** (*to prefer*), and **se lever** (*to get up*). Here's how to proceed with the future tense of verbs like these:

1. **Start with the infinitive and drop the -er.**

   For example, **amener** turns into **amen-**.

2. **Change the e/é + consonant to è+ consonant.**

   Here, **amen-** becomes **amèn-**.

3. **Put the -er back on.**

   Amèn- now becomes **amèner-**.

4. **Add the future ending that matches your subject: -ai, -as, -a, -ons, -ez, or -ont.**

   If you want to use the first person singular in this case, **amèner** + **-ai** (for **je**) = **amènerai**.

As another example, here's the complete conjugation for **acheter**.

acheter *(to buy)*	
j'**achèterai**	nous **achèterons**
tu **achèteras**	vous **achèterez**
il/elle/on **achètera**	ils/elles **achèteront**

Note: These verbs used to keep the **-é** in future, but they don't any more according to spelling reform issued in 1990. But many books still show the old way, so don't be surprised to find both versions.

In each of the following sentences, change the irregular verb in parentheses to the future tense, making sure it matches the subject(s) in the sentence. Here's an example:

O. Vous _____ le pain. (acheter)

A. achèterez

21. Elle _____ tard dimanche. (se lever)

22. Vous _____ votre chien au pique-nique. (amener)

23. Il _____ un cadeau pour toi. (acheter)

24. Tu _____ le chien. (promener)

25. Nous _____ partir avant vous. (préférer)

26. Je _____ les enfants pour l'école. (lever)

27. Ils _____ ensemble. (répéter)

28. Tu _____ ton manteau dans la maison. (enlever)

29. Cet hiver le lac _____. (geler)

30. Elles _____ sûrement une solution. (suggérer)

Introducing verbs with a completely irregular stem in the future

Some irregular verbs are such oddballs that you just have to memorize them. Table 17-1 lists some of the most common verbs that have a completely different stem in the future tense.

Table 17-1	Irregular Future Stems	
Infinitive	*Translation*	*Future-Tense Stem*
aller	*to go*	ir-
avoir	*to have*	aur-
devoir	*to have to*	devr-
envoyer	*to send*	enverr-
être	*to be*	ser-
faire	*to do*	fer-
pleuvoir	*to rain*	pleuvr-
pouvoir	*to be able to*	pourr-
recevoir	*to receive*	recevr-
savoir	*to know*	saur-

(continued)

Table 17-1 (continued)

Infinitive	Translation	Future-Tense Stem
tenir	*to hold*	tiendr-
venir	*to come*	viendr-
voir	*to see*	verr-
vouloir	*to want*	voudr-

To form the future of these irregular verbs, proceed as follows:

1. **Start from the stem given to you in Table 17-1.**

   For instance, for **voir** (*to see*), take **verr-**.

2. **Add the usual future endings to it, choosing the one that matches your subject: -ai, -as, -a, -ons, -ez, or -ont.**

   For example, if you want to use the first person singular of **verr-**, just add **-ai** to get **je verrai**.

Here are some other examples in action:

J'aurai bientôt une nouvelle voiture. (*I will soon have a new car.*)

Cet été, tu enverras des cartes postales à tes amis. (*This summer, you will send post-cards to your friends.*)

In each of the following sentences, I provide an irregular verb in the infinitive. Put it in the future tense and make sure your ending matches the subject. Here's an example:

Q. Je _____ partir. (pouvoir)

A. **pourrai**

31. **Nous** _____ **la cuisine. (faire)**

32. **Mon fils** _____ **dans une bonne école. (aller)**

33. **Ils ne** _____ **jamais la vérité. (savoir)**

34. **Dans 10 ans tu** _____ **marié. (être)**

35. **Vous** _____ **des cartes postales pendant le voyage. (envoyer)**

36. **Elle** _____ **des choses intéressantes. (voir)**

37. **Elles** _____ **assez de temps pour finir leur travail. (avoir)**

38. **Je** _____ **avec toi. (venir)**

39. **Demain, il** _____ **. (pleuvoir)**

40. **Je** _____ **partir. (pouvoir)**

Exploring Other Ways of Talking about the Future

Like in English, in French the simple future is not the only way to express that something is coming. In the following sections, you discover what several other ways are, how to form them, and when to use them as opposed to the simple future.

Adding expressions of time

Because the simple future expresses a rather vague future, it's rarely used on its own. You can use expressions of time to anchor down your future action with more precision. Table 17-2 lists common French expressions of time.

Table 17-2	Common Expressions of Time
Expression of Time Used with the Future Tense	*English Translation*
après	*after*
puis	*then/next*
ensuite	*then/next*
plus tard	*later*
tout à l'heure	*in a little bit*
bientôt	*soon*
dans + [amount of time]	*in + [amount of time]*
cet après-midi	*this afternoon*
ce soir	*tonight/this evening*
demain	*tomorrow*
demain matin	*tomorrow morning*
demain après-midi	*tomorrow afternoon*
demain soir	*tomorrow night/evening*
après-demain	*the day after tomorrow*
[day of week] + prochain	*next [day of the week]*
la semaine prochaine	*next week*
le mois prochain	*next month*
le weekend prochain	*next weekend*
l'année prochaine	*next year*
la prochaine fois (que)	*next time (that)*
l'été prochain	*next summer*
le printemps prochain	*next spring*
l'automne prochain	*next fall*
l'hiver prochain	*next winter*
un jour	*one day*

Some of the expressions in Table 17-2 are used with both present tense and past tense. In that case, the verb tense changes the meaning of the expression like **ce weekend** in a future tense sentence indicates *this weekend*, but in a past sentence it would mean *last weekend*.

Here are some expressions of time in action with the simple future tense:

> **Il fera la vaisselle plus tard, ensuite il regardera la télé.** (*He will do the dishes later; then he will watch television.*)

> **Le weekend prochain nous irons au zoo.** (*Next weekend, we'll go to the zoo.*)

> **Un jour, on inventera les voyages dans le temps.** (*One day, they will invent time travel.*)

When you use a conjugated verb after **la prochaine fois** (*next time*) to indicate the next time that you do a particular action, insert **que** between the two. To say just *next time*, leave the **que** out. The following examples illustrate the difference.

> **La prochaine fois que tu iras en vacances, prends des photos.** (*The next time that you go on vacation, take pictures.*)

> **La prochaine fois, je n'oublierai pas mon appareil photo!** (*Next time, I won't forget my camera.*)

Put the following sentences in the future by conjugating the verb in simple future and changing the present expression of time to a future one. Regular and irregular verb forms are fair game here, and each sentence must have a different expression of time (for instance, **maintenant** [*now*] has several future options). Consult a French-English dictionary if you need help with any of the following vocabulary. Here's an example:

Q. **Tu es ici aujourd'hui.**

A. **Tu seras ici demain.**

41. **Je vais en vacances maintenant.**

_____

42. **Ils parlent avec leurs amis ce soir.**

_____

43. **Tu joues au foot lundi.**

_____

44. **Scarlett pense à son problème aujourd'hui.**

_____

45. Il pleut cet après-midi.

_____

46. Nous sommes en vacances cette semaine.

_____

47. Vous nettoyez votre bureau maintenant.

_____

48. Elles s'ennuient ce mois-ci.

_____

49. On voit nos amis samedi.

_____

50. Tu as ton diplôme cette année.

_____

Combining aller and an infinitive when the future is certain

You use a special form of future tense to express what will happen in the near future, the **futur proche** _(near future)_. For example, when the sky is very, very dark and full of menacing clouds, you pretty much know that it's about to rain, and you'd say **Il va pleuvoir** _(It is going to rain)_. The **futur proche** is very easy to form: You conjugate **aller** _(to go)_ in present, with the subject you need, and add the actual verb in the infinitive as shown here:

Subject + conjugated form of **aller** in the present tense + verb in the infinitive

Je + vais + dormir. _(I am going to sleep.)_

Nous + allons + danser. _(We are going to dance.)_

To make this construction easy for you, here's the conjugation of **aller** in the present tense.

aller _(to go)_	
je **vais**	nous **allons**
tu **vas**	vous **allez**
il/elle/on **va**	ils/elles **vont**

Compare the difference in usage between **futur** and **futur proche** in these two sentences. Your friends just got married, and you think that one day they will probably have kids.

> **Ils auront un bébé un jour.** (*They will have a baby one day.*)

Then nine months later, you run into them. The woman is enormously pregnant, so you can safely say:

> **Ils vont avoir un bébé.** (*They're going to have a baby.*)

Proceed like this to negate a verb in the **futur proche**:

1. **Isolate the auxiliary verb aller.**

   Conjugate this verb. For example, **va** is the third person singular conjugation of **aller**.

2. **Put ne and pas (or another negative word) around it.**

   In this example, you now have: **ne va pas**.

3. **Put the infinitive after pas.**

   Here is your completed sentence: **Elle ne va pas dormir.** (*She is not going to sleep.*)

The negative words **personne** (*no one*), **nulle part** (*nowhere*), **ni** (*neither/nor*), and **aucun** with a noun (*none*) don't follow this rule; they go after the infinitive, not before. Here's the formula:

> Subject + **ne** + conjugated form of **aller** + infinitive + **personne/nulle part/ni/aucun** with a noun

Here they are in action:

> **Je ne vais écrire à personne.** (*I'm going to write to no one.*)
>
> **Ils ne vont partir nulle part pour Noël.** (*They are going nowhere for Christmas.*)
>
> **Elle ne va voir ni sa soeur, ni sa mère.** (*She's going to see neither her mother nor her sister.*)
>
> **Nous n'allons prendre aucun médicament.** (*We're going to take no medication.*)

Using the present tense in certain cases

Sometimes, in the right context, you can simply use the present tense to express an idea that is future (flip to Chapter 6 for more about the present tense). If you talk about something that is clearly in the future, like an appointment, or if you add a time reference to the future, like **ce soir** (*tonight*) or **demain** (*tomorrow*), you can use the present tense instead of **le futur** or **le futur proche**. In fact, you will sound very French doing so.

Here are some examples in action:

> —**Quand as-tu rendez-vous chez le dentiste?** (*When is your dentist appointment?*)
> —**J'y vais demain.** (*I'm going tomorrow.*)

> —**Qu'est-ce que tu fais ce soir?** (*What are you doing tonight?*)
> —**Je garde ma petite soeur.** (*I'm baby-sitting my little sister.*)

Discovering Other Uses of the Future Tense

In French, people very commonly use **le futur** to discuss something other than the future. For example, you can describe a cause-effect relationship using the future tense, and you can also tell someone what you intend do *when* you finish your work early. Furthermore, the verbs **espérer** (*to hope*) and **prédire** (*to predict*) are typically used with the future tense. See what it's all about in the following sections.

Describing a cause-effect relationship

"If you finish your work early, you will go home early." This type of "if" sentence expresses a logical link between the two parts of the sentence, which have equal weight (unlike a hypothesis statement such as "If you finished early, you would go home early.") In the cause-effect sentence, the effect, or result half, is expressed with a verb in the future, whereas the cause half has **si** (*if*) + present tense. These two halves are called *clauses,* and you can switch the two clauses around — but don't switch the tenses from one clause to another. In other words, the verb in future should never be in the same clause as **si**.

To be sure you keep the tenses separate, follow this little formula:

> Clause 1 [**si** + present tense (cause)] + Clause 2 [future tense alone (effect)]
>
> *Or*
>
> Clause 1 [future tense alone (effect)] + Clause 2 [**si** + present tense (cause)]

Here are some examples of this formula in action:

> **Si tu viens à Austin, tu resteras chez nous.** (*If you come to Austin, you will stay with us.*)

> **Tu auras plus de temps pour jouer ce soir si tu finis ton travail maintenant.** (*You will have more time to play tonight if you finish your work now.*)

Expressing what you'll do when something else happens

In a sentence with two clauses separated by **quand** (*when*) or a similar expression, you need to use the future in both clauses — that is, in both parts of the sentence. For example:

> **Qu'est-ce que tu feras quand il fera très chaud cet été?** (*What will you do when it is really hot this summer?*)

> **Quand je serai grand, je serai pilote de Formule 1.** (*When I grow up, I will be an F1 driver.*)

Make sure you remember this major difference between French and English. In English, you use present tense after *when*, but in French, the future is used after **quand**. It goes like this:

French: [**Quand** + verb conjugated in future], [other verb conjugated in future]

English: [*When* + verb conjugated in present], [other verb conjugated in future]

But the two clauses can be switched around as well, like this:

French: [Other verb conjugated in future] [**quand** + verb conjugated in future]

English: [Other verb conjugated in future] [*when* + verb conjugated in present]

Here are common expressions to use in such sentences instead of **quand**:

lorsque (*when* [more formal])

dès que (*as soon as*)

aussitôt que (*as soon as* [more formal])

Put the following sentences into French. You can use a French-English dictionary if needed. All the sentences use a future expression of time, so use the future tense in both clauses. Note that when English uses present tense, French uses **futur simple**. Here's an example:

0. *When you finish your work, you will leave.*

A. **Quand tu finiras ton travail, tu partiras.**

51. *As soon as he arrives in Paris, he will phone his parents.*

_____

52. *We will go to Houston when we have a new car.*

_____

53. *When you* (singular informal) *arrive at the intersection, you will turn left.*

_____

54. *When the weather is nice next summer, I will go to the beach.*

_____

55. *You will have an ice cream when you* (plural informal) *are good.*

_____

Discussing hopes and predictions

The future tense is also used after verbs like **espérer** (*to hope*) and **prédire** (*to predict*), because they indicate something that hasn't yet happened and is therefore in the future. Here are some examples:

Elle espère qu'il fera beau demain. (*She hopes that the weather will be nice tomorrow.*)

La voyante prédit que nous aurons une fille. (*The clairvoyant predicts that we will have a daughter.*)

Answer Key

1 fermeront

2 téléphonerai

3 partirez

4 habiteras

5 changera

6 se marieront

7 étudiera

8 nourrira

9 réagirons

10 choisiront

11 prendrons

12 diras

13 mettrai

14 lirons

15 attendront

16 paiera/payera

17 t'ennuieras

18 emploieront

19 nettoierez

20 essaiera/essayera

21 se lèvera

22 amènerez

23 achètera

24 **promèneras**

25 **préfèrerons**

26 **lèverai**

27 **répèteront**

28 **enlèveras**

29 **gèlera**

30 **suggèreront**

31 **ferons**

32 **ira**

33 **sauront**

34 **seras**

35 **enverrez**

36 **verra**

37 **auront**

38 **viendrai**

39 **pleuvra**

40 **pourrai**

41 **J'irai en vacances plus tard.**

42 **Ils parleront avec leurs amis demain soir.**

43 **Tu joueras au foot lundi prochain.**

44 **Scarlett pensera à son problème demain.**

45 **Il pleuvra demain après-midi.**

46 **Nous serons en vacances la semaine prochaine.**

47 **Vous nettoierez votre bureau tout à l'heure.**

48 **Elles s'ennuieront le mois prochain.**

49 **On verra nos amis samedi prochain.**

50 **Tu auras ton diplôme l'année prochaine.**

51 Dès qu'il arrivera à Paris, il téléphonera à ses parents.

52 Nous irons à Houston quand nous aurons une nouvelle voiture.

53 Quand tu arriveras à l'intersection, tu tourneras à gauche.

54 Quand il fera beau l'été prochain, j'irai à la plage.

55 Vous aurez une glace quand vous serez sages.

Part V

Expressing Conditions, Subjectivity, and Orders

Imperatives of Some Moody -er Verbs

Infinitive	Imperative Tu	Imperative Nous	Imperative Vous
appeler (*to call*)	**appelle** (*call*)	**appelons** (*let's call*)	**appelez** (*call*)
balayer (*to sweep*)	**balaie** (*sweep*)	**balayons** (*let's sweep*)	**balayez** (*sweep*)
célébrer (*to celebrate*)	**célèbre** (*celebrate*)	**célébrons** (*let's celebrate*)	**célébrez** (*celebrate*)
commencer (*to begin*)	**commence** (*begin*)	**commençons** (*let's begin*)	**commencez** (*begin*)
effacer (*to erase*)	**efface** (*erase*)	**effaçons** (*let's erase*)	**effacez** (*erase*)
envoyer (*to send*)	**envoie** (*send*)	**envoyons** (*let's send*)	**envoyez** (*send*)
épeler (*to spell*)	**épelle** (*spell*)	**épelons** (*let's spell*)	**épelez** (*spell*)
jeter (*to throw*)	**jette** (*throw*)	**jetons** (*let's throw*)	**jetez** (*throw*)
lancer (*to throw*)	**lance** (*throw*)	**lançons** (*let's throw*)	**lancez** (*throw*)
manger (*to eat*)	**mange** (*eat*)	**mangeons** (*let's eat*)	**mangez** (*eat*)
menacer (*to threaten*)	**menace** (*threaten*)	**menaçons** (*let's threaten*)	**menacez** (*threaten*)
nager (*to swim*)	**nage** (*swim*)	**nageons** (*let's swim*)	**nagez** (*swim*)
payer (*to pay*)	**paie** (*pay*)	**payons** (*let's pay*)	**payez** (*pay*)
refléter (*to reflect*)	**reflète** (*reflect*)	**reflétons** (*let's reflect*)	**reflétez** (*reflect*)
répéter (*to repeat*)	**répète** (*repeat*)	**répétons** (*let's repeat*)	**répétez** (*repeat*)
voyager (*to travel*)	**voyage** (*travel*)	**voyageons** (*let's travel*)	**voyagez** (*travel*)

Try out pointers for forming and using the conditional in a free article at www.dummies.com/extras/frenchgrammar.

In this part . . .

- ✔ Talk about a daydream, a wish, or a hypothetical situation with the conditional.

- ✔ Express feelings about an event with the subjunctive.

- ✔ Tell people to do things with the imperative, which is the verb form that expresses commands.

- ✔ Discuss an action that's further in the past than the main action of a sentence with two-word forms called *compound tenses*.

Chapter 18

Wondering with the Conditional

Where *would you go* on vacation if you *could choose* any destination? *Would you choose* the beach or the mountains? In English, the conditional tense allows you to express a daydream, a wish, or a hypothesis. It is a two-word verbal form that uses an auxiliary word (*would, could*) along with the verb. The French **conditionnel**, on the other hand, is a single-word form, and the conditional is built from the infinitive of the verb itself. This chapter tells you how to form the conditional and how to put those forms to good use.

Forming the Conditional of Regular Verbs

The following sections take you through the conditional forms of regular verbs, which are very similar to the future forms of regular verbs (see Chapter 17). Both the conditional and the future use the whole infinitive as their stem; they only differ in their endings. The conditional endings actually resemble those of the **imparfait** (*imperfect*). They are: **-ais**, **-ais**, **-ait**, **-ions**, **-iez**, and **-aient** (see Chapter 16 for more on the **imparfait**). Now get ready to put stems and endings together to form the conditional of regular **-er**, **-ir**, and **-re** verbs.

All infinitives (**-er**, **-ir**, and **-re**) have an **-r**, and because the stem for a verb's conditional form is the infinitive, all forms of the conditional have that **-r** from the infinitive. If you don't see that **-r**, you're not dealing with the conditional!

Regular -er and -ir verbs

To form the conditional of regular **-er** and **-ir** verbs, proceed like this:

1. **Start with the complete infinitive (don't drop any part of it).**

2. **Add one of the following endings, depending on the subject you're using: -ais, -ais, -ait, -ions, -iez, or -aient.**

   Be sure to choose the ending that matches the subject you need: for **je**, choose the **-ais** ending; for **nous**, choose **-ions**; and so on.

Would you like to see these steps in action? Here's the complete conjugation of the conditional for **parler** (*to speak*), a regular **-er** verb, indicating that someone *would speak*.

parler (*to speak*)	
je **parlerais**	nous **parlerions**
tu **parlerais**	vous **parleriez**
il/elle/on **parlerait**	ils/elles **parleraient**

To say that someone *would finish,* you need the complete conjugation for **finir** (*to finish*), a regular **-ir** verb.

finir (*to finish*)	
je **finirais**	nous **finirions**
tu **finirais**	vous **finiriez**
il/elle/on **finirait**	ils/elles **finiraient**

Regular -re verbs

For the conditional of regular **-re** verbs, things are almost the same as they are for regular **-er** and **-ir** verbs, except the **-e** of the **-re** infinitive is dropped. Follow these steps:

1. **Start with the infinitive and drop the final -e only.**

2. **Add one of the following endings, depending on the subject you're using: -ais, -ais, -ait, -ions, -iez, or -aient.**

    Be sure to choose the ending that matches the subject you need: for **je**, choose **-ais**; for **tu**, choose **-ais**; and so on.

Need an example? Here's the complete conjugation for **comprendre** (*to understand*), a regular **-re** verb.

comprendre (*to understand*)	
je **comprendrais**	nous **comprendrions**
tu **comprendrais**	vous **comprendriez**
il/elle/on **comprendrait**	ils/elles **comprendraient**

In each of the following phrases, change the infinitive in parentheses into the appropriate form of the conditional tense. Here's an example:

Q. Tu _____ à l'heure. **(finir)**

A. finirais

1. Je _____ avec toi. (**déjeuner**)

2. Ils _____ visite à Mamie. (**rendre**)

3. Nous _____. (**attendre**)

4. Elles _____. (**agir**)

5. Ils _____ mieux. (**danser**)

6. Tu _____. (**réussir**)

7. Vous _____ des sandwiches. (**préparer**)

8. Il _____. (**grossir**)

9. On _____ des champignons. (**chercher**)

10. Elle _____ sa voiture. (**vendre**)

Tackling Irregular Forms in the Conditional

Like any conjugation in French, the conditional has its share of irregular forms. But the good thing about these forms in the following sections is that they may look familiar to you, because the irregular verbs in the conditional are the same ones as the irregular verbs of the future (see Chapter 17). Two for one!

Verbs ending in -yer and -ayer

All verbs that have an infinitive in **-yer** like **employer** (*to employ/to use*) and **nettoyer** (*to clean*) have a slight irregularity in the conditional: Their **y** turns to **i**. Here's how to proceed:

1. **Start from the infinitive and change the y of the infinitive to an i, without dropping anything.**

   For example: **employer** changes to **emploier**.

2. **Add the usual conditional endings to it, choosing the one that matches your subject: -ais, -ais, -ait, -ions, -iez, or -aient.**

   Here's an example: For **je** choose **-ais**: **j'emploierais**.

Here's the complete conjugation for **employer** so you can see the change from **y** to **i**.

employer (*to employ*)	
j'**emploierais**	nous **emploierions**
tu **emploierais**	vous **emploieriez**
il/elle/on **emploierait**	ils/elles **emploieraient**

For **-ayer** verbs, the **y** also changes to **i**, but you also have the option of keeping it. I show you the complete conjugation of **payer** (*to pay*) with both options:

payer (*to pay*)	
je **paierais/payerais**	nous **paierions/payerions**
tu **paierais/payerais**	vous **paieriez/payeriez**
il/elle/on **paierait/payerait**	ils/elles **paieraient/payeraient**

Because **-yer** and **-ayer** are such similar endings, I suggest following the route of the common denominator, which goes from **y** to **i**. This way, you always get it right.

In each of the following phrases, change the infinitive in parentheses into the appropriate form of the conditional tense. Here's an example.

0. tu _____ (**payer**)

A. **paierais/payerais**

11. ils _____ (**employer**)

12. nous _____ (**tutoyer**)

13. je _____ (**nettoyer**)

14. elle _____ (**essayer**)

15. on _____ (**s'ennuyer**)

The verbs appeler and jeter

For **appeler** (*to call*) and **jeter** (*to throw*), all you need to do is double the consonant that precedes the infinitive ending and then add the conditional endings. Here's how to proceed to form the conditional of these two verbs:

1. **Start with the infinitive and drop the -er ending.**

   Appeler turns into **appel-**, and **jeter** turns into **jet-**.

2. **Double the last consonant you see (l for appeler, t for jeter) and put the -er ending back on.**

   appel +l + er

   jet + t + er

3. **Add the conditional ending that matches your subject: -ais, -ais, -ait, -ions, -iez, or -aient.**

   Here's an example: For **nous**, choose **-ions**: **appellerions/jetterions**.

Here's the complete conditional conjugation for **appeler**.

appeler (*to call*)	
j'**appellerais**	nous **appellerions**
tu **appellerais**	vous **appelleriez**
il/elle/on **appellerait**	ils/elles **appelleraient**

Here's the complete conditional conjugation for **jeter**.

jeter (*to throw*)	
je **jetterais**	nous **jetterions**
tu **jetterais**	vous **jetteriez**
il/elle/on **jetterait**	ils/elles **jetteraient**

Verbs ending in e/é plus a consonant plus -er

For all verbs that have an **e/é** + consonant immediately before the infinitive ending of **-er**, you change that **e/é** to an **è** on all forms of the conditional. Verbs of this kind include **acheter** (*to buy*), **enlever** (*to remove*), **répéter** (*to repeat*), **préférer** (*to prefer*), and **espérer** (*to hope*). Here's how to proceed to form the conditional of verbs like these:

1. **Start from the infinitive and drop the -er.**

   For example, **répéter** turns into **répét-**.

2. **Change the e/é + consonant to an è + consonant.**

   Here, **répét-** becomes **répèt-**.

3. **Put the -er back on.**

   In this example, **répèt-** becomes **répèter-**.

4. **Add the conditional ending that matches your subject: -ais, -ais, -ait, -ions, -iez, or -aient.**

   Here's an example: For **je**, choose **-ais: répèterais**.

Another example: Here's the complete conditional conjugation for **acheter**.

acheter (*to buy*)	
j'**achèterais**	nous **achèterions**
tu **achèterais**	vous **achèteriez**
il/elle/on **achèterait**	ils/elles **achèteraient**

Put the verbs in parentheses into the conditional. Check out this example to get started:

0. je _____ (amener)

A. j'amènerais

16. tu _____ (espérer)

17. il _____ (geler)

18. nous _____ (posséder)

19. vous _____ (répéter)

20. ils _____ (enlever)

Verbs with completely different stems in the conditional

For some irregular forms of the conditional, you can forget using the whole infinitive as the stem. A completely different stem replaces the good old infinitive, and your best bet is probably to plan on memorizing all the irregular stems. I put the most common ones in Table 18-1 for you.

Table 18-1	Irregular Verbs with Conditional Stems	
Infinitive	*Translation*	*Conditional Stem*
aller	*to go*	ir-
avoir	*to have*	aur-
devoir	*to have to*	devr-
envoyer	*to send*	enverr-
être	*to be*	ser-
faire	*to do*	fer-
pleuvoir	*to rain*	pleuvr-
pouvoir	*to be able to*	pourr-
recevoir	*to receive*	recevr-
savoir	*to know*	saur-
tenir	*to hold*	tiendr-
venir	*to come*	viendr-
voir	*to see*	verr-
vouloir	*to want*	voudr-

To form the conditional of these irregular verbs, proceed as follows:

1. **Start with the stem provided in Table 18-1.**

   For instance, for **venir** (*to come*), take **viendr-**.

2. **Add the usual conditional endings to it, choosing the one that matches your subject: -ais, -ais, -ait, -ions, -iez, or -aient.**

   For example, if you want to use the first person singular of **viendr-**, just add **-ais** to end with **je viendrais**.

Here are some other examples in action:

Je ferais la vaisselle maintenant si je n'étais pas occupé. (*I would do the dishes now if I were not busy.*)

Nous irions à la plage s'il faisait beau. (*We would go to the beach if the weather were nice.*)

Ils auraient plus de temps s'ils regardaient moins la télé. (*They would have more time if they watched TV less.*)

Put the infinitive in parentheses into the correct form of the conditional for each sentence. The verbs are all irregular.

0. S'il faisait beau, je _____ à la plage. (aller)

A. irais

21. Si elles avaient 90 ans, elles _____ vieilles! (être)

22. Qu'est-ce que vous _____ si vous n'aviez plus d'argent? (faire)

23. Si nous avions le temps nous _____ chez vous. (venir)

24. Si on achetait des billets on _____ voir le spectacle. (pouvoir)

25. Si j'avais mal aux dents, j'_____ chez le dentiste. (aller)

26. Si tu étais poli, tu _____ la porte. (tenir)

27. S'ils allaient à Paris, ils _____ la Tour Eiffel. (voir)

28. S'il était riche, il _____ un chateau. (avoir)

29. Si elle avait un chien, elle _____ le promener! (devoir)

30. Si tu étais le prof, tu _____ les réponses. (savoir)

Knowing When to Use the Conditional

Like in English, the conditional in French enables you to describe a hypothetical event (*it would happen if . . .*); politely express advice, offers, and wishes; and express a future event from a past context (*he said he would do that*). In the following sections, I show you how to say all those things in French.

Make sure you understand the context of a sentence in English before translating it into the conditional in French. Some English conditional words don't actually express the conditional:

- ✔ *Could* can mean *was able to*, which requires the **passé composé** (*present perfect*) in French. For example: *He could not do it* translates to **il n'a pas pu le faire.** Flip to Chapter 15 for more about the present perfect.

- ✔ *Would* can express a habitual action in the past, which requires the **imparfait** (*imperfect*) in French. For example: *He would see his grandmother every Thursday* translates to **Il allait voir sa grand-mère chaque jeudi.** See Chapter 16 for more about the imperfect.

Daydreaming about different situations

And now you find out why the conditional is called that. Any guesses? Yes, because it involves a condition! You state something conditional, like *if the weather were nice* or *if you didn't have to work*, and then you state what *would happen* if those conditions were met. But because it's all based on conditions, it's not likely to become reality, so I call it a daydream.

The condition is expressed in a **si** (*if*) clause with a verb in the imperfect, like this: **s'il faisait beau** (*if the weather was nice*). (Flip to Chapter 16 for details on the imperfect.) The other clause of the sentence, the part with the would-be result, uses the conditional. See it all at work in these examples:

> **Si elle avait une moto, elle achèterait un casque.** (*If she had a motorcycle, she would buy a helmet.*)

> **Si tu avais mal à la tête, tu prendrais une aspirine.** (*If you had a headache, you would take an aspirin.*)

The two clauses can switch order, but don't switch the verbs! Never put the conditional in a **si** clause. The verb in the conditional isn't part of the condition. For example:

> **Si nous étions trés riches nous aurions un château.** (*If we were very rich, we would have a castle.*) = **Nous aurions un château si nous étions trés riches.** (*We would have a castle if we were very rich.*)

The following situations are not good. *If* the conditions *were* different, then the results *would be* better. Use the conditional to improve these situations, and consult a French-English dictionary if you need help with vocabulary. Here's an example:

0. **Pierre n'étudie pas assez. Il a de mauvaises notes.** (*Pierre doesn't study enough. He has bad grades.*)

A. **Si Pierre étudiait assez, il n'aurait pas de mauvaises notes.** (*If Pierre studied enough, he wouldn't have bad grades.*)

31. **Je n'ai pas de moto. Je n'achète pas de casque!** (*I don't have a motorcycle. I'm not buying a helmet!*)

_____

32. **Albert ne travaille pas. Il est fauché.** (*Albert doesn't work. He's broke.*)

_____

33. **Elle est occupée. Elle ne vient pas.** (*She's busy. She's not coming.*)

_____

34. **Nous n'avons pas de livre. Nous ne lisons pas.** (*We don't have a book. We don't read.*)

_____

35. **Paul ne dort pas assez. Il est fatigué.** (*Paul doesn't sleep enough. He's tired.*)

_____

36. **Il pleut. Je reste à la maison.** (*It's raining. I'm staying home.*)

_____

37. **Elle a peur en avion. Elle ne prend jamais l'avion.** (*She's scared in planes. She never takes a plane.*)

_____

38. **La maison est sale. Nous faisons le ménage.** (*The house is dirty. We clean up.*)

_____

39. **Julie n'aime pas Paul. Elle ne se marie pas avec lui.** (*Julie is not in love with Paul. She isn't marrying him.*)

_____

40. **Il ne fait pas beau. Valérie ne va pas à la plage.** (*The weather is not nice. Valérie doesn't go to the beach.*)

_____

Giving friendly advice

Your good friend Paul is trying to grow a beard, but it really doesn't look good on him. You try to let him know (in a nice way) by saying something like, *Maybe you should shave it off. Should* is what allows you to soften the verb *shave* into advice rather than a command. The French equivalent of *should* is the conditional of **devoir** (*to have to/must*). (Note that **devoir** is completely irregular in the conditional; see the earlier section "Verbs with completely different stems in the conditional" for details.)

To give advice in French, use the conditional of **devoir** like this:

> Subject + **devoir** (in the conditional) + other verb (in infinitive)

For example: **Tu devrais raser ta barbe.** (*You should shave your beard.*)

The subject of **devoir** depends on who you're giving advice to. Table 18-2 helps you pick the right subject.

Table 18-2	Conditional Forms of Devoir to Use with Different People
Person(s) You're Advising	*Form of Devoir*
Yourself	**je devrais**
A familiar, singular person (speaking directly to)	**tu devrais**
A singular person (speaking indirectly about)	**il/elle devrait**
A group that includes you	**nous devrions**
A singular stranger (speaking directly to)	**vous devriez**
Several familiar people or strangers (speaking directly to)	**vous devriez**
A group of people (speaking indirectly about)	**ils/elles devraient**

Here are some examples:

> **Tu devrais manger moins de sucre.** (*You should eat less sugar.*)
>
> **Nous devrions prendre des vacances.** (*We should take some vacation.*)
>
> **Vous devriez penser aux autres!** (*All of you should think of others.*)

Making a polite request

To make a polite request of the *Could you . . .?* type, French uses the conditional of the verb **pouvoir** (*to be able to*) followed by the infinitive of the other verb. (Note that **pouvoir** is completely irregular in the conditional; see the earlier section "Verbs with completely different stems in the conditional" for details.) Here's how to proceed to express a polite request in French:

> Subject + conditional of **pouvoir** + infinitive of other verb + ?

The subject of **pouvoir** is the person you're asking a favor from, so I exclude **je** (*I*). Table 18-3 helps you pick the right subject.

Table 18-3	Conditional Forms of Pouvoir to Use with Different People
Person(s) You're Asking	*Form of Pouvoir*
A familiar, singular person (asking directly)	**tu pourrais**
A singular person (speaking indirectly about)	**il/elle pourrait**
A group that includes you	**nous pourrions**
A singular stranger (speaking directly to)	**vous pourriez**
Several familiar people or strangers (speaking directly to)	**vous pourriez**
A group of people (speaking indirectly about)	**ils/elles pourraient**

Here are some examples (see Chapter 9 for more about forming questions):

> **Est-ce que tu pourrais me prêter ta voiture demain?** (*Could you lend me your car tomorrow?*)

> **Pourriez-vous fermer la porte s'il vous plaît?** (*Could you close the door, please?*)

> **Est-ce que les étudiants pourraient venir plus tôt demain?** (*Could the students come earlier tomorrow?*)

Expressing offers and wishes

Depending on their subject, the verbs **vouloir** (*to want*) and **aimer** (*to like*) can express either an offer or a wish when they're in the conditional. Here's the conditional conjugation for **vouloir**:

vouloir (*to want*)	
je **voudrais**	nous **voudrions**
tu **voudrais**	vous **voudriez**
il/elle/on **voudrait**	ils/elles **voudraient**

Here's the complete conditional conjugation for **aimer**:

aimer (*to like*)	
j'**aimerais**	nous **aimerions**
tu **aimerais**	vous **aimeriez**
il/elle/on **aimerait**	ils/elles **aimeraient**

To express an offer like *Would you like some water?*, French has two options. They both use the conditional:

- ✔ Use **vouloir** in the conditional + whatever you're offering. For example:

  Voudrais-tu de l'eau? (*Would you like some water?*)

- ✔ Use **aimer** in the conditional + whatever you're offering. For example:

  Aimerait-il de l'aide? (*Would he like some help?*)

In both cases, the subject of the verb is the person you're offering something to, not you, the speaker. (See Chapter 9 for more details about the structure of questions.)

The verbs **vouloir** and **aimer** also can be used interchangeably to express a wish, and this time the subjects determine whose wish it is. If the subject is **je**, the wish of the speaker is expressed; if the subject is **ils**, that person's wish is expressed; and so on. Sentences should be constructed this way: Subject + verb in the conditional + infinitive and/or item wished for. Here are some examples:

> **Je voudrais commander s'il vous plait.** (*I'd like to order, please.*)
>
> **Bébé voudrait un ours en peluche pour Noël.** (*Baby would like a stuffed bear for Christmas.*)
>
> **Nous aimerions gagner le loto.** (*We would like to win the lottery.*)

Vouloir and **aimer** can be used interchangeably, but **vouloir** is the most common.

Discussing the future in a past context

The conditional is especially useful for talking about the future in a past context. Consider the following sentence: **Elle nous a dit que ce serait facile et c'était vrai.** (*She told us it would be easy, and it was.*) In this sentence, **serait** (*would be*) is the conditional expressing the future from a past context.

You can recognize such sentences by their introductory verb, which is always in a past tense: *They said yesterday that . . .* or *He promised that. . . .* Here are several examples:

> **Le maire a dit qu'il n'y aurait pas de marathon dimanche prochain.** (*The mayor said there would not be a marathon next Sunday.*)
>
> **Maman a promis qu'elle m'achèterait une voiture l'an prochain.** (*Mom promised that she would buy me a car next year.*)
>
> **Sherlock pensait qu'il pourrait arrêter l'assassin.** (*Sherlock thought he would be able to stop the murderer.*)
>
> **Hier, ils nous ont dit qu'il ferait froid aujourd'hui.** (*Yesterday they told us it would be cold today.*)

Determine whether the following sentences express polite advice, a polite request, a wish, or the future in a past context. Consult a French-English dictionary if you need help with any of the vocabulary.

Q. **Pourrais-tu parler plus fort?**

A. polite request

41. **La radio a annoncé qu'il ferait beau demain.** _____

42. **Elle voudrait se reposer.** _____

43. **Pourrais-tu m'expliquer le problème?** _____

44. **Vous devriez suivre sa recommandation.** _____

45. **Ils aimeraient visiter la France.** _____

46. **Pourriez-vous ouvrir la porte?** _____

47. **Tu devrais dormir plus.** _____

48. **Nous avons parié que ce candidat perdrait les élections.** _____

49. **Je savais que tu réussirais!** _____

50. **Tu ne devrais pas manger tout ce chocolat.** _____

Answer Key

1 déjeunerais

2 rendraient

3 attendrions

4 agiraient

5 danseraient

6 réussirais

7 prépareriez

8 grossirait

9 chercherait

10 vendrait

11 emploieraient

12 tutoierions

13 nettoierais

14 essaierait

15 s'ennuierait

16 espèrerais

17 gèlerait

18 possèderions

19 répèteriez

20 enlèveraient

21 seraient

22 feriez

23 viendrions

24 pourrait

25 irais

26 tiendrais

27 verraient

28 aurait

29 devrait

30 saurais

31 Si j'avais une moto, j'achèterais un casque! (*If I had a motorcycle, I would buy a helmet!*)

32 Si Albert travaillait, il ne serait pas fauché. (*If Pierre worked, he would not be broke.*)

33 Si elle n'était pas occupée, elle viendrait. (*If she wasn't busy, she would come.*)

34 Si nous avions un livre, nous lirions. (*If we had a book, we would read.*)

35 Si Paul dormait assez, il ne serait pas fatigué. (*If Paul slept enough, he would not be tired.*)

36 S'il ne pleuvait pas, je ne resterais pas à la maison. (*If it wasn't raining, I wouldn't stay at home.*)

37 Si elle n'avait pas peur en avion, elle prendrait l'avion. (*If she wasn't scared in the plane, she would take the plane.*)

38 Si la maison n'était pas sale, nous ne ferions pas le ménage. (*If the house wasn't dirty, we would not clean up.*)

39 Si Julie aimait Paul, elle se marierait avec lui. (*If Julie loved Paul, she would marry him/get married with him.*)

40 S'il faisait beau, Valérie irait à la plage. (*If the weather was nice, Valérie would go to the beach.*)

41 future in the past

42 wish

43 polite request

44 polite advice

45 wish

46 polite request

47 polite advice

48 future in the past

49 future in the past

50 polite advice

Chapter 19

Surveying the Subjunctive

· ·

· ·

*L*e subjonctif (*the subjunctive*) is a verb form that expresses the speaker's subjectivity, and it isn't exactly a tense. It's called a *mood,* and it has a present tense and a past tense. But for simplicity's sake, I just call the present subjunctive *the subjunctive* in this chapter.

Note: French has several super categories of tenses called moods. The *indicative* is the mood of facts, and it includes most of the common tenses like the present (see Chapter 6), the **passé composé** (*present perfect*; see Chapter 15), the **imparfait** (*imperfect*; see Chapter 16), and the future (see Chapter 17). Other moods are the conditional, which denotes hypothetical situations (see Chapter 18), and the imperative, used for commands (see Chapter 20).

The subjunctive is never by itself in a sentence. It has to be triggered by the main verb, and a sentence with a verb in the subjunctive must have two elements that other sentences don't have:

✔ It must begin with a specific phrase ending with the word **que** (*that*), which triggers the subjunctive in the second clause.

✔ It has two clauses, each with a different subject.

For example, in **j'ai peur qu'il pleuve** (*I'm afraid it may rain*) and **il veut que tu partes** (*He wants you to leave*), **j'ai peur que** (*I'm afraid that*) and **il veut que** (*he wants that*) are the trigger phrases, and the second clauses have different subjects.

The subjunctive form is uncommon in English, so English speakers need to recognize the triggers in order to get the hang of using the subjunctive in French. The forms and uses of the subjunctive are easy, as I show you in this chapter, so you can focus on those triggers and practice, practice, practice!

Familiarizing Yourself with Subjunctive Forms

If you're familiar with the present tense conjugations (see Chapter 6), you can be very comfortable conjugating the subjunctive, because it is formed from the third person plural of the present (**ils/elles**), for regular and irregular verbs alike.

Table 19-1 presents the subjunctive endings for each of the subjects of the conjugation. The subjunctive endings for **je**, **tu**, **il/elle/on**, and **ils/elles** are the same as those for the **je**, **tu**, **il/elle/on**, and **ils/elles** forms of present tense of regular **-er** verbs.

Table 19-1	Verb Endings Used in the Subjunctive
Subject	*Subjunctive Verb Ending*
je	-e
tu	-es
il/elle/on	-e
nous	-ions
vous	-iez
ils/elles	-ent

The following sections cover both regular and irregular subjunctive conjugations. ***Note:*** For clarity's sake, each time I list a subjunctive form, it's preceded by **que** to differentiate it from the regular present tense form.

Forming the subjunctive of regular verbs

To form the subjunctive of regular verbs, follow these easy steps:

1. **Find the ils/elles form of the present tense and drop the -ent.**

   For example, the present tense third person plural of the verb **parler** (*to speak*) is **parlent**. Drop the **-ent** ending to get **parl-**.

2. **Replace the -ent with the correct ending (see Table 19-1), making sure the ending corresponds to the subject you chose.**

   If you want the **nous** form of **parler**, add the ending **-ions** to the stem from Step 1 so you're left with **parlions**.

Here's the subjunctive conjugation of **aimer** (*to like*), a regular **-er** verb whose present tense **ils/elles** form is **aiment**.

aimer (*to like*)	
que j'**aime**	que nous **aimions**
que tu **aimes**	que vous **aimiez**
qu'il/elle/on **aime**	qu'ils/elles **aiment**

Regular verbs that end in **-ier**, like **étudier** (*to study*), end up with a double **i** in the **nous** and **vous** forms of the subjunctive, like this: **que nous étudiions**, **que vous étudiiez**.

Here's the subjunctive conjugation of **finir** (*to finish*), a regular **-ir** verb whose present tense **ils/elles** form is **finissent**.

finir (*to finish*)	
que je **finisse**	que nous **finissions**
que tu **finisses**	que vous **finissiez**
qu'il/elle/on **finisse**	qu'ils/elles **finissent**

Here's the subjunctive conjugation of **vendre** (*to sell*), a regular **-re** verb whose present tense **ils/elles** form is **vendent**.

vendre (*to sell*)	
que je **vende**	que nous **vendions**
que tu **vendes**	que vous **vendiez**
qu'il/elle/on **vende**	qu'ils/elles **vendent**

For each regular verb, give the **ils/elles** form of the present tense and then the **je** and **nous** forms of the subjunctive preceded by **que**. (Flip to Chapter 6 for information on the present tense if you need help.) Here's an example:

0. **chanter**

A. **ils chantent, que je chante, que nous chantions**

1. **manger**

_____   _____   _____

2. **choisir**

_____   _____   _____

3. **attendre**

_____   _____   _____

4. **réussir**

_____   _____   _____

5. **arriver**

_____   _____   _____

6. répondre

_____ _____ _____

7. penser

_____ _____ _____

8. finir

_____ _____ _____

9. travailler

_____ _____ _____

10. rendre

_____ _____ _____

Creating irregular subjunctive conjugations

Verbs with irregular subjunctive conjugations include verbs with two stems, such as **boire** (*to drink*); verbs that keep their irregular stems in the subjunctive; and verbs that are completely irregular in the subjunctive, such as the "fatal four" of **être** (*to be*), **avoir** (*to have*), **aller** (*to go*), and **faire** (*to do*), along with a few more that follow their own subjunctive tune!

Two-stem verbs

Two-stem verbs verbs are conjugated in the present tense with one stem for the **je**, **tu**, **il/elle/on**, and **il/elles** forms and another one for the **nous** and **vous** forms. This stem change carries over into the subjunctive.

For the **je**, **tu**, **il/elle/on**, and **il/elles** forms (stem 1), follow these steps for the subjunctive:

1. **Take the ils/elles form of the present and drop the -ent.**
2. **Replace -ent with the subjunctive ending that matches the subject you chose: -e for je, -es for tu, -e for il/elle/on, and -ent for ils/elles.**

For the **nous** and **vous** forms (stem 2), follow these steps for the subjunctive:

1. **Start with the nous form of the present and drop the -ons.**
2. **Replace -ons with the subjunctive ending that matches the subject you chose: -ions for nous, and -iez for vous.**

Table 19-2 shows you the stem change from present to subjunctive for some common two-stem verbs.

Table 19-2	The Subjunctive for Two-Stem Verbs			
Infinitive	*Stem 1: Present Tense ils/elles*	*Subjunctive je*	*Stem 2: Present Tense nous*	*Subjunctive nous*
acheter (*to buy*)	**achètent**	**que j'achète**	**achetons**	**que nous achetions**
appeler (*to call*)	**appellent**	**que j'appelle**	**appelons**	**que nous appelions**
boire (*to drink*)	**boivent**	**que je boive**	**buvons**	**que nous buvions**
payer (*to pay*)	**paient**	**que je paie**	**payons**	**que nous payions**
prendre (*to take*)	**prennent**	**que je prenne**	**prenons**	**que nous prenions**
venir (*to come*)	**viennent**	**que je vienne**	**venons**	**que nous venions**

Verbs that keep their irregular stems in the subjunctive

Some -**ir** and -**re** verbs are irregular in the present because they don't play fair and don't follow the pattern indicated by their ending. Good news for the subjunctive, though: No matter what the **ils** form looks like in present, it's still your stem for the subjunctive, and you use the same endings as I outline in the earlier section "Forming the subjunctive of regular verbs."

Table 19-3 gives you the present tense **ils** form of the most common of these irregular verbs, followed by the stem for the subjunctive.

Table 19-3	Stems for Irregular Verbs Used in the Subjunctive	
Infinitive	*Third Person Plural Form in the Present Tense*	*Stem for the Subjunctive*
dire (*to say*)	**ils disent**	**dis-**
dormir (*to sleep*)	**ils dorment**	**dorm-**
écrire (*to write*)	**ils écrivent**	**écriv-**
mettre (*to put*)	**ils mettent**	**mett-**
offrir (*to offer*)	**ils offrent**	**offr-**
partir (*to leave*)	**ils partent**	**part-**
sortir (*to write*)	**ils sortent**	**sort-**

Unfriendly irregular verbs

When you try to make them subjunctive, some irregular verbs are unfriendly because

✔ They don't follow any pattern at all in the present.

✔ They don't use their (already irregular) **ils/elles** form of the present to form their subjunctive stem.

So your best bet is to just memorize them! These verbs include the "fatal four": **être** (*to be*), **avoir** (*to have*), **aller** (*to go*), and **faire** (*to do*). They also include **pouvoir** (*to be able to*), **vouloir** (*to want*), and **savoir** (*to know*).

être (*to be*)	
que je **sois**	que nous **soyons**
que tu **sois**	que vous **soyez**
qu'il/elle/on **soit**	qu'ils/elles **soient**

avoir (*to have*)	
que j'**aie**	que nous **ayons**
que tu **aies**	que vous **ayez**
qu'il/elle/on **ait**	qu'ils/elles **aient**

aller (*to go*)	
que j'**aille**	que nous **allions**
que tu **ailles**	que vous **alliez**
qu'il/elle/on **aille**	qu'ils/elles **aillent**

faire (*to do/to make*)	
que je **fasse**	que nous **fassions**
que tu **fasses**	que vous **fassiez**
qu'il/elle/on **fasse**	qu'ils/elles **fassent**

pouvoir (*to be able to*)	
que je **puisse**	que nous **puissions**
que tu **puisses**	que vous **puissiez**
qu'il/elle/on **puisse**	qu'ils/elles **puissent**

vouloir (*to want*)	
que je **veuille**	que nous **voulions**
que tu **veuilles**	que vous **vouliez**
qu'il/elle/on **veuille**	qu'ils/elles **veuillent**

savoir (to know)	
que je **sache**	que nous **sachions**
que tu **saches**	que vous **sachiez**
qu'il/elle/on **sache**	qu'ils/elles **sachent**

The verbs **pleuvoir** (*to rain*) and **falloir** (*to be necessary*) are also unfriendly irregular verbs, but they have only the third singular form: **qu'il pleuve** (*that it may rain*) and **qu'il faille** (*that it may be necessary*).

For each irregular verb, give the irregular subjunctive for the indicated subjects. Here's an example:

0. aller: que j'_____, qu'elles _____

A. **que j'aille, qu'elles aillent**

11. avoir: que tu _____, que nous _____

12. être: que je _____, qu'ils _____

13. faire: que tu _____, que nous _____

14. pouvoir: que je _____, qu'ils _____

15. boire: qu'il _____, que vous _____

16. écrire: que tu _____, que vous _____

17. dire: qu'elle _____, que nous _____

18. sortir: que je _____, qu'ils _____

19. venir: que tu _____, qu'on _____

20. payer: qu'il _____, que nous _____

Recognizing Phrases That Trigger the Subjunctive

A number of phrases can trigger the subjunctive. They can have a personal subject, as in **Anne veut que** (*Anne wants that*) or **je préfère que** (*I prefer that*), or they can have an impersonal one, like **il faut que** (*It's necessary that*) or **il est bon que** (*It's good that*). Here is what you need to know about those triggers:

- ✔ The verb in a trigger phrase can be in any tense. For example, **je voudrais que** (*I would like that*) is in the conditional (see Chapter 18).

- ✔ A trigger phrase always ends in **que** (*that*). If it doesn't, then you can't use the subjunctive in the next clause.

In the following sections, I separate triggers into several categories:

- Personal and impersonal triggers of want/need/advice
- Personal and impersonal triggers of emotion/reaction
- Personal and impersonal triggers of doubt

Expressing wants, needs, and advice

French uses the subjunctive when one person wants, needs, prefers, recommends, or advises another person to do something.

This type of trigger is called expressions of want, need, and advice. Here's a list of the triggers of the personal variety (meaning a specific person or group of people is the subject):

- **apprécier que** (*to appreciate that*)
- **attendre que** (*to wait for*)
- **avoir besoin que** (*to need that*)
- **exiger que** (*to demand that*)
- **ne pas supporter que** (*to not being able to stand that*)
- **préférer que** (*to prefer that*)
- **proposer que** (*to propose to do*)
- **recommender que** (*to recommend that*)
- **refuser que** (*to refuse to do*)
- **souhaiter que** (*to wish that*)
- **suggérer que** (*to suggest that*)
- **vouloir que** (*to want that*)

The verb **espérer** (*to hope*) is not one of those trigger verbs, and it is never followed by the subjunctive. Instead, you use the present (although that option is rather uncommon), the future, or the **passé composé**.

Here are a few personal triggers in action:

> **Elle ne supporte pas que les enfants désobéissent.** (*She can't stand that the children disobey.*)

> **Le prof apprécie que nous parlions français en classe.** (*The professor appreciates that we speak French in class.*)

Here are a few impersonal trigger expressions of want/need/advice:

- **il est important que** (*it is important that*)
- **il faut que** (*it's necessary that*)
- **il ne faut pas que** (*one must not*)

> ✔ **il se peut que** (*it's possible that*)
>
> ✔ **il vaut mieux que** (*it's better that*)

In an impersonal trigger such as **il est important que**, any adjective expressing need can replace the adjective **important**: **essentiel** (*essential*), **utile** (*useful*), **indispensable** (*indispensible*), **bon** (*good*), and more.

Here are some impersonal triggers of want, need, and advice in action:

> **Il est important que les étudiants écoutent bien.** (*It's important that the students listen well.*)
>
> **Il vaut mieux que tu ailles voir le docteur.** (*It's better that you go see the doctor.*)

Translate the trigger expression in parentheses with the help of the preceding lists to complete the subjunctive sentences. Here's an example:

0. (*It's necessary that*) _____ tu sois à l'heure.

A. **Il faut que**

21. (*It's better that*) _____ nous disions la vérité.

22. (*I prefer that*) _____ tu viennes demain.

23. (*It's possible that*) _____ vous ayez raison.

24. (*He suggests that*) _____ nous commencions demain.

25. (*They want that*) _____ tu te dépêches.

Discussing feelings about what's happening

In the following sections, I give you a good number of phrases that you can use to express emotions like sadness, joy, surprise, or anger about an event that is occurring or will occur.

Trigger verbs that express emotion

Triggers can be regular verbs that express an emotion such as fear or a preference. They are conjugated with a personal subject (such as **je** or **tu**). Here are a few common ones:

> ✔ **admirer que** (*to admire that*)
>
> ✔ **aimer que** (*to like that*)
>
> ✔ **avoir peur que** (*to fear that*)
>
> ✔ **comprendre que** (*to understand that*)
>
> ✔ **craindre que** (*to fear that*)
>
> ✔ **s'inquiéter que** (*to worry that*)
>
> ✔ **se réjouir que** (*to rejoice that*)

Here are some of them in action:

> **J'ai peur qu'il pleuve demain**. (*I fear that it may rain tomorrow.*)
>
> **Nous admirons que tu puisses faire ça.** (*We admire that you can do that.*)
>
> **Il comprend que vous soyez déçus.** (*He understands that you may be disappointed.*)

Personal expressions with être + adjective

When personal expressions are involved, the subject of the verb **être** is the speaker reacting to a situation. In that case, use a personal subject like **je** or **tu** + the matching form of **être** + a matching adjective. (See Chapter 6 for the conjugation of this verb.) For example:

> **Elle est surprise que tu n'aimes pas le chocolat.** (*She is surprised that you don't like chocolate.*)
>
> **Nous sommes contents que tu viennes nous voir.** (*We are happy that you're coming to see us.*)

Here are some adjectives you can use in such triggers: **surpris** (*surprised*), **content** (*happy*), **triste** (*sad*), **désolé** (*sorry*), **inquiet** (*worried*), **flatté** (*flattered*), **fier** (*proud*), **déçu** (*disappointed*), and **choqué** (*shocked*).

Expressions starting with ça

To say that it annoys/surprises you or him or them that something is happening, French uses an impersonal phrase that begins with **ça** (*it/that*) and includes one of the following object pronouns to refer to the subject (the person *surprised*, *annoyed*, or what have you; see Chapter 13 for more about object pronouns): **me** (*me*), **te** (*you*), **le** (*him*), **la** (*her*), **nous** (*us*), **vous** (*you*), or **les** (*them*). For example: **Ça me surprend que tu sois là.** (*It surprises me that you're here.*)

Ça can be the subject of verbs like **déranger** (*to bother*), **intéresser** (*to interest*), **amuser** (*to amuse*), **surprendre** (*to surprise*), **plaire** (*to please*), **inquiéter** (*to worry*), **énerver** (*to annoy*), and **rendre** (+ adjective) (*to make* + adjective).

Here are some examples:

> **Ça vous dérange que je fume?** (*Does it bother you that I smoke?*)
>
> **Ça la rend triste que tu sois malade.** (*It makes her sad that you're sick.*)

Note: Ça is an impersonal trigger but it nonetheless tells how the personal speaker feels.

Expressions with il est/c'est + adjective

Use the impersonal **il est** or **c'est** (*it is*) followed by the masculine singular form of a (relevant) adjective to describe a situation (see Chapter 3 for details on knowing when to use each phrase). For example:

> **Il est étonnant qu'il fasse si chaud en décembre.** (*It is surprising that it's so warm in December.*)
>
> **C'est bizarre qu'il n'y ait pas de bruit. . . .** (*It's strange that there are no noises. . . .*)

Here's a sampling of such adjectives: **dommage** (*too bad*), **bizarre** (*strange*), **fou** (*crazy*), **amusant** (*funny*), **triste** (*sad*), **honteux** (*shameful*), **étonnant** (*astonishing*), **bête** (*silly*), **inquiétant** (*worrysome*), **triste** (*sad*), **surprenant** (*surprising*), **super** (*great*), and **regrettable** (*regrettable*).

Put the following sentences, which express feelings, into English. Check out a French-English dictionary if you need help with any vocabulary. Here's an example:

Q. **Nous sommes contents que tu viennes.**

A. *We're happy that you're coming.*

26. **J'ai peur que vous ne compreniez pas.**

_____

27. **Ça les surprend que tu chantes bien.**

_____

28. **Il est honteux qu'ils ne disent pas la vérité.**

_____

29. **Ça m'inquiète que les enfants soient en retard.**

_____

30. **Il est dommage qu'il habite si loin.**

_____

Showing doubt

When you want to express doubt about something that is happening or is going to happen (or not), use one of the following trigger verbs followed by the subjunctive: **douter que** (*to doubt that*), **nier que** (*to deny that*), **ne pas croire que** (*to not believe that*), **ne pas penser que** (*to not think that*), or **ne pas trouver que** (*to not find that*).

Here are some examples:

> **Je ne trouve pas que vous vous ressembliez.** (*I don't find that you look alike.*)

> **Le juge doute que tu sois coupable.** (*The judge doubts that you're guilty.*)

A number of impersonal expressions with **il est/c'est** + *[relevant adjective]* also indicate doubt. Such adjectives include: **impossible** (*impossible*), **impensable** (*unthinkable*), **douteux** (*doubtful*), and **faux** (*false*). For example: **Il est impossible que tu puisses manger tout ça!** (*It's impossible that you can eat all that.*)

Keeping the Number of Subjects in Mind

The subjunctive cannot happen on its own, so the subjunctive construction requires two clauses, each one with a subject. For example, **il faut que tu partes** (*it's necessary for you to leave*) has two different subjects, and **que** separates the trigger from the second clause. Sentences with one subject but two verbs don't use the subjunctive. Get the scoop in the following sections.

Sticking with the subjunctive in two-subject sentences

Here is the formula for a French sentence with a verb in subjunctive:

> Trigger with subject 1 + **que** + subject 2 + verb in subjunctive.

For example: **Je voudrais que tu viennes demain soir.** (*I would like for you to come tomorrow night.*)

As you can see from this example, the English sentence equivalent to a French subjunctive sentence follows a different formula, one that goes more like this: Trigger with subject 1 + object pronoun + verb in infinitive. And if you try to literally apply that same pattern in French (something like **je te veux m'aider**), the sentence will fail.

For the following English sentences, indicate whether the subject of the trigger expression is different from the subject of the other verb and therefore would require the subjunctive in French. Write **oui** (*yes*) if they are different and if you would use subjunctive in French; write **non** (*no*) if it's not the case.

0. *They want me to come.*

A. **oui**

31. *I would like to go on vacation.* _____

32. *They need to help me.* _____

33. *It's better that we work together.* _____

34. *I'm happy to see you.* _____

35. *It's necessary to go to the library.* _____

36. *The teacher wants the students to succeed.* _____

37. *I'm afraid it's going to rain.* _____

38. *I don't like that you come home after 12.* _____

39. *He's afraid he's going to meet the wolf.* _____

40. *What do you want me to do?* _____

Using the infinitive rather than the subjunctive in one-subject sentences

After you are more familiar with the trigger phrases (see the earlier section "Recognizing Phrases That Trigger the Subjunctive"), you can't get carried away! I simply mean that you can't use the subjunctive every time an expression like **je veux** (*I want*) or **j'ai peur** (*I'm afraid*) comes around. Keep in mind the second requirement for the subjunctive: two distinct subjects, one for each clause of the sentence.

If you *want to go on vacation*, or if *you're afraid you're going to be late*, the same subject (that's you) does all the actions. Therefore you don't need **que** to introduce the second subject, and so you can't have the subjunctive in this type of sentence. Instead, French uses the infinitive, like this:

> **Je voudrais partir en vacances.** (*I'd like to go on vacation.*)

> **Il vaut mieux se protéger du soleil.** (*It's better to protect oneself from the sun.*)

The formula for a single subject sentence is: Trigger phrase (without **que**) + infinitive. Now, depending on the trigger, you need to tweak that formula just a little:

- ✔ When the trigger is **être** (*to be*) + adjective, use **de** before the next infinitive. For example:

  > **Elle est énervée d'être malade.** (*She is annoyed to be sick.*)

  > **Il est important de boire de l'eau.** (*It's important to drink water.*)

- ✔ When the trigger is an expression with **avoir** (*to have*), such as **avoir envie** (*to feel like*), use **de** before the next infinitive. For example:

  > **J'ai peur d'être en retard.** (*I'm afraid I'm going to be late.*)

- ✔ When the trigger is the verb **regretter** (*to regret*), use **de** before the next infinitive. For example:

  > **Il regrette de ne pas pouvoir t'aider.** (*He regrets that he is unable to help you.*)

Avoiding a Few Pitfalls

After you're familiar with subjunctive constructions, you need to be sure that you're using them properly. The following sections tell you what to look for in order to not fall in the traps.

Picking out false triggers

False triggers are tricky verbs that dress up just like trigger verbs with a **que** (which is the first requirement for the subjunctive) and sneak into a sentence with two distinct subjects (the second requirement for the subjunctive), such that the whole sentence looks like the formula of the subjunctive even though it's not! Here's one example: **J'espère que vous comprenez.** (*I hope that you understand.*) In this sentence, **comprenez** is not in the subjunctive, even though it follows what seems to be a trigger phrase.

A number of very common verbs fall into this false trigger category: These verbs often express reported speech, such as *he said that* and *you answered that*:

- **dire que** (*to say that*)
- **écrire que** (*to write that*)
- **entendre dire que** (*to hear that*)
- **espérer que** (*to hope that*)
- **être sûr que** (*to be certain that*)
- **expliquer que** (*to explain that*)
- **il paraît que** (*it seems that/rumor has it*)
- **promettre que** (*to promise that*)
- **raconter que** (*to tell that*)
- **répondre que** (*to answer that*)
- **savoir que** (*to know that*)
- **se souvenir que** (*to remember that*)

Entendre dire is always conjugated in the present perfect (see Chapter 15) and it introduces a verb in the pluperfect (see Chapter 21). For example, **J'ai entendu dire que Pierre avait eu un accident.** (*I heard that Pierre had an accident.*)

Here they are in action:

Nous savons que tu dis la vérité. (*We know you're telling the truth.*)

Je suis sûr que j'ai oublié de fermer à clé. (*I am certain I forgot to lock up.*)

Il a répondu qu'il ne savait pas. (*He answered that he didn't know.*)

Staying aware of turncoat verbs

Some verbs alternate between subjunctive and indicative depending on whether they're affirmative, negative, or interrogative. They are verbs of opinion, like **penser que** (*to think that*), and verbs that express certainty, like **il est certain que** (*it's certain that*). Here's what you need to know:

✔ When a trigger of this type is affirmative, the verb that follows is not in the subjunctive (it can be in any tense). For example:

>**Je pense qu'il fera beau demain.** (*I think it will be nice tomorrow.*)

In this example, the second verb is in the future tense.

✔ When a trigger of this type is negative or interrogative (inversion only), the verb that follows is in the subjunctive. For example:

>**Je ne pense pas qu'il fasse beau demain.** (*I don't think it will be nice tomorrow.*)

Verbs of this kind include personal expressions like **penser que** (*to think that*), **croire que** (*to believe that*), and **trouver que** (*to find that*), and impersonal expressions like **il semble que** (*it seems that*), **il est vrai que** (*it is true that*), and **il est évident que** (*it is obvious that*).

The following practice questions are to help you recognize true subjunctive sentences from the others. Look at each sentence and put the verb in parentheses in the subjunctive or in the present or future, like in the following example. (See Chapter 6 for details on the present tense and Chapter 17 for more about the future tense.)

0. Je pense qu'il _____ raison. (avoir)

A. a

41. Je sais que tu _____ toujours. (réussir)

42. Il est important que nous _____ bien. (écouter)

43. Il n'est pas sûr que nous _____ venir samedi. (pouvoir)

44. Tu te souviens qu'ils _____ au premier étage? (habiter)

45. Mes parents veulent que je _____ des études. (faire)

46. Ils pensent que je _____ sérieux. (être)

47. Pensez-vous qu'il y _____ des habitants sur Mars? (avoir)

48. Je ne trouve pas qu'ils _____ très intéressants. (être)

49. Il comprend que vous _____ tôt. (partir)

50. Je te promets que je _____ l'histoire plus tard. (raconter)

Answer Key

1 ils mangent, que je mange, que nous mangions

2 ils choisissent, que je choisisse, que nous choisissions

3 ils attendent, que j'attende, que nous attendions

4 ils réussissent, que je réussisse, que nous réussissions

5 ils arrivent, que j'arrive, que nous arrivions

6 ils répondent, que je réponde, que nous répondions

7 ils pensent, que je pense, que nous pensions

8 ils finissent, que je finisse, que nous finissions

9 ils travaillent, que je travaille, que nous travaillions

10 ils rendent, que je rende, que nous rendions

11 que tu aies, que nous ayons

12 que je sois, qu'ils soient

13 que tu fasses, que nous fassions

14 que je puisse, qu'ils puissent

15 qu'il boive, que vous buviez

16 que tu écrives, que vous écriviez

17 qu'elle dise, que nous disions

18 que je sorte, qu'ils sortent

19 que tu viennes, qu'on vienne

20 qu'il paie, que nous payions

21 Il vaut mieux que

22 Je préfère que

23 Il se peut que

24 Il suggère que

`25` **Ils veulent que**

`26` *I'm afraid that you don't understand.*

`27` *It surprises them that you can sing well.*

`28` *It's a shame that they don't tell the truth.*

`29` *It worries me that the kids are late.*

`30` *It's too bad that he lives so far.*

`31` **non**

`32` **non**

`33` **oui**

`34` **non**

`35` **non**

`36` **oui**

`37` **oui**

`38` **oui**

`39` **non**

`40` **oui**

`41` **réussis**

`42` **écoutions**

`43` **puissions**

`44` **habitent**

`45` **fasse**

`46` **suis**

`47` **ait**

`48` **soient**

`49` **partiez**

`50` **raconterai**

Chapter 20

Giving Orders with the Imperative

· ·

In This Chapter

▶ Commanding something to happen

▶ Telling people *not* to do something

▶ Combining commands and pronouns

· ·

When something is *imperative,* that means it must be done. The **impératif** is the verb form of commands. For example, when you want children to listen to your instructions, you say **Écoutez bien**! (*Listen carefully!*) (Of course, using an exclamation mark isn't required, but it adds punch to your command.) The imperative is also the verb form you use when you want to prohibit someone from doing something — in other words, a negative command. For example, **Ne regarde pas la télé!** (*Don't watch TV!*)

In this chapter, I explain how to create commands, both affirmative and negative, and I show you how to add an object pronoun to any command so you can be more specific.

Making Affirmative Commands

An affirmative command is when you directly tell someone to do something. You can tell a single person, as in **écoute** (*listen*), or a group of people, as in **écoutez** (*listen*); or you can include yourself in a group of people, as in **écoutons** (*let's listen*). This section presents regular commands and irregular commands and shows you how to make a command for a pronominal verb.

Grasping the three forms

Before you give an order, target your subject. Who are you ordering? One person? Several? Are you including yourself in the command? The imperative has three forms (unlike English, which has two), and the one you choose depends on who you're talking to:

▸ Second person singular corresponds to **tu**

▸ Second person plural corresponds to **vous**

▸ First person plural corresponds to **nous**

But you don't actually use those subject pronouns (**tu**, **vous**, or **nous**) when uttering the command. The imperative is the only French verb form that doesn't use a subject. The verb endings are the only clue as to who the command is directed at (see Chapter 6 for an introduction to verb endings). For example, here are the commands for the regular **-er** verb **danser** (*to dance*):

✔ When you hear **Danse!** (*Dance!*), you know it's a singular *you* command because of the **-e** ending.

✔ When you hear **Dansons!** (*Let's dance!*), the command is undoubtedly addressed to a group that includes yourself because of the **-ons** ending.

✔ When you hear **Dansez!** (*Dance!*), you know the command is addressed to **vous** because of the **-ez** ending. You still have to determine which **vous** it is, but the context surely tells you that. (The three meanings of **vous** are the formal singular, the formal plural, and the informal plural; see Chapter 6 for details.)

Here are the guidelines for using the different forms:

✔ **Tu:** Use the **tu** form of the imperative to order a person you normally say **tu** to: a friend, a family member, your spouse, a child, or anyone else you speak informally to. Here are a couple of examples:

> To your sister: **Allume la lumière s'il te plaît.** (*Turn on the light, please.*)

> To a child: **Fais tes devoirs.** (*Do your homework.*)

✔ **Nous:** Use the **nous** form of the imperative to order a group of people that includes yourself. Here are some examples:

> **Allons au restaurant ce soir.** (*Let's go to the restaurant tonight.*)

> **Prenons le bus au lieu de la voiture.** (*Let's take the bus instead of the car.*)

✔ **Vous:** Use the **vous** form of the imperative in the following situations:

- To order a single person you normally say **vous** to: a professor, a person you don't know, a sales clerk, or anyone else you speak formally to. For example, if you were giving directions to a stranger on the street, you'd say: **Prenez la première rue à gauche.** (*Take the first left.*)

- To give a direction to more than one person you normally say vous to. For example, **Mesdames et messieurs, entrez dans la salle de conférence, s'ils vous plaît.** (*Ladies and gentlemen, please enter the conference room.*)

- To order more than one person you normally say **tu** to. For example, if speaking to a group of children, you might say, **Rentrez tout de suite!** (*Come in right now!*)

Forming the imperative of regular verbs

You'll be pleased to know that the conjugation of the imperative is fairly easy. In fact, it's not even a conjugation per se, because it borrows its forms from the present tense for the most part. (If you want to brush up on the present tense, go to Chapter 6.) The following sections provide information on how to form the imperative of regular **-er**, **-ir**, and **-re** verbs.

Regular -er verbs

To form the imperative of regular **-er** verbs and the irregular **-er** verb **aller** (*to go*), take the present tense form of the verb that corresponds to **tu** (minus the **s** of the **-es** ending), **nous** (**-ons**) or **vous** (**-ez**), and drop their subject pronouns. As an example, the following list shows you the **tu**, **nous**, and **vous** present tense forms of **parler** (*to speak*), side by side with the corresponding imperative forms.

Present Tense	*Imperative*
tu parles (*you speak*)	**parle** (*speak*)
nous parlons (*we speak*)	**parlons** (*let's speak*)
vous parlez (*you speak*)	**parlez** (*speak*)

Give the English translation for the following French commands. To distinguish between the two forms of *you*, write *you singular* and *you plural*.

0. **Parlons.**

A. *Let's talk.*

1. **Dansez.** _____

2. **Écoute.** _____

3. **Regarde.** _____

4. **Allons.** _____

5. **Mange.** _____

Regular -ir verbs

To form the the imperative of regular **-ir** verbs, take the present tense forms for **tu** (**-is**), **nous** (**-issons**), and **vous** (**-issez**) and drop the subject pronouns. Unlike **-er** verbs, you don't drop the **-s** of the second person singular; all three forms are borrowed exactly from the present tense. For example, the following list shows you the **tu**, **nous**, and **vous** present tense forms of **finir** (*to finish*), side by side with the corresponding imperative forms.

Present Tense	*Imperative*
tu finis (*you finish*)	**finis** (*finish*)
nous finissons (*we finish*)	**finissons** (*let's finish*)
vous finissez (*you finish*)	**finissez** (*finish*)

Regular -re verbs

To form the the imperative of regular **-re** verbs, proceed the same way as for **-er** and **-ir** verbs. Take the present tense forms for **tu** (**-s**), **nous** (**-ons**), and **vous** (**-ez**) and drop the subject pronouns. All three forms are borrowed exactly from the present tense. For example, the following list shows you the **tu**, **nous**, and **vous** present tense forms of **vendre** (*to sell*), side by side with the corresponding imperative forms.

Present Tense	*Imperative*
tu vends (*you sell*)	**vends** (*sell*)
nous vendons (*we sell*)	**vendons** (*let's sell*)
vous vendez (*you sell*)	**vendez** (*sell*)

Complete the sentences below, conjugating the infinitive in parentheses into a command that matches the subject in parentheses.

Q. _____ ta vieille voiture. (**vendre**; to your mother)

A. **Vends**

6. _____ aux questions. (**répondre**; to the students)

7. _____ nos livres à la bibliothèque. (**rendre**; you and your fellow students)

8. _____ dans la vie. (**réussir**; to your children)

9. _____ les bons conseils. (**écouter**; to a family member)

10. _____ l'artiste. (**applaudir**; you and your friend)

11. _____ vite! (**agir**; to the students)

12. _____ le bip sonore. (**attendre**; to a stranger)

13. _____ de crier. (**arrêter**; to your children)

14. _____ ensemble. (**jouer**; you and your fellow students)

15. _____ bien! (**réfléchir**; to a family member)

Introducing irregular forms

Most irregular verbs form their imperative regularly, by borrowing their three forms directly from the present tense (see the preceding section). As a result, the following sections are really a refresher of the irregular present tense conjugations that I provide in Chapter 6. And who couldn't use one? (But watch out — some verbs don't form the imperative from their present tense conjugations. I cover these verbs in this section as well.)

Moody -er verbs

The **-er** verbs that I consider to be moody are

- Verbs ending in **-cer** or **-ger**
- Verbs ending in **-yer**
- Verbs ending in **é/e** + consonant + **-er**
- The verb **appeler** (*to call*)

To form the the imperative of moody **-er** verbs, use the present tense forms for **tu** (minus the **s** of the **-es** ending), **nous** (**-ons**), and **vous** (**-ez**) without their subject pronouns. All the tweaking you apply to moody **-er** verbs for the present tense transfers to the imperative (see Chapter 6 for details). Table 20-1 gives you examples of these verbs and the imperative for each kind.

Table 20-1	Imperatives of Some Moody -er Verbs		
Infinitive	*Imperative Tu*	*Imperative Nous*	*Imperative Vous*
appeler (*to call*)	**appelle** (*call*)	**appelons** (*let's call*)	**appelez** (*call*)
lancer (*to throw*)	**lance** (*throw*)	**lançons** (*let's throw*)	**lancez** (*throw*)
manger (*to eat*)	**mange** (*eat*)	**mangeons** (*let's eat*)	**mangez** (*eat*)
payer (*to pay*)	**paie** (*pay*)	**payons** (*let's pay*)	**payez** (*pay*)
répéter (*to repeat*)	**répète** (*repeat*)	**répétons** (*let's repeat*)	**répétez** (*repeat*)

Put the following moody -er verbs into the commands forms indicated in parentheses.

0. **payer** (tu)

A. Paie!

16. envoyer (vous) _____

17. voyager (nous) _____

18. commencer (tu) _____

19. régler (vous) _____

20. nettoyer (tu) _____

Three -ir verbs that act like -er verbs

Three **-ir** verbs behave like regular **-er** verbs in the present tense. They are **ouvrir** (*to open*), **offrir** (*to offer*), and **souffrir** (*to suffer*). To conjugate them, you drop the **-ir** ending and replace it with one of the **-er** verb endings, depending on the subject: **-e, -es, -e, -ons, -ez, -ent**. By extension, their imperative is also the same as for **-er** verbs. For example, here are the three imperative forms of **ouvrir: ouvre** (*open*), **ouvrons** (*let's open*), and **ouvrez** (*open*).

A variety of irregular verbs

The same thing you do for moody -**er** verbs earlier in this chapter is true for the more irregular verbs, like short -**ir** verbs, such as **partir** (*to leave*), **sortir** (*to go out*), **dormir** (*to sleep*); -**ir** verbs behaving like -**er** verbs, such as **ouvrir** (*to open*) and **offrir** (*to offer*); and other irregular verbs listed in Table 20-2. (Also see Chapter 6 for details).

In other words, use the present tense forms for **tu**, **nous**, and **vous** without their subject pronouns. All the tweaking you apply to these verbs for the present tense transfers to the imperative.

Table 20-2	Imperatives of Common Irregular Verbs		
Infinitive	*Imperative Tu*	*Imperative Nous*	*Imperative Vous*
apprendre (*to learn*)	**apprends** (*learn*)	**apprenons** (*let's learn*)	**apprenez** (*learn*)
boire (*to drink*)	**bois** (*drink*)	**buvons** (*let's drink*)	**buvez** (*drink*)
dire (*to tell*)	**dis** (*tell*)	**disons** (*let's tell*)	**dites** (*tell*)
écrire (*to write*)	**écris** (*write*)	**écrivons** (*let's write*)	**écrivez** (*write*)
faire (*to do/make*)	**fais** (*do*)	**faisons** (*let's do*)	**faites** (*do*)
mettre (*to put*)	**mets** (*put*)	**mettons** (*let's put*)	**mettez** (*put*)
partir (*to leave*)	**pars** (*leave*)	**partons** (*let's leave*)	**partez** (*leave*)
venir (*to come*)	**viens** (*come*)	**venons** (*let's come*)	**venez** (*come*)
voir (*to see*)	**vois** (*see*)	**voyons** (*let's see*)	**voyez** (*see*)

Four verbs that don't use the present tense for the imperative

Four verbs don't borrow the present tense forms to make their imperative. They are **avoir** (*to have*), **être** (*to be*), **savoir** (*to know*), and to some extent **vouloir** (*to want*). In fact, their forms come from the subjunctive conjugation (see Chapter 19 for more on the subjunctive).

The following list shows you the **tu**, **nous**, and **vous** present tense forms of **avoir** with the corresponding imperative forms:

Present Tense	*Imperative*
tu as (*you have*)	**aie** (*have*)
nous avons (*we have*)	**ayons** (*let's have*)
vous avez (*you have*)	**ayez** (*have*)

In the imperative **nous** and **vous** forms of **avoir**, the **a** sounds like **é**. (Flip to Chapter 2 for an introduction to sounding out French words.)

The following list shows you the **tu**, **nous**, and **vous** present tense forms of **être** with the corresponding imperative forms.

Present Tense	*Imperative*
tu es (*you are*)	**sois** (*be*)
nous sommes (*we are*)	**soyons** (*let's be*)
vous êtes (*you are*)	**soyez** (*be*)

The following list shows you the **tu**, **nous**, and **vous** present tense forms of **savoir** with the corresponding imperative forms.

Present Tense	*Imperative*
tu sais (*you know*)	**sache** (*know*)
nous savons (*we know*)	**sachons** (*let's know*)
vous savez (*you know*)	**sachez** (*know*)

Vouloir behaves a little differently from the previous three verbs. It is used in fixed phrases of extreme formality and therefore doesn't have a **tu** form, because **tu** is the informal address. As to the **nous** form, well, it just isn't used in French. So you're left with only the **vous** form! Here it is: **veuillez**.

The best way to translate **veuillez** in English is to say *please*, as in **veuillez patienter** (*please wait*) or even more formal, *if you would*. The funny thing is that in French, you also often add **s'il vous plaît** (*please*) at the end of such a command. Here are a few more examples of very formal **veuillez**:

> **Veuillez me suivre, s'il vous plaît.** (*If you would, follow me please.*)

> **Veuillez remplir ce formulaire.** (*If you would, fill out this form.*)

Using the imperative of **savoir** and **vouloir** makes your request/command very formal. In an informal everyday context, avoid using them. You always have an alternative way to form the imperative available.

Dealing with pronominal verbs

Pronominal verbs are conjugated with an extra pronoun called a reflexive pronoun. (For the lowdown on pronominal verbs, go to Chapter 7). For example, **je m'amuse** (*I have fun*) has the subject pronoun **je** and also the reflexive pronoun **me**. All pronominal verbs, like the verbs earlier in this chapter, borrow their imperative forms directly from the present tense. You drop the subject pronoun but keep the reflexive pronoun. Now the question is, where do you put it? In the present tense, reflexive pronouns come before the verb they're attached to, like this:

> **Vous vous dépêchez.** (*You hurry.*)

However, in a command form, the reflexive pronoun follows the verb and is attached to it by a hyphen, like this:

Dépêchez-vous! (*Hurry up!*)

And in the command form, the reflexive pronoun **te** is replaced by **toi**, which is attached to the verb with a hyphen like this: **Lève-toi tôt** (*Get up early*) and **Réveille-toi!** (*Wake up!*)

Here's an example: The following list shows you the **tu**, **nous**, and **vous** present tense forms of **s'amuser** (*to have fun*) with the corresponding imperative forms.

Present Tense	*Imperative*
tu t'amuses (*you have fun*)	**amuse-toi** (*have fun*)
nous nous amusons (*we have fun*)	**amusons-nous** (*let's have fun*)
vous vous amusez (*you have fun*)	**amusez-vous** (*have fun*)

Here are more examples.

Repose-toi. Tu as l'air fatigué. (*Rest up. You look tired.*)

Dépêchons-nous! Nous allons être en retard. (*Let's hurry! We're going to be late.*)

Arrêtez-vous quand il y a un bus scolaire. (*Stop when there's a school bus.*)

Please be quiet. Go away! Sit down! Aren't those very common expressions? And yet, the French equivalents of those pronominal verbs are super irregular! So for reference, because they're so useful and rather difficult to handle, I give you their full imperative forms in Table 20-3.

Table 20-3	Imperative of Some Irregular Prominal Verbs		
Infinitive	*Tu Form*	*Nous Form*	*Vous Form*
s'asseoir (*to sit down*)	**assieds-toi** (*sit down*)	**asseyons-nous** (*let's sit down*)	**asseyez-vous** (*sit down*)
se taire (*to be quiet*)	**tais-toi** (*be quiet*)	**taisons-nous** (*let's be quiet*)	**taisez-vous** (*be quiet*)
s'en aller (*to leave*)	**va-t'en** (*leave*)	**allons-nous en** (*let's leave*)	**allez-vous en** (*leave*)

Here they are in action:

Asseyez-vous tout de suite. (*Sit down immediately.*)

Tais-toi! Je travaille. (*Be quiet. I'm working.*)

Ce film est ennuyeux. Allons-nous en. (*This movie is boring. Let's leave.*)

Give the French equivalent of the following commands (consult a French-English dictionary if you're unfamiliar with any vocabulary).

0. *Be good in class.* (plural)

A. **Soyez sages.**

21. *Be quiet!* (singular) _____

22. *Relax during the holidays.* (plural) _____

23. *Let's get up early today!* _____

24. *Do the dishes please.* (plural) _____

25. *Have fun.* (singular) _____

Forming Negative Commands

Somebody is about to cross the street, oblivious of a speeding car. You shout, **Ne traversez pas!** (*Don't cross!*) That's a negative command, which must start with *don't* in English and **ne** in French. French negative imperatives are formed by borrowing the corresponding negative present tense forms for all verbs (whether they're regular or irregular).

To form the negative commands for **-er**, **-ir**, and **-re** verbs, proceed exactly like with affirmative commands (which I cover earlier in this chapter): Take the present tense verb form of **tu**, **nous**, and **vous** and drop the subject. Then add **ne** in front of it all and **pas** at the end.

For example, here are the three negative imperative forms for the regular **-er** verb **parler** (*to speak*), with the negative present tense next to it for comparison.

Present Tense, Negative	*Negative Imperative*
tu ne parles pas (*you don't speak*)	**ne parle pas** (*don't speak*)
nous ne parlons pas (*we don't speak*)	**ne parlons pas** (*let's not speak*)
vous ne parlez pas (*you don't speak*)	**ne parlez pas** (*don't speak*)

Here are more examples of negative commands in action:

> **Ne parlez pas fort quand bébé dort.** (*Don't talk loud when Baby is asleep.*)
>
> **Je n'aime pas cet endroit. Ne restons pas ici.** (*I don't like this place. Let's not stay here.*)
>
> **Ne finis pas ton dessert.** (*Don't finish your dessert.*)

When using pronominal verbs, you have to remember a big difference between affirmative commands and negative ones: The pronoun is switched back to the front. Here's how you tell someone to not worry (**s'inquiéter**), for instance. For the **tu** form, take the negative of the present tense: **Tu ne t'inquiètes pas.** Drop the **s** (because it's an **-er** verb) and drop the subject pronoun: **Ne t'inquiète pas** (*Don't worry*). Do the same thing with the **nous** and **vous** forms: **Ne nous inquiétons pas** (*Let's not worry*) and **Ne vous inquiétez pas** (*Don't worry*). Et voilà!

Change the following commands into negative commands. The practice includes **-er** verbs (regular and moody) and also **-ir** and **-re** verbs.

Q. **Prends ce livre.** (*Take that book.*)

A. **Ne prends pas.**

26. **Mangeons ces biscuits.** (*Let's eat those cookies.*)

_____

27. **Ouvrez la porte!** (*Open the door.*)

_____

28. **Avançons lentement.** (*Let's progress slowly.*)

_____

29. **Posez des questions.** (*Ask questions.*)

_____

30. **Arrive en retard.** (*Arrive late.*)

_____

Adding an Object Pronoun to Your Command

If you want Julie to pass you the salt, you say *Pass me the salt, please* (**Passe-moi le sel s'il te plaît**). In this command, *me* is an object pronoun. And if someone looks at you funny, you may want to tell them: *Don't look at me like that* (**Ne me regardez pas comme ça**). Again, you've used an object, but in a negative command this time. French object pronouns are **me**, **te**, **le**, **la**, **les**, **lui**, **leur**, **nous**, **vous**, **en**, and **y** and they follow specific rules of placement. I fill in all the details in this section. (For all the details about object pronouns, flip to Chapter 13.)

In affirmative commands

In a regular affirmative sentence, you place the object pronouns (the pronouns that receive the action) before the verb, as in **Nous le regardons** (*We're looking at him*). However, in the imperative, object pronouns are placed behind the verb and attached to it with a hyphen, like so: **Regardons-le!** (*Let's look at him!*). For English speakers, this order seems natural. But even so, a few things need to happen that are not so natural, I'm afraid:

✔ The pronouns **me** and **te** change to **moi** and **toi** when they are after the verb. For example:

Excusez-moi. (*Excuse me.*)

Regarde-toi! (*Look at yourself!*)

✔ With the pronouns **y** and **en**, two things can happen to the verb:

- If it's a **tu** command the verb ends in an **e** (regular **-er** verbs and **aller**), you have an issue with the possible collision of two vowels. (French really doesn't like that!) For example: The **e** of **mange** (*eat*) shouldn't bump against the **e** of **en**. To avoid the collision, just put back the **s** (of the **-er** verb present tense **tu** form), like this: **manges-en** (*eat some*).

  Here are a few more examples:

  Regular command: **Cherche des champignons.** (*Look for mushrooms.*)

  Command with **en**: **Cherches-en.** (*Look for some.*)

  Regular command: **Entre dans la maison.** (*Enter the house.*)

  Command with **y**: **Entres-y.** (*Enter it.*)

- With the **nous** or **vous** commands for all verbs and the **tu** commands for **-ir** and **-re** verbs, the preceding problem doesn't exist because these forms all end in a consonant and you can do the **liaison** that I describe in Chapter 2. Just attach the pronoun after the verb, like **parlons-en** (*let's talk about it*), **parlez-en** (*talk about it*), **prends-en** (*take some*), and **réfléchis-y** (*think about it*), with a *z* sound before **en** and **y**.

Attach the pronoun in parentheses to the following imperatives. Be sure to put the **-s** of the **tu** form back on when necessary.

Q. **prends** (en)

A. **prends-en**

31. **écoute** (les) _____

32. **va** (y) _____

33. **finissez** (en) _____

34. **rentrons** (y) _____

35. **parlons** (lui) _____

In negative commands

If you read the preceding section, put aside what I just said about the place of the object pronoun in affirmative commands. In negative commands (like *don't take it*), you're back to the French way of placing pronouns: before the verb! Use a regular negative command like **Ne prends pas ce sac** (*Don't take this bag*) and place the pronoun right before the verb, like this: **Ne le prends pas!** (*Don't take it!*) Here are a few more examples:

N'oublions pas nos affaires (*Let's not forget our things*) becomes **Ne les oublions pas** (*Let's not forget them*).

N'écoute pas les mauvais conseils (*Don't listen to bad advice*) becomes **Ne les écoute pas** (*Don't listen to them*).

Ne téléphonez pas à vos professeurs (*Don't call your professors*) becomes **Ne leur téléphonez pas.** (*Don't call them*).

Before the pronouns **en** and **y**, **ne** becomes **n'**. Here are some examples:

N'en mange pas. (*Don't eat any.*)

N'y va pas. (*Don't go there.*)

Add the pronoun in parentheses to the following negative imperatives. Pay attention to whether you need the **-s** for the **tu** commands.

Q. **Dites!** (me)

A. **Ne me dites pas.**

36. **Ne prépare pas.** (en) _____

37. **Ne déjeunons pas.** (y) _____

38. **Ne regardons pas.** (les) _____

39. **Ne cherchez pas.** (en) _____

40. **N'écoute pas.** (me) _____

Answer Key

1 *Dance!* (you plural)

2 *Listen!* (you singular)

3 *Look!* (you singular)

4 *Let's go!*

5 *Eat!* (you singular)

6 **Répondez**

7 **Rendons**

8 **Réussissez**

9 **Écoute**

10 **Applaudissons**

11 **Agissez**

12 **Attendez**

13 **Arrêtez**

14 **Jouons**

15 **Réfléchis**

16 **Envoyez!**

17 **Voyageons!**

18 **Commence!**

19 **Réglez!**

20 **Nettoie!**

21 **Tais-toi!**

22 **Détendez-vous pendant les vacances.**

23 **Levons-nous tôt aujourd'hui.**

24 **Faites la vaisselle, s'il vous plait.**

25 Amuse-toi.

26 Ne mangeons pas.

27 N'ouvrez pas.

28 N'avançons pas.

29 Ne posez pas.

30 N'arrive pas.

31 écoute-les

32 vas-y

33 finissez-en

34 rentrons-y

35 parlons-lui

36 N'en prépare pas.

37 N'y déjeunons pas.

38 Ne les regardons pas.

39 N'en cherchez pas.

40 Ne m'écoute pas.

Chapter 21

Discovering Compound Tenses

In This Chapter
▶ Picking out the pluperfect
▶ Focusing on the future perfect
▶ Considering the past conditional

Temps composés (*compound tenses*) are two-word verb forms that express an action that's farther in the past than the main action of a sentence. As a result, they are often found in complex sentences (sentences with two clauses). Of course, they can also appear in simple sentences, so you'd better know them!

The cool thing about compound tenses is that you don't need to worry too much about their conjugation. Why? All you need to conjugate is the auxiliary **être** (*to be*) or **avoir** (*to have*); the main verb is the past participle. Here's the formula you use to form a basic compound tense:

> Subject + conjugated form of **être** or **avoir** + past participle

French has eight compound tenses. The most widely used ones are the **passé composé** (*present perfect*), the **plus-que-parfait** (*pluperfect*), the **futur anterieur** (*future perfect*), and the **conditionnel passé** (*past conditional*). Chapter 15 goes into detail on the present perfect, including the full scoop on forming past participles, and this chapter discusses the others.

Some verbs use **être** to form their compound; in Chapter 15, I call these verbs the "house of **être**" verbs. They are verbs of motion, like **aller** (*to go*), and all pronominal verbs, like **se réveiller** (*to wake up*). (Chapter 7 has details on pronominal verbs.) When the auxiliary is **être**, the past participle must agree in number and gender with the subject of the verb. For example, in **elles sont sorties** (*they went out*), the past participle **sorties** is feminine plural to match the subject **elles**.

Most verbs form their compound with **avoir** and a past participle, as you find out in Chapter 15. Those verbs include impersonal verbs like **pleuvoir** (*to rain*), **être** and **avoir**, and all other verbs that aren't included in the house of **être**. When the auxiliary is **avoir**, the past participle must agree in number and gender with the object of the verb when it comes before **avoir**. For example, in **il a aimé les histoires** (*he liked the stories*), the past participle **aimé** doesn't agree, but if you say **il les a aimées** (*he liked them*), with the object pronoun **les** referring to **les histoires** (feminine plural), now the past participle agrees in number and gender with **les** because it is now in front of **avoir**: **aimées**.

A Long Time Ago: The Pluperfect

The **plus-que-parfait** (*pluperfect*) describes an action that is further in the past than another past action in the **passé composé** or **imparfait** (*imperfect*; see Chapter 16). In a complete sentence, the clause with the pluperfect indicates what *had already happened* before the main action took place. For example: **Il faisait froid ce matin parce qu'il avait neigé pendant la nuit.** (*It was cold this morning because it had snowed during the night.*) The clause **parce qu'il avait neigé pendant la nuit** (*because it had snowed during the night*) is in the pluperfect tense.

The English expression *by* [a certain time], as in *I was all finished with work by 4*, doesn't have an equivalent in French. You can't use **par** (*by*) for this application. The only way to render this very common phrase is to use the pluperfect with **à** (*at*) or **avant** (*before*) + [the time]. You can add **déjà** (*already*) if you really want to insist, like this: **J'avais déjà fini tout mon travail à 4 heures.** (*I had already finished all my work at/by 4:00.*)

The **plus-que-parfait** can also be combined with the past conditional (which I discuss later in this chapter) in a sentence about missed opportunities, like this: **S'il avait suivi tes conseils, il aurait réussi.** (*If he had followed your advice, he would have succeeded.*) The clause with **si** + the pluperfect tells what did not happen, while the other one, with the past conditional, expresses what could have been.

To form the **plus-que-parfait**, take the imperfect of the auxiliary **être** (*to be*) or **avoir** (*to have*) and the past participle of the verb (see Chapter 16 for more on the imperfect and Chapter 15 for details on how to form past participles). For your reference, here's the imperfect conjugation of **être**.

être (*to be*)	
j'**étais**	nous **étions**
tu **étais**	vous **étiez**
il/elle/on **était**	ils/elles **étaient**

And here's the imperfect conjugation of **avoir**:

avoir (*to have*)	
j'**avais**	nous **avions**
tu **avais**	vous **aviez**
il/elle/on **avait**	ils/elles **avaient**

You often find expressions such as **déjà** (*already*) or **pas encore** (*not yet*) or **la veille** (*the day before*) in the pluperfect. Here are some examples:

Anne avait sommeil ce matin parce qu'elle s'était couchée tard la veille. (*Anne was sleepy this morning because she had gone to bed late the previous night.*)

Quand nous sommes arrivés sur le quai, le train avait déjà quitté la gare! (*When we arrived on the platform, the train had already left the station!*)

Put the verb in parentheses in pluperfect. Be sure to use the correct auxiliary, **être** or **avoir**. Here's an example.

Q. Le train _____. (**partir**)

A. était parti

1. Elle _____. (**se coucher tard**)

2. Nous _____. (**dîner**)

3. Tu _____. (**arriver**)

4. Ils _____. (**finir**)

5. J' _____. (**comprendre**)

Back to the Future: The Future Perfect

It may sound a bit strange for me to talk about the future, because I say earlier in this chapter that compound tenses are all past tenses. But sometimes you need to refer to something that's both future and past tense: The future perfect describes a future action or event that *will have been done* before another one occurs.

A complete sentence in **le futur antérieur** (*the future perfect*) has the following two clauses, which can go in either order:

Expression of time with the verb in the future perfect + clause in the future

The future perfect is formed with the future tense of the auxiliary **être** (*to be*) or **avoir** (*to have*) and the past participle (Chapter 17 talks about the future tense, and Chapter 15 explains how to form past participles). For your reference, here's **être** in the future tense.

être (*to be*)	
je **serai**	nous **serons**
tu **seras**	vous **serez**
il/elle/on **sera**	ils/elles **seront**

And here's the future conjugation of **avoir**:

avoir (*to have*)	
j'**aurai**	nous **aurons**
tu **auras**	vous **aurez**
il/elle/on **aura**	ils/elles **auront**

Here are some examples of the future perfect with literal English translations:

Quand je serai parti . . . (*When I will have left . . .*)

Quand il se sera excusé . . . (*When he will have apologized . . .*)

Quand vous aurez fini . . . (*When you will have finished . . .*)

Here are some examples of complete French sentences featuring the future perfect and their correct English translation, which does not necessarily include the future perfect:

Tu pourras lire mon livre quand je l'aurai fini. (*You'll be able to read my book when I am done with it.*)

Dès que nous serons rentrés de vacances, nous vous téléphonerons. (*As soon as we have returned from our vacation, we will call you.*)

English tends to use the present perfect where French uses the future perfect. Don't use the present perfect like that in French.

Here are a few of expressions of time can help you tell when to use the future perfect:

- **aussitôt que** (*as soon as*)
- **dès que** (*as soon as*)
- **lorsque** (*when*)
- **quand** (*when*)

Put the verb in parentheses in future perfect. Be sure to use the correct auxiliary, **être** or **avoir**. Here's an example.

Q. Le train _____. (partir)

A. sera parti

6. Elles _____. (se laver)

7. Nous _____. (manger)

8. Tu _____. (partir)

9. Ils _____. (entrer)

10. J' _____. (apprendre)

Missed Opportunities: The Past Conditional

Could you have done it differently? Should they have listened to you? If only. In expressions of missed opportunities like these, you use **le conditionnel passé** (*the past conditional*) in French, like in English, to express a missed opportunity. It is typically found in a two-clause sentence with **si** (*if*) and a verb in pluperfect in the other clause, to express a situation that did not happen (I discuss the pluperfect earlier in this chapter). The past conditional then expresses the missed opportunity. Here is what a sentence with a past conditional looks like:

Si + pluperfect clause + past conditional clause

The past conditional is formed with the conditional of the auxiliary **être** (*to be*) or **avoir** (*to have*) and the past participle. (Check out Chapter 18 for more about the conditional and Chapter 15 for details on past participles.) For your reference, here's the conditional of **être**.

être (*to be*)	
je **serais**	nous **serions**
tu **serais**	vous **seriez**
il/elle/on **serait**	ils/elles **seraient**

And here's the conditional conjugation of **avoir**.

avoir (*to have*)	
j'**aurais**	nous **aurions**
tu **aurais**	vous **auriez**
il/elle/on **aurait**	ils/elles **auraient**

Here are some examples of the past conditional in action:

Si j'avais su, j'aurais écouté tes conseils! (*If I had known, I would have listened to your advice!*)

Si tu m'avais aidé, j'aurais pu finir mon travail à temps. (*If you had helped me, I could have finished my work on time.*)

Elle serait partie tôt si elle avait pu. (*She would have left early if she had been able to.*)

Put the verb in parentheses in past conditional. Be sure to use the correct auxiliary, **être** or **avoir**. Here's an example.

O. Le facteur _____. (**arriver**)

A. **serait arrivé**

11. Elles _____. (**s'amuser**)

12. Vous _____. (**parler**)

13. Tu _____. (**danser**)

14. Ils _____. (**réussir**)

15. J' _____. (**vendre**)

Give the French compound equivalent to the following English verb forms. Keep in mind that French compounds only have one auxiliary and one past participle. Check out a French-English dictionary if you need help with any vocabulary. Here's an example.

0. *I had been*

A. **j'avais été**

16. *you* (singular informal) *will have finished* _____

17. *we had come* _____

18. *she would have listened* _____

19. *they had* (already) *left* _____

20. *you* (plural) *had spoken* _____

21. *I will be/have finished* _____

22. *he could have* _____

23. *we will have seen* _____

24. *you'd have come* _____

25. *they* (feminine) *had been waiting* _____

Reacting to the Past: The Past Subjunctive

When the structure of a sentence calls for the subjunctive (meaning it includes a trigger phrase and two subjects; see Chapter 19), you have two options: using the present subjunctive or using the past subjunctive. The past subjunctive expresses a desire, emotion, or doubt about something that has happened before. The choice is a little tricky, so let me walk you through the process.

✔ If the action in the subjunctive is simultaneous (at the same time) to the trigger verb or happens after it, use the present subjunctive. Here's an example of simultaneous actions:

    Papa veut que nous réussissions. (*Dad wants us to succeed.*)

Here is an example of an action (*may rain*) that will come after the trigger verb (*afraid*):

    J'ai peur qu'il pleuve demain. (*I'm afraid it may rain tomorrow.*)

✔ If the action in the subjunctive happened before the trigger verb, you use the past subjunctive. Here's an example:

    Julie est triste que sa meilleure amie ne soit pas venue à son anniversaire. (*Julie is sad that her best friend didn't come to her birthday.*)

In this example, Julie is sad now, because her best friend didn't come to her birthday that ocurred some time ago.

Don't automatically use the past subjunctive in the subjunctive clause, even if the verb of the trigger is in the past. For example, in this sentence you need the present subjunctive even when the trigger is in the past:

Il était content que ses amis soient là. (*He was happy that his friends were there.*)

To form the past subjunctive, you use the auxiliary **être** (*to be*) or **avoir** (*to have*) in the subjunctive and add the past participle. Here's the complete conjugation of **danser** (*to dance*) in the past subjunctive with **avoir:**

avoir (*to have*) with **danser** (*to dance*)	
que **j'aie dansé**	que nous **ayons dansé**
que tu **aies dansé**	que vous **ayez dansé**
qu'il/elle/on **ait dansé**	qu'ils/elles **aient dansé**

Here's the complete conjugation of **aller** (*to go*) in the past subjunctive with **être:**

être (*to be*) with **aller** (*to go*)	
que je **sois allé(e)**	que nous **soyons allé(e)s**
que tu **sois allé(e)**	que vous **soyez allé(e)s**
qu'il/elle/on **soit allé(e)**	qu'ils/elles **soient allé(e)s**

Consider whether the bold verb requires the past subjunctive or the present subjunctive. Write *past* or *present* in the blank accordingly.

0. I'm happy you're here.

A. present

26. I am sorry **you didn't understand** my questions on the last test. _____

27. In the '60s it was important for Americans **to go** to the moon. _____

28. Are you proud that the American athletes **won** so many medals in the Olympics? _____

29. It's too bad that **you didn't wait for** us; we arrived ten minutes after you left. _____

30. It's important for you **to drink** plenty of water. _____

Answer Key

1	s'était couchée tard
2	avions dîné
3	étais arrivé(e)
4	avaient fini
5	avais compris
6	se seront lavées
7	aurons mangé
8	seras parti
9	seront entrés
10	aurai appris
11	se seraient amusées

12	auriez parlé
13	aurais dansé
14	auraient réussi
15	aurais vendu
16	tu auras fini
17	nous étions venus
18	elle aurait écouté
19	ils étaient déjà partis
20	vous aviez parlé
21	j'aurai fini

22	il aurait pu
23	nous aurons vu
24	tu serais venu(e)
25	elles avaient attendu
26	past
27	present
28	past
29	past
30	present

Part VI

The Part of Tens

In this part . . .

✔ Discover how to avoid making ten common French grammar mistakes.

✔ Enjoy a list of ten (or so) French idioms whose meanings you may have a hard time guessing!

Chapter 22

Ten Common French Grammar Mistakes (And How to Avoid Them)

. . . .

In This Chapter

▶ Staying clear of common beginner errors

▶ Refining a few vocabulary issues

. . . .

This chapter assumes that you're going to make French grammar mistakes. You know it's true. In fact, the best way to learn a language is to try it out and get corrected when necessary! And the more chances you get to try out a language, the faster you'll learn. This chapter presents ten common mistakes made in French grammar and how to avoid them.

Using Definite Articles Incorrectly

Le, la, and **les** (*the*) are not the default articles in French. The indefinite and partitive articles are. Article usage is quite different between French and English, and this is one area where you need to be careful. Table 22-1 highlights major differences in usage between French and English definite articles. (See Chapter 3 for more about definite articles.)

Table 22-1	Using French and English Definite Articles	
French	*English*	*Usage*
Definite article	(no equivalent)	Naming a category
Definite article	(no equivalent)	Naming a preference
Definite article	(no equivalent)	Referring to an entire category
Definite article	Definite article	Referring to something previously mentioned

Confusing Indefinite and Partitive Articles

French uses different articles for nouns that can be counted, such as **un livre** (*a book*), and nouns that can't be counted, like **de l'eau** (*some water*).

- ✔ Use indefinite articles to introduce a noun that can be counted. For example, you can say **une maison** (*a/one house*) or **cinq maisons** (*five houses*).
- ✔ Use partitive articles to introduce a noun that can't be counted. For example, you can say **du sable** (*some sand*), but you can't say **trois sables** (*three sands*).

Check out Chapter 3 for a full discussion of indefinite and partitive articles.

Using the Wrong Word for "Time"

Le temps is a singular word always spelled with an **-s** that has a narrower meaning in French than in English.

- ✔ **Temps** is the French equivalent of the word *weather*, as in **Quel temps fait-il?** (*What's the weather like?*)
- ✔ **Temps** is also the French equivalent of the word *time*, as in **Je n'ai pas le temps.** (*I don't have time.*)

If you need to translate the word *time* into French in any other context, here are some examples:

What time is it?	**Quelle heure est-il?**
three times	**trois fois**
in the times of	**à l'époque de**
at the time of	**au moment de**
many times	**souvent**

Flip to Chapter 5 for the basics of dealing with times in French.

Incorrectly Translating Means of Transportation

When they refer to means of transportation, verbs like *to fly*, *to drive*, *to swim*, and *to walk* can't be translated directly into French. You can say **j'aime marcher** (*I like to walk*) referring to the action of walking per se, as opposed to running for instance. But to say that *you walked to work*, indicating how you went to work, you need a sentence with the verb **aller** (*to go*) plus the means of transportation. This is how to do it:

Aller + **à** or **en** + means of transportation

And here are some examples:

> To fly: **aller en avion** (literally *to go in a plane*)
>
> To drive: **aller en voiture** (literally *to go in a car*)
>
> To swim: **aller à la nage** (literally *to go by swimming*)
>
> To walk: **aller à pied** (literally *to go by foot*)

Chapter 6 explains how to conjugate **aller** in the present tense. Watch out — it's pretty unusual!

Trying to Find an Equivalent for the -ing Verb Form in French

English uses two different verb forms to express present tense; you can say *I talk to the postman* or *I am talking to the postman*. In French, however, don't look for the *-ing* form of a verb in the present tense, because it doesn't exist! French has only one form of the present tense, and it is a simple tense: **Je parle au facteur.** (*I'm talking to the postman.*) Don't say **Je suis parler**, which literally means *I am to speak* but has no meaning in French because you can't have an infinitive after **être.** Here are a few examples (see Chapter 6 for more about the present tense):

> *We are having lunch.* (**Nous déjeunons.**)
>
> *He's waiting for you.* (**Il t'attend.**)

With an *-ing* form in the past tense, use the **imparfait** (*imperfect;* see Chapter 16). The **imparfait** can indicate an ongoing past activity (that you *were doing* something). Here are a few examples:

> *He was thinking about the problem.* (**Il pensait au problème.**)
>
> *They were sleeping when the phone rang.* (**Ils dormaient quand le téléphone a sonné.**)

In English, the *-ing* form of a verb is called the *gerund.* French has a gerund, but it has different uses from those in English; see Chapter 14 for details.

Using Possessives with Pronominal Verbs to Refer to Body Parts

In expressions that involve body parts, like **les mains** (*the hands*) and **les cheveux** (*the hair*), French uses a pronominal verb, like **se laver** (*to wash*) or **se brosser** (*to brush*). A pronominal verb indicates that the subject is doing whatever the action is to him- or herself. So if you want to say *I wash my hands* in French, you can't use both the pronominal verb **je me lave** and the possessive **mes mains** (*my hands*)! It would be redundant: *I am washing* *myself's hands.* Instead, you use a definite article like **le**, **la**, or **les** (see Chapter 3). The correct way to say *I wash my hands* is **Je me lave les mains.** Here are a few more examples:

> **Il s'est cassé la jambe.** (*He broke his leg.*)
>
> **Elles se brossent les cheveux.** (*They're brushing their hair.*)

Find the full details of pronominal verbs in Chapter 7.

Putting the Wrong Verb Form after Avoir or Être

The verbs **avoir** (*to have*) and **être** (*to be*) are helper verbs; as that name implies, these two verbs often help to form a new tense. The tenses formed with the help of **avoir** and **être** are called compound, and they usually indicate a past tense. For example:

- ✔ The phrase **nous avons fini** (*we finished*) is made of the auxiliary **avoir** followed by a past participle; the combination of the two is a compound tense, the **passé composé** (*present perfect*) in this case (see Chapter 15 for more about the present perfect and past participles).

- ✔ In **tu étais déjà parti** (*you had already left*), the auxiliary is **être**, followed by a past participle to form the **plus-que-parfait** (pluperfect) this time. (For more on the pluperfect and other compound tenses, see Chapter 21.)

English often expresses obligation by using *to have* plus an infinitive, as in *we have to listen.* French, however, never uses **avoir** or **être** with an infinitive. To express obligation in French, use **devoir** (*to have to*) as the helper verb: **nous devons écouter** (*we have to listen*). Use only a past participle like **arrivé** (*arrived*), **dansé** (*danced*), **fini** (*finished*), or **vendu** (*sold*) after **être** or **avoir** used as auxiliaries.

Mixing Up Similar Verbs

Dire (*to say/tell*) and **parler** (*to talk*) have to do with producing sounds, but like in English the two verbs have different usage.

- ✔ Use **dire** alone when quoting someone's words, as in **Il a dit "allons-y"!** (*He said "let's go"!*); or to report speech, as in **Il a dit que nous partirions demain.** (*He said that we would leave tomorrow.*)

  You can also use **dire** followed by a noun (its direct object), as in **tu dis un mensonge.** (*You're telling a lie.*)

- ✔ Use **parler** alone (no direct object) to say *to talk*, as in **Vous parlez trop!** (*You talk too much*), or followed by the preposition **à** to indicate an indirect object to whom the subject speaks as in **Le prof parle à ses étudiants.** (*The teacher talks to his/her students.*)

  Parler is never followed by **que** + another clause, or by a direct object.

Voir and **regarder** each have an English equivalent: *to see* and *to watch*.

> ✔ Use **voir** (*to see*) alone to express that you understand: **je vois** (*I see*), or most commonly, use it with a direct object to say that you see something: **Nous avons vu des choses surprenantes.** (*We saw some surprising things.*)

> ✔ Use **regarder** (*to watch*) when you are actively looking at something, as in **Il regarde la télé.** (*He watches TV.*)

Entendre and **écouter** also have English equivalents: *to hear* and *to listen to*. The difference between them is the same as between **voir** and **regarder**: **entendre** (*to hear*) is accidental, as in **Tu as entendu ce bruit?** (*Did you hear that noise?*), whereas **écouter** (*to listen to*) is intentional, as in **Nous écoutons le prof.** (*We are listening to the teacher.*)

Confusing Connaître and Savoir

French has two different verbs for the verb *to know*, **connaître** and **savoir**, but they are not interchangeable!

To say that you know a place, a book, or a person, as in being familiar with those, use **connaître**. Here are some examples:

> **Je connais bien l'endroit où tu es né.** (*I know very well the place where you were born.*)

> **Tu connais les livres?** (*Are you familiar with the books?*)

> **Vous connaissez Pierre?** (*Do you know Pierre?*)

For everything else, use **savoir**. Here are some examples:

> **Tu sais nager?** (*Do you know how to swim?*)

> **Elle sait que vous arriverez bientôt.** (*She knows that you will arrive soon.*)

Being Tricked by False Cognates

A *cognate* is a word that looks and means the same in French and in English. For example, *an animal* is **un animal** in French. The English adjective *patient* is **patient** in French also. However, some tricky words look the same in both languages but don't mean the same! They are called *false cognates* and are often refered to as "false friends" for obvious reasons. Table 22-2 gives you a sampling of some common such words.

Table 22-2	Common False Cognates	
English Word	*French Cognate*	*Meaning of the French Word*
actually	actuellement	currently
a demand	une demande	a request
assist	assister	to attend
college	collège	junior high
commode	commode (adj)	practical
deception	déception	disappointment
entrée	entrée	appetizer/starter
eventually	éventuellement	possibly
gross	gros	fat
location	location	rental
to pass (an exam)	passer (un examen)	to take an exam
patron	patron	boss
to rest	rester	to stay
rude	rude	harsh

Chapter 23

Ten (Or So) Useful French Idioms

In This Chapter

▶ Taking a bridge to a vacation

▶ Knowing that something isn't too difficult

▶ Using idioms that involve the body

*E*very language has *idioms* — expressions whose literal meanings are quite different from their common-usage meanings. For instance, when you are *in a pickle*, you're faced with a delicate situation that has nothing to do with pickles!

Idioms find their roots pretty deep in the culture of a language, and sometimes even native speakers don't know the reason for idioms they use and understand. This chapter presents a few colorful and common French idioms that you can use right away.

Faire le pont

Literally, **faire le pont** means *to do the bridge,* but French speakers use it to describe a particular type of vacation. For instance, when a holiday falls on a Thursday and you take the following day (Friday) off work, you're *doing the bridge* over to the weekend to get a four-day vacation! Here's this idiom in action:

> **Cette année, Noël tombe un jeudi, alors nous allons faire le pont jusqu'à lundi!**
> (*This year Christmas falls on a Thursday, so we are going to "do the bridge" over to Monday.*)

The verb **faire** (*to do*), along with **être** (*to be*), **avoir** (*to have*), and **aller** (*to go*), have unusual conjugations in the present tense; see Chapter 6 for details.

Ce n'est pas la mer à boire

If someone tells you to do something that you find hard to do, she may add, **Ce n'est pas la mer à boire** (*It's not the whole sea to drink*), meaning that it could be worse. (Maybe you should tell her to try it herself! *To drink the sea* would be an impossible challenge, but saying that something *isn't as bad as that* doesn't necessarily mean it's easy, right?) Here's an example of how you use this idiom:

—**Il faut faire la lessive, passer l'aspirateur et préparer le dîner! Quel travail!** (*It's necessary to do the laundry, vacuum, and prepare dinner. What a job!*)

—**Mais non, ce n'est pas la mer à boire.** (*Nah! It's not the sea to drink.*)

Ça me prend la tête

Literally **Ça me prend la tête** means *it takes my head*, which definitely makes no sense as is! In fact, it refers to an annoying situation that is driving you crazy, or to use an English idiom, *it gets your goat*. For example, you've been waiting for the bus for 30 minutes now, and you say:

Ça fait 30 minutes que j'attends le bus. Ça commence à me prendre la tête! (*I've been waiting for the bus for 30 minutes now. It's starting to get my goat!*)

Faire la tête

Faire la tête literally means *to make the head*. If someone is *making the head*, they're simply pouting. For example, if your friend forgot your birthday and you're not happy about it, someone else may say to you:

Ne fais pas la tête! Ça arrive. (*Don't pout! It happens.*)

Avoir la gueule de bois

La gueule is an animal's face, so **avoir la gueule de bois** literally means that you have *a wooden animal face*. The reason? You had too much to drink the night before and now your head really hurts! You would probably whisper:

Oh là là . . . j'ai trop bu hier soir. J'ai la gueule de bois ce matin! (*Oh la la . . . I drank too much last night. I have a hangover this morning.*)

Comme un cheveu sur la soupe

Have you ever found a hair floating in your soup? It's gross, because a hair has no place on a plate of food. And that's exactly what this expression means: **Comme un cheveu sur la soupe** indicates that, *like a hair on soup,* something is not in the right place. For example, in the middle of a conversation about your summer plans, the person you're talking with says, "And what about Christmas?" You'd probably be tempted to tell him:

> **Tu parles de Noël quand je parle de cet été?! Ça, ça tombe comme un cheveu sur la soupe.** (*You talk about Christmas when I'm talking about this summer?! That's very incongruous.*)

Au pif

The **pif** is slang for *nose,* and doing something **au pif** indicates that you are doing it by following instinct, or by guesstimation, instead of thinking. For instance:

> **Je ne savais pas la réponse alors j'ai écrit quelque chose au pif.** (*I didn't know the answer, so I wrote something kind of guessing.*)

Donner sa langue au chat

The expression **donner sa langue au chat** literally means *to give your tongue to the cat,* but you use it when you don't know the answer to a particular riddle and want the person who asked the question to finally give you the answer. For example:

> **Si tu ne trouves pas la réponse, donne ta langue au chat!** (*If you don't find the answer, give up!*)

Être sur les charbons ardents

If you had to stand on red hot coals, you'd be hopping from one foot to the other, unable to stay in place. Use **être sur les charbons ardents** (which literally means *to stand on red hot coals*) when you're expecting news that is so important to you that you can't stay still. Imagine a future dad in a delivery room:

> **Le bébé est sur le point d'arriver. Papa est sur les charbons ardents.** (*The baby is about to arrive. Papa can't stay still.*)

Bête comme ses pieds

Can feet be dumb? The French seem to think so, because that's what **bête comme ses pieds** means: that you're *as dumb as your feet*! It's not a terribly insulting expression, except maybe if you really like your feet. Check out this idiom in use:

> **Cet étudiant ne donne jamais la bonne réponse; ou il le fait exprès, ou il est bête comme ses pieds!** (*This student never gives the right answer; either he does it on purpose, or he is dumb as an ox.*)

Tirer le diable par la queue

No one has ever actually tried to pull the devil's tail, but **tirer le diable par la queue** is the French colorful way of saying that someone is having financial difficulties and can't make ends meet. For example:

> **Pierre est au chômage et maintenant il tire le diable par la queue.** (*Pierre is unemployed and now he has trouble making ends meet.*)

Index

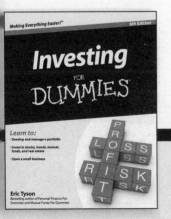
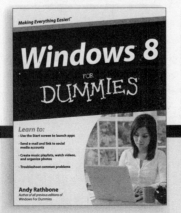

Math & Science

Algebra I For Dummies,
2nd Edition
978-0-470-55964-2

Anatomy and Physiology
For Dummies,
2nd Edition
978-0-470-92326-9

Astronomy For Dummies,
3rd Edition
978-1-118-37697-3

Biology For Dummies,
2nd Edition
978-0-470-59875-7

Chemistry For Dummies,
2nd Edition
978-1-1180-0730-3

Pre-Algebra Essentials
For Dummies
978-0-470-61838-7

Microsoft Office

Excel 2013 For Dummies
978-1-118-51012-4

Office 2013 All-in-One
For Dummies
978-1-118-51636-2

PowerPoint 2013
For Dummies
978-1-118-50253-2

Word 2013 For Dummies
978-1-118-49123-2

Music

Blues Harmonica
For Dummies
978-1-118-25269-7

Guitar For Dummies,
3rd Edition
978-1-118-11554-1

iPod & iTunes
For Dummies,
10th Edition
978-1-118-50864-0

Programming

Android Application
Development For Dummies,
2nd Edition
978-1-118-38710-8

iOS 6 Application
Development For Dummies
978-1-118-50880-0

Java For Dummies,
5th Edition
978-0-470-37173-2

Religion & Inspiration

The Bible For Dummies
978-0-7645-5296-0

Buddhism For Dummies,
2nd Edition
978-1-118-02379-2

Catholicism For Dummies,
2nd Edition
978-1-118-07778-8

Self-Help & Relationships

Bipolar Disorder
For Dummies,
2nd Edition
978-1-118-33882-7

Meditation For Dummies,
3rd Edition
978-1-118-29144-3

Seniors

Computers For Seniors
For Dummies,
3rd Edition
978-1-118-11553-4

iPad For Seniors
For Dummies,
5th Edition
978-1-118-49708-1

Social Security
For Dummies
978-1-118-20573-0

Smartphones & Tablets

Android Phones
For Dummies
978-1-118-16952-0

Kindle Fire HD
For Dummies
978-1-118-42223-6

NOOK HD For Dummies,
Portable Edition
978-1-118-39498-4

Surface For Dummies
978-1-118-49634-3

Test Prep

ACT For Dummies,
5th Edition
978-1-118-01259-8

ASVAB For Dummies,
3rd Edition
978-0-470-63760-9

GRE For Dummies,
7th Edition
978-0-470-88921-3

Officer Candidate Tests,
For Dummies
978-0-470-59876-4

Physician's Assistant Exa
For Dummies
978-1-118-11556-5

Series 7 Exam
For Dummies
978-0-470-09932-2

Windows 8

Windows 8 For Dummies
978-1-118-13461-0

Windows 8 For Dummies,
Book + DVD Bundle
978-1-118-27167-4

Windows 8 All-in-One
For Dummies
978-1-118-11920-4

e Available in print and e-book formats.

Take Dummies with you everywhere you go!

Whether you're excited about e-books, want more from the web, must have your mobile apps, or swept up in social media, Dummies makes everything easier .